BEING IRISH

BEING IRISH

Personal Reflections on Irish Identity Today

Edited by Paddy Logue

Oak Tree Press
Dublin

Oak Tree Press
Merrion Building
Lower Merrion Street
Dublin 2, Ireland
www.oaktreepress.com
www.BeingIrish.com

A catalogue record of this book is
available from the British Library.

ISBN 1 86076 176 3 Paperback
ISBN 1 86076 187 9 Hardback

The essays in this volume by Brian Dooley, Jill Fergus, Andrew Greeley, Colum McCann, Cormac MacConnell and Frank McCourt originally appeared in *Irish America* magazine's 15th Anniversary issue in October/November 2000. Reprinted with permission.

A version of the essay by Louis le Brocquy originally appeared in *The Recorder*, Volume 42, The American Irish Historical Society, 1981.

The essay by Ronit Lentin originally appeared in *The Irish Times*, 16 June 1998.

While every effort has been made to trace copyright of photographs, the Publishers will be happy to correct any omissions in future printings of this book.

Printed in the Republic of Ireland by Colour Books Ltd.

Contents

Acknowledgements .... *xi*

Introduction by Paddy Logue... *xv*

Taoiseach Bertie Ahern TD 1

Mike Allen.. 4

Dr. Moosajee Bhamjee.. 7

Dr. Esmond Birnie MLA 10

Prime Minister Tony Blair MP 12

Professor John Bradley 15

John Bruton TD 18

Bishop Pat Buckley 20

Anne Cadwallader... 24

Gregory Campbell MLA 27

Norah Casey.. 30

Mary Boylan Clarke 34

Martin Collins 37

Peter Cosgrove 40

Polly Devlin 42

Ken Doherty 45

Brian Dooley 47

Sammy Douglas 50

Jill Fergus 53

Fr Aengus Finucane 56

Hugh Frazer 59

Lord Anthony Gifford 63

Fr Andrew Greeley 66

Hon. Desmond Guinness 69

Professor Fred Halliday 72

Patricia Harty 75

Tom Hayden 78

David Hewitt 81

John Hume MP, MEP 84

Fionnuala Hunt 86

Garry Hynes 89

Jennifer Johnston 90

Brian Kennedy 92

Dennis Kennedy 96

Sr Stanislaus Kennedy 99

Tony Kennedy 102

Lainey Keogh 105

Virginia Kerr 106

Avila Kilmurray 109

Maeve Kyle 115

Louis le Brocquy 118

Professor Joe Lee 121

Ronit Lentin 124

Fee Ching Leong 127

Gretta Logue 130

Nell McCafferty 133

Sean McCague 136

Colum McCann 138

Felicity McCartney 142

Muiris Mac Conghail 145

Cormac MacConnell 148

Inez McCormack 151

Frank McCourt 155

Ian McCracken 158

Geoff MacEnroe 162

Ann McGeeney 165

Barry McGuigan 168

Martin McGuinness MP, MLA 171

Tommy McKearney 174

Ann Madden 177

Martin Mansergh 179

Paddy Moloney 182

Paddy Monaghan 184

Austen Morgan 188

Jane Morrice MLA 191

Bruce Morrison 194

Liam Mulvihill 197

Dervla Murphy 200

Niamh Murray 204

Rabbi Julia Neuberger 207

Doireann Ní Bhriain 210

Senator David Norris 213

Barbara Nugent 217

Brendan O'Carroll 219

Conor O'Clery 221

Niall O'Dowd 224

Josephine Olusola 227

Amal Omran 230

John O'Shea 232

Andy Pollak 236

Terry Prone 239

Janet Quilley 242

Ruairi Quinn TD 245

Mary Reid 248

Adi Roche...250

Brendan Parsons, Earl of Rosse 253

Dana Rosemary Scallon MEP.. 256

Elizabeth Shannon.. 258

Peter Shirlow 261

Gaye Shortland 264

Darina Shouldice 267

Shalini Sinha.. 270

Marie Smyth 273

Nell Stewart-Liberty 276

His Excellency Michael J. Sullivan.. 279

Peter Sutherland.. 282

Professor Alan Titley 285

David Trimble MP, MLA 288

Niall Williams 291

Father Desmond Wilson.. 293

Acknowledgements

First and foremost, I would like to thank all of the contributors who put so much time and energy into wrestling with such a difficult topic, and for producing such a varied and insightful collection of essays. Thank you also to all the contributors and photographic agencies who supplied photographs for the book; three contributors requested that their photographs be excluded.

I am most grateful to Patricia Harty, Editor of *Irish America*, for introducing me to Irish-American writers and for her generosity in allowing us to reproduce a number of articles from the magazine; to Philip Watt, Director of the National Consultative Committee on Racism and Interculturalism, and to Niall Crowley, Chief Executive Officer of the Equality Authority, for introducing me to writers from minorities; to all the staff at Oak Tree Press, particularly David Givens and Brian Langan, for their hard work and diligence in bringing the book to press; to Liz Mitchell for typing a number of the essays; and to my wife Marian and family for their good-humoured tolerance of my long absences at the computer.

For Stephen

Introduction

For the past year, the idea of "being Irish" has been my constant companion.

It came with me even during my holiday in Crete in July when I visited the ancient palace of Knossos. I took the opportunity of relating to my two youngest children, Marie-Claire and Deirdre, the story of King Minos and the Minotaur, half-man and half-bull. How Daedalus, the clever craftsman, was commissioned by Minos to build a Labyrinth to contain the Minotaur and ended up being imprisoned in it himself, along with his son Icarus. And how he fashioned wings from birds' feathers and beeswax to enable himself and his son to fly out of the Labyrinth. How young Icarus ignored his father's cautious advice and began to perform aerial rolls and double loops and eventually soared too near to the sun, which melted the wax holding his wings together. He plunged into the sea while Daedalus made good his escape. A myth from the very beginning (the twentieth century BC) of the Greeks', and the Europeans', preoccupation with their identity.

Standing there in the courtyard of the Minoan palace, I thought of James Joyce's Stephen Daedalus and his wrestling with the challenge of being Irish at the start of the twentieth century AD. To Stephen, the birth of the Irish soul is slow, dark and mysterious. And eventually when it is born, nets are flung at it to hold it back from flight. The nets are "nationality, language and religion". He is determined to fly past these nets and to "forge in the smithy of my soul the uncreated conscience of my race". His mother urges caution and humility. She prays that away from home and friends he may learn what the heart is and what it feels. Daedalus escapes from the labyrinth of Ireland. We are left to wonder whether he manages to escape from the Irish condition.

Half a century later, Sean O'Faolain examined what being Irish meant to him in the middle years of the twentieth century. Ireland had experienced the effects of two World Wars, the Easter Rising and Partition in the intervening years and was much changed. In his 1947 book *The Irish*, O'Faolain draws on Celtic mythology and early Irish literature "to see what sort of people the Irish were in the infancy of the race". He charts their development through the age of Saints and Scholars, the Norman period and the Reformation and identifies five representative types of the Irish that have emerged from this history. They are the peasantry, the Anglo-Irish, the rebels, the priests and the writers. He hints at a sixth type, which he calls the new middle classes or native bourgeoisie and remarks that it is too soon to say whether they are really the peasantry in the process of development or in the process of final decay. There is a curiously narrow picture of Irish identity in this scholarly book.

Another half century later, I have been moved by the radical developments that have occurred in Ireland in recent years to undertake this examination of Irish identity. Following the wars in the century that has just ended and 30 years of conflict at home, I am uncomfortable with the exclusive categories of "race" and "nationality" used by Joyce and O'Faolain. What is Irish identity today? Has it changed in the last, say, 50 or 100 years? What changes are likely to happen to it in the coming century? What makes us what we are? What makes us different from other people? Who are we?

The developments that prompted me onto the road that has led to this book are our involvement in Europe, the Celtic Tiger economy, the Good Friday Agreement and the crisis in religion. These are the political events and social forces that, more than any others, constitute the context for this examination and many of the contributors refer to them.

Europe

There are some milestones in Ireland's journey to the centre of European economic and social life. Ireland voted by four to one to join the European Economic Community (EEC), as it was then called, in 1974. In 1979, Ireland broke the link with sterling and joined the European Monetary Scheme (EMS). Finally on 1 January 1999 Ireland joined the European single currency. The process has brought huge economic benefits to Ireland, advanced the pace of social policy legislation and given Ireland a stage on which it displays the talents of its people in all walks of life. Psychologically, it has transformed a small, introspected, backward-looking, peripheral country overshadowed by Britain into a confident, modern society that looks to Europe and beyond for fresh conquests.

The Celtic Tiger

In tandem with the European adventure, the move at home towards changes in fiscal policy, in inward investment strategy and in developing social partnership which began in the late 1980s led to the economic boom in the 1990s which has become known as the Celtic Tiger. There's now a highway linking Irish economic life to the centre of the global economy and the traffic is two-way. There's a new, wild excitement and energy. Training and managing this tiger is presenting an unprecedented economic and social challenge. It must be met if we are to become a prosperous and inclusive society and not one with a wealthy and selfish core surrounded by poor communities and alienated minorities.

The end to introspection, the turning outwards to the world and the new self-confidence which are results of both the Celtic Tiger experience and the involvement in Europe have had other remarkable effects. Our cultural influence extends throughout the whole world in many different forms. This process has been called the hibernisation of Europe but it is fair now to talk about the hibernisation of the world. Our music, dance, films, pubs, literature, theatre, athletes are everywhere. I have heard the word "riverdance" used on an American television programme as a verb meaning to do an Irish dance.

At home, these global successes have emboldened civic society to demand the highest standards in public and business life. The public has taken on some of the most powerful people and interests in the country and the Tribunals are simultaneously flushing out some of the corrupt from the body politic and making it more difficult for corruption to take hold again in the future.

Another effect has been immigration. Many Irish, both first and second generation, are returning home to find work and thousands of foreigners are attracted by our success to seek a home and a job here. (Many of our immigrants, of course, do not come here by choice, but are forced by often-tragic circumstances from their own countries.) There is an uncanny reversal of roles: for centuries, the Irish travelled the world looking for those basic means of survival that immigrants to Ireland now seek here. It presents a new challenge to the Irish. Is Irish identity confident enough, broad enough and caring enough to accord to these immigrants the same rights that the Irish demanded on many a foreign shore?

The Good Friday Agreement

Those of us who have lived through the conflict in the North still sometimes have to convince ourselves and each other that we are not dreaming. The ceasefires of 1994 led to the process of talks and breakdowns and more talks and the Good Friday Agreement and the overwhelmingly positive referendums of 1998 and then more talks and more breakdowns and now, in this first year of the twenty-first century, we have a power-sharing Executive taking tentative steps towards political normality. The situation is changed utterly.

The peace process has allowed us to snap out of the trance of the two traditions, that mutual obsession of nationalists and unionists, the hypnotic focus of a cobra and a mongoose about to attack each other. As the shouts and din of the ancient quarrel begin to subside, we hear other voices. In Ireland today there are atheists, Jews, Sikhs, Buddhists, socialists, Chinese, Travellers, blacks, Moslems, gays, asylum-seekers, feminists and others, all of whom locate themselves outside the two traditions and are entitled to parity of esteem and equality of treatment. And cutting horizontally across all these traditions and groupings is the division between rich and poor, the included and the excluded, the conservative and the progressive, the right and the left. A political discourse of reason, social justice, rights and duties is replacing the politics of rhetoric, prejudice, nods and winks.

Crisis in Religion

The Catholic Church in Ireland survived the external attacks from the global process of secularisation which followed in the trail of industrialisation, liberalism and democracy, right up to the 1990s. Then it was the enemy within that did the damage. A series of sexual scandals involving bishops, religious orders and parish clergy hit it hard. Hardest of all was the seemingly endless stories of child sexual abuse and cover-up. Although it is still a powerful organisation in Irish society, its claim to be the authoritative source of morality and the cement of the social edifice is no longer accepted. An increasing number of people now depend on their own judgement and that of their peers, on the law and the courts, on social policy and human rights legislation and on community action and the power of the media for decent public and private morality and social cohesion. In this respect, Ireland has taken her place among the societies of the modern world.

The Protestant Churches were hit by different problems. The association of some of their clergy and church property with anti-Catholic demonstrations by the Orange Order undermined the authority of their leaders in their appeals for peace and tolerance. Their argument is now just one of many competing for the soul of Protestantism.

As a former priest, I hope that the leaders of these churches can raise their heads from internal preoccupations and rally their large memberships behind the campaign for justice, equality and human rights for all in Ireland. And as someone from Northern Ireland, I am pleased that northern Protestants responded to my challenge of reflecting on what being Irish means to them. Their articles are an authoritative return of serve.

The Contributors

The method I chose for the examination was to invite a balanced cross-section of Irish people to contribute a short personal article of around 800 words on what being Irish meant to them at this time in their lives and in our common history. The invitations were sent to the famous and not so famous, to people at the centre of things and to people at the margins, to men and women, to nationalists and unionists, to those who live in Ireland and to those who live abroad. I also sought several "views from the side", that is, from people who are not Irish but who have an obvious interest or connection. I asked them to identify and give expression to that special something that is (more or less) instantly recognisable as Irish; to detect and describe changes in it; and to record for the present and future generations the rich tapestry that is Irish identity today.

The editorial aim was to create a debate about our identity, to acknowledge difference and to encourage tolerance. I asked the contributors to blow away the dust from our sacred cows and take a fresh look at them; to examine the stereotypical images of Ireland and the Irish and test their accuracy and relevance to the actual Irish of the twenty-first century. I asked them to report sightings of Holy Ireland, the cute hoor, peasant Ireland, Father O'Flynn, leprechauns, martyred Ireland, the begrudger, shillelaghs, a United Ireland, Cathleen Ní Houlihan, wild rovers. I asked the contributors to be as honest and personal as possible. I was asking a lot.

It is not an easy thing to put on public record your personal thoughts about the identity of yourself and your fellow Irish. We can be touchy. Many invitees chose to ignore the invitations. Others declined mostly because of sheer pressure of work and wished the project well. One said the whole question was upsetting him and he was beginning to lose sleep over it; another thought Irish identity was like money . . . if you have it, you don't have to talk about it. Many of the contributors spoke to me of the difficulty they experienced in getting their heads, and hearts, around this question of what being Irish actually meant to them. One said he regretted not dashing off an immediate reply because the more he pondered, the more difficult the task became; another frightened the bejasus out of me by telling me that I was a "brave man" to address such a controversial subject.

In the end, we reached our target of 100 articles. I am not claiming, and the contributors certainly don't claim, that this selection of essayists are a group truly and fully representative of contemporary Irish identity. Nor am I claiming that this is as balanced a group as I had hoped to assemble; for example, the 59 male contributors outnumbered the 41 female. (Why were the men more ready to write about Irish identity than the women?) What I am saying is that this group is one cross-section of Irish people who have taken the time to reflect on their identity and have had the courage to publish their reflections in order to stimulate public debate on the various manifestations of Irish identity current today.

I know many of the contributors personally. Others I invited in the interests of breadth and balance. Some are practised speakers and writers. Some are articulate in their chosen fields of business, art, music, politics, community development. Some are visionaries. Some come up with practical suggestions. Some are seeing their thoughts published for the first time. My overall impression is of a group of individuals conscious that they are living in a time of change, a time of opportunity, challenges and threats. Had an examination of Irish identity similar to this been published 10 years ago, I believe it would have contained more backward glances, more blaming others for our situation; more smugness, escapism and hypocrisy. While some of that remains, this collection is characterised more by an orientation to the future, by acceptance of responsibility to deal with whatever it brings; by confidence, realism and honesty.

In these articles, you will recognise familiar themes from Irish literature, ancient and modern, such as attachment to place, the pain of exile. You will encounter new themes like the economy, cultural diversity, the diaspora, racism, the global village. At the end of the day, the contributors speak for themselves and I wouldn't presume to summarise or highlight all the points contained here. However, at the risk of abusing my editorial authority, I will mention the point that struck me most forcibly. Several contributors, especially those from the estimated 70 million strong Irish diaspora, make the point that there are many ways of being Irish. We can be Irish by birth; Irish by ancestry; Irish by geography; Irish with European links; Irish by accident; Irish by necessity; Irish with British links; Irish by association; Irish by culture; Irish by history; Irish with American links; and Irish by choice. One writes that he is Irish by "choice of allegiance" and describes the magic in raising identity from the "bloodlines of ethnicity to the lifelines of human rights". Now there's a vision for the Irish in the twenty-first century.

To further facilitate the debate, I have established a website, **www.BeingIrish.com**. On this site, I have posted a selection of the articles in this volume and invited the "invisible" Irish anywhere in the globe to get involved. Write your own personal reflection on what being Irish means to you. Do what we Irish are supposed to be good at: discuss, disagree, argue about it, but in a spirit of tolerance. I intend publishing a second volume of articles taken from the website and including some of the people who couldn't contribute this time due to other commitments.

The Irishness in these pages is palpable. We are not an elusive people. If our birth has been slow, dark and mysterious and our adolescence moody, introspective, furtive and violent, our arrival at maturity has been attended by peace and prosperity, omens of good fortune. We have come of age.

Paddy Logue
September 2000

Bertie Ahern

Bertie Ahern is Taoiseach of the Republic of Ireland.

The one constant over many generations and centuries through all tribulations has been our pride in being Irish. Yeats described this as "the indomitable Irishry". What it means to be Irish has nonetheless developed dramatically over the past 50 years.

The historic Irish nation were the inheritors of an ancient culture and civilisation the equal of any in Europe. But in later centuries the mass of the people experienced dispossession and dislocation. The native dynasties were gone.

"'s is atuirse trím chroí gan a dtuairisc ann." *

It was a long struggle to re-establish political and religious freedom, with terrible tragedies along the way. Irish people often had more opportunity to show their talent and vigour in the countries that received them as emigrants. But in the end, amidst gradual progress, we won back our country — relatively poor, reasonably self-sufficient and determined to lead a national life of its own, but shorn of the most developed part of the country in North-East Ulster, which remained with Britain.

The Ireland into which I was born was relatively homogenous, with a strong sense of community, little natural wealth and struggling to maintain its viabil-

---

* Aogán Ó Rathaille, "Is fada liom oíche fhirfhliuich" from *An Duanaire: Poems of the Dispossessed*, ed. Seán Ó Tuama, transl. Thomas Kinsella ("It is bitterness through my heart they have left no trace").

ity. I was brought up on a farm in a city. Because of the central importance of agriculture for employment and exports, we were slow to realise the potential of an export-oriented industrial base, or that the future of the country would lie largely in the development of its towns and cities. We valued education, we played and followed sport — in my case especially Gaelic Games and soccer — and family and religion played a big part in all our lives.

As far as I was concerned and in the inner city in which I live, greater employment opportunities, better working conditions and improved housing, health and social welfare, as well as a drug- and crime-free environment, were and are the priorities. Initially, I was a trade union activist, more than I was a political one, and if there is any group of citizens to whom Ireland owes much of its present prosperity it is the trade union wing of the labour movement.

Joining the EEC gave us a European identity that took us out from under the shadow of Britain and enabled a much healthier relationship to emerge. We were of course on the side of Northern Nationalists, but not approving from any quarter the horrific violence, which hit our capital city twice, as well as Monaghan, with terrible force. Gradually, we came to realise that there are two communities and traditions that have to be peacefully accommodated.

We have learnt and are still learning from our mistakes. Overoptimistic expectations of the EEC in the 1970s led to a stagnant economy for much of the 1980s. But since we collectively took decisive remedies from 1987, we have not looked back. Indeed, we have astonished ourselves at the huge pace of progress, which has catapulted us towards the front line of the global economy. We are tackling as rapidly as possible the big backlog in infrastructure. Our self-confidence is also reflected in culture and sport.

There are, to be sure, big pressures in our society. Our success is attracting people from other countries to work here. We now need to see ourselves not just as a pluralist society but as a multicultural one. The best qualities of the Irish are natural ability, tolerance, friendliness and sociability and an instinctive egalitarianism and solidarity. Our instincts are non-confrontational and pragmatic, because we know how tenaciously we fight when we are confronted. We are naturally optimistic and our people are prepared to work very hard, once there is a point to it and a reasonable reward. We have a unique opportunity for progress, now that we have the means to solve our most pressing problems. The dreams of our patriots are finally coming true.

The peace process is a marvellous boost to the country. We look forward to the challenge of working more closely with both communities in the North, as well as with other parts of these islands. We are also strengthening Ireland's international engagement, in the United Nations, with the applicant countries of Eastern Europe and with the developing world, because our whole history over the past 2,000 years indicates that we are an adventurous and outward-looking people, seeking not to conquer, but to carry a message of hope and solidarity.

Mike Allen

Mike Allen is General Secretary of the Irish Labour Party. He was General Secretary of the Irish National Organisation of the Unemployed (INOU) for 12 years.

Sometimes I want to explain it all: my grandparents' reasons for leaving; my mother's half-remembered rebel songs; my father's reluctance to tell the stories; my own reasons for coming back; the decision to stay. Other times I just leave it stand — why should I have to prove my right to my nationality? There is an ambivalence about asserting my sense of being Irish.

"My family had more honourable reasons for leaving than yours did for staying," I once told the scion of a Galway merchant family who accused me of, "coming over here with your English, welfare state assumptions." But I knew I had let myself down by saying it, by feeling I had to. I had accepted the bigoted assumption that the value of your opinions depends upon your nationality.

My family did not make much of the stories of our departure from Ireland. I only heard the full account years after I had made my home here. Perhaps my father, particularly after 1969, felt that to retell these stories would ignite old hatreds. After I moved to Ireland, my mother sent me a fragile, yellowed newspaper page from before the First World War. It had a picture of a group of men in Irish Volunteer uniforms carrying flags. One faceless figure is circled in blue pen with "your grandfather" scrawled beside it. I had never known such history existed, let alone that we possessed its relics.

My grandfather had been a rare thing, a draughtsman in Harland and Wolff who was also a Catholic. He also took photographs of the shipyard and my aunt has one of him standing beside the hull of the *Titanic*. In 1922, during anti-Catholic riots, my grandfather was one of those driven out. There are stories of my pregnant grandmother escaping to a safehouse in the Antrim Glens with the children while safe passage was arranged to Glasgow.

My grandfather's brothers, who had also worked in Belfast, fled south to Dublin at the same time. My grandparents talked of coming back to Ireland but they never did. My father was born a few weeks after they arrived in Glasgow and grew up there. My mother's family had arrived in Glasgow from Antrim over a generation earlier. My father always accused them of acclimatising — they celebrated Hogmanay instead of Christmas.

I was born in Wales because that was where my father was working. I went to school on the edge of the coal and steel belt of what was then industrial South Wales. It was an area which had retained its Welshness against wave after wave of economic immigration. National identity in school was, to borrow from the Irish debate, a matter of "Welsh, Welsher and Welshest". I didn't play rugby, couldn't speak Welsh and couldn't sing. It was made very clear to me that I was not Welsh. Being Catholic — sorry, Roman Catholic — had something to do with it too.

For a variety of reasons, my sisters and my brother did not experience this dismissal of any claim to Welshness and they all feel some affinity to the country of their upbringing. It is difficult to reconstruct how a sense of "being Irish" developed. After all, I don't play GAA or speak Irish — and I still can't sing.

Then, once I moved to Ireland, there was my family's yielding up of the stories which made sense of my want to be here. After I lost my job and decided to stay and work against unemployment rather than return to London, my sense of being Irish hardened from a feeling into a commitment, a loyalty.

In two years' time, I will have lived here half my life. I've already lived here longer than I've lived anywhere else. I carry an Irish passport. My children's Irishness is not disputed. But I still speak in an accent that many Irish people consider "English". For the twelve years I worked with organisations campaigning against unemployment, people said my words "gave voice to the voiceless". Once, as I stood in O'Connell Street addressing the largest demonstration the Irish National Organisation of the Unemployed ever organised, a drunk made his way to the front of the crowd. "Tell that Englishman to go back where he came from," he roared.

There have been more serious challenges to "my right" to "come over here and tell us what to do". It makes me sad and angry that a country which sent so many of its people to live in other countries retains these exclusive assumptions. Former President Mary Robinson's talk of the Irish diaspora improved things. The brief glory of our football team and "'allo, moy name's Tow-nee Cascarino" made a difference too.

Now our streets, shops and cafés are filling up with French and Spanish and Nigerian and Romanian voices. We are deeply challenged to accept the participation of people with different voices in our society — without first submitting them to the test of their Irishness. Until we face that challenge, and stop trying to cut people out, I will continue to feel unease about whether I am explaining or justifying.

Moosajee Bhamjee

Dr Moosajee Bhamjee is a consultant psychiatrist in Our Lady's Hospital, Ennis, County Clare. Born in Pietermaritzburg, South Africa, he moved to Ireland in 1965. He represented Clare as a Labour TD from 1992 to 1997.

I am writing these words to give a personal account of how I feel about being Irish in the year 2000.

I moved to Ireland in 1965 as a medical student and upon marriage took up permanent residence. I am a naturalised Irish citizen since 1978, having sworn my loyalty to the State in a court of law. This certificate allowed me to stand for election to Dáil Éireann. Thus I was elected as the first Labour TD for Clare since the early 1950s, and became known as the first "Indian" in the Dáil. Though I was born in South Africa, my parental ancestry is Indian.

From being a relatively unknown student and doctor it can be surprising to be recognised in all the villages of Ireland and to be called "Bhamjee", a name I personally adopted when answering the phone or introducing myself to people. I seem to have lost my first name since becoming a TD, but I am proud to have retained my original name and not adjusted or changed it.

Today one can buy the spices to cook a curry in any supermarket and to see people eating "curry and rice" regularly at home shows how the staple diet has changed; pastas, spaghetti and chow mein are also cooked in many homes. But one must love burgers and fish fingers, and the Sunday roast is still the most important meal of the week when all the family are together.

I am proud to have read Irish history, Irish folklore and Irish literature but I still have not been able to grasp the Irish language, nor have I been able to pronounce any phrases in Irish; my wife Clare was able to help the children with their Irish homework. I have a good interest in sport and like to read about the national team and the major sporting heroes and attend as many GAA matches as possible. Presently I am coaching the local under-16 girls' football team. To be passionate for County Clare comes naturally to me and I can be heard roaring at all their matches. Whenever Ireland play against South Africa, the land of my birth, I find my loyalty is to Ireland. My children speak fluent Irish and, being born in Ireland, do not feel different in any way, and they think and feel Irish. But I feel guilty about not increasing their knowledge of my ancestry and teaching them my language.

I find it hard not to be honest and straightforward and to speak openly and frankly about my feelings over certain issues, be it in a group or at official meetings. Thus I find it hard to meet people who will be critical over a decision pre- and post-meeting but will never express their views at the meeting, when it matters most. There is still a lot of "*plámás*" at meetings, which can be annoying. The person who speaks openly is seen as being odd or strange. Also, meetings rarely start on time and this can be frustrating as other appointments might be scheduled and people left waiting, or other appointments cancelled; to accept this as "normality" I find difficult to accommodate. To comply with modern bureaucratic needs, people are still long-winded and irrelevant rather than being succinct, to the point, getting the message across in the minimal of words.

I love reading my *Irish Times*, as it contains analysis, factual information and international news, but there is no substance to the Sunday newspapers, even though they have a lot of print. So I have lost interest in the Sunday papers, which I loved reading and looked forward to in the 1960s and 1970s.

Driving a big fast car seems to be the fashion at present, but I still enjoy driving a small car with a low horsepower, which motors along at a steady pace. Unfortunately, the Sunday drive is not as popular as it used to be.

Being Irish can be worrying with regards to drinking and drug abuse, as both are occurring at a young age and people do not seem to be able to control themselves when drinking. I am also concerned with the increased number of racist attacks and vandalism throughout the country.

It is good to see magazines writing on "taboo subjects" like mental illness, divorce, euthanasia, and now people are willing to discuss these topics. I am pleased to have helped bring divorce into Ireland, as people now have a second chance and a new beginning.

I find it difficult to make people see ahead or a different viewpoint. Thus the thinking is still confined, narrow and indoctrinated. I enjoy meeting the person who is different, as society does not cater for them; being eccentric seems like an abnormality now and the "village character" is gone. It is all about conforming.

Esmond Birnie

Dr Esmond Birnie, MLA, is an Ulster Unionist Member of the Northern Ireland Assembly for South Belfast, Chairman of the Committee for the Department of Higher and Further Education, Training and Employment and UUP spokesman on North-South and the British-Irish Council.

I am grateful as a unionist to have this opportunity to explain some of my feelings about "being Irish". At the outset I concede that as someone who was born in Edinburgh, I have as much (or as little) right to be considered Irish as the 1916 leader James Connolly, who was also born in the Scottish capital.

First of all, some negative points. What "Irishness" does not mean to me. It has no necessary connection to republicanism in either its classical (i.e. anti-monarchical) or modern Irish (i.e. physical force tradition) forms. I would also reject the old perceived one-to-one congruence of Irishness with Catholicism, nationalism, Gaelic speaking and certain types of sport and music. It is not that I have an irrational prejudice against any of those forms of cultural expression. It is simply that I do not want them to be the exclusive property of one political camp. Sadly, traditional Irishness has sometimes been reduced to hatred for England or Britain. This is another thing which I would repudiate.

Positively, I acknowledge a certain level of "geographical Irishness". I have lived on this island for most of my life and this gives me a certain sense of space and locality, which is shared with others, be they nationalists, republicans or unionists. Furthermore, the history of the island is, to some extent, my history too. Heroes and hero worship may have become somewhat discredited in the period since Thomas Carlyle. Nevertheless, I still admire the evangelism of Patrick, Burke's liberal conservatism, the symphonies of C.V. Stanford, Wellington and Montgomery's victories, Lord Kelvin's science, Thomas Sinclair's liberal unionism, the constitutionalism of Kevin O'Higgins and the paintings of Daniel Maclise and John Lavery.

Any valid, valuable and viable sense of Irishness must acknowledge the East–West links. The island has so often benefited from infusions of talent from the outside. Conversely, Irish people of whatever hue have as emigrants so often stamped their impact on the wider world. (Incidentally, this is one reason why both Northern Ireland and the Republic of Ireland should show generosity to genuine asylum seekers.) To take one very tangible example: architecture. A.W. Pugin decorated Westminster's Houses of Parliament and also designed a large number of the chapels and cathedrals of Catholic Ireland.

Finally, there is no incompatibility between my sense of Irishness and my Britishness. The geographical, historical or cultural Irishness which I feel can be accommodated within the diversity of the United Kingdom, which has worked fairly well for centuries as a multinational state. As Tony Blair said recently (28 March 2000): "Blood alone does not define our national identity. How can we separate out the Celtic, the Roman, the Saxon, the Norman, the Huguenot, the Jewish, the Asian and the Caribbean and all the other nations that have come and settled here?"

Tony Blair

Tony Blair is Prime Minister of the United Kingdom.

Ireland is in my blood. My mother was born in the flat above her grandmother's hardware shop in the main street of Ballyshannon in Donegal. She lived there as a child, started school there and only moved when her father died, her mother remarried and they crossed the water to Glasgow. But I still spent virtually every childhood summer holiday, up to when the troubles really took hold, usually at Rosnowlagh. It was there in the seas off the Irish coast that I learned to swim and my father took me to my first pub, a remote little house in the country, for a Guinness, a taste I have never forgotten and which is always a pleasure to repeat.

Even now in my constituency of Sedgefield, which at one time had 30 pits or more, all now gone, virtually every community remembers that its roots lie in Irish migration to the mines of Britain. When we look around other parts of Britain, we see the influence of the Irish people in almost every facet of British life. We have a shared history, some of it painful, but by the same token some of it good. So like it or not, the British and the Irish are irredeemably linked.

But we need not be prisoners of our history. My generation in Britain sees Ireland differently today and probably the same generation in Ireland feels differently about Britain. We can understand the emotions generated by Northern Ireland's troubles, but we cannot really believe, in the twenty-first century, that there is not a better way forward to the future than through murder, terrorism and sectarian hatred. Thankfully, we are now beginning to see the fruits of the Good Friday Agreement. There remains a long way to go, but little by little we can draw together in closer mutual co-operation.

The changes in Ireland have been seen by all across Europe. Today Ireland has a modern, open economy. After long years of emigration, people are coming back for the quality of life offered. Ireland is a part of Europe's mainstream and has some of the best business brains in the world. Ireland has also become a leader in popular culture, bringing us U2, The Corrs, Boyzone, Westlife and B*witched. We hope that the Irish people can see the changes taking place in Britain as we emerge from our post-Empire malaise, modernising and becoming confident of our future as we once were of our past.

It is precisely the dramatic changes in both countries that allow us to see the possibilities of change in our relationship with each other. It will require vision, but no more than the vision that has transformed Ireland. It will require imagination, but no more than that shown by the British people over the last few years.

Old ways are changing between London and Dublin. And this can spur the change and healing in Northern Ireland too. The old notions of Unionist supremacy and of narrow nationalism are gradually having their fingers prised from their grip on the future. My point is very simple. Those urges to belong, divergent as they are, can live together more easily if we, Britain and Ireland, can live closer together too. Down through the centuries, Ireland and Britain have inflicted too much pain on each other. But now the UK and Ireland as two modern countries can try to put our histories behind us and try to forgive and forget those age-old enmities.

We have both grown up. A new generation is in power in each country. We now have a real opportunity to put our relations on a completely new footing, not least through working together in Europe. I know that is what our peoples want and I believe we can deliver it. Our ties are already rich and diverse:

- The UK is the largest market for Irish goods. Ireland is our fifth most important market in the world;

- In trade unions, professional bodies and the voluntary sector, our people work together to help their communities;

- In culture, sport and academic life, there is an enormous crossover. Our theatres are full of Irish plays. Our television is full of Irish actors and pre-senters. The Irish national football team has a few English accents too;

- Above all, at the personal level, millions of Irish people live and work in Britain, and hundreds of thousands of us visit Ireland every year.

But none of this threatens our separate identities. Co-operation does not mean losing distinctiveness. What we seek is a new dimension to our relationship — a real partnership between Governments and peoples which will engage our societies at every level.

What I welcome above all is that, after keeping the United Kingdom and Ireland apart for so long, Northern Ireland is now helping to bring us closer together. But I do not believe Northern Ireland can or should any longer define the relationship between our countries. Our common interests, what we can achieve together go much, much wider than that. Our two countries can look to the future with confidence in our separate ways. But we will be stronger and more prosperous working together. I believe we should confront the challenge of the twenty-first century with confidence and together give our children the future they deserve.

John Bradley

*John Bradley is a Professor at the Economic and So-
cial Research Institute (ESRI) in Dublin, where his
research centres on European issues. He has carried
out a wide range of international consultancy assignments for the Irish government, the European
Commission and other international organisations.*

A child's view of identity and place is centred on its immediate and familiar
environment. Which of us in middle age, when rummaging in dusty attics,
has not happened on a storybook with our name written in a childish hand,
followed by something like: *Dublin, Ireland, Europe, the World, the Universe*?
To a child, the rest of the world is seen as through the wrong end of a tele-
scope, and other places and identities are remote and incomprehensible. As
children, we do not choose our identity consciously. A real sense of what it
means to be Irish only comes with age and experience, when we interact with
people of other nationalities, cultures and identities.

For most of my adult life, I have worked as an economist. This is a challenging and attractive profession, built on language and concepts that invite —
even compel — international comparisons. My work takes me mainly to
Northern Ireland, to the countries of Europe, both East and West, and I have
seen a little of the USA. As I grew older, I gradually came to develop an understanding of what it meant to be Irish.

To be Irish is a bit like being in an inter-tidal zone between alternative
worlds. We are suspended between two cultures: one, British, made us citizens
of the modern hard-nosed urban world of trade and commerce; the other, a
gentler Gaelic heritage, made us spiritual and rural. We live in a society that is
at once traditional and modern, and the tension between these forces serves to

animate our thought and artistic expression. We gave up our language (a deep symbol of our uniqueness), yet retained a strong and distinct cultural identity that we express (however imperfectly) in two languages. As a child I learned the names of flowers, crops and animals in Irish and the dry facts of commerce, geography and science in English.

We are comfortable in the global economy, yet are in many ways inward-looking. We are both insiders and outsiders. We can be deeply religious, with a tendency towards asceticism, yet our hedonism has been exported all over the world in the phenomenon of ubiquitous Irish Pubs. We leave Ireland in droves, but usually return.

This delicate balance between different Irish cultures has interesting consequences, even in the dismal science of economics. Some years ago, I gave a lecture in Ljubljana on the Irish experience of foreign direct investment, and as I related the story of how our manufacturing sector has come to be largely owned by foreign multinationals, I became aware of how unpalatable the Slovenians found this notion. Afterwards, my Slovenian colleagues explained to me that they had not won independence in order to give their economy away to foreigners. How convenient, I thought, to live on an island far away from the battlefields of marauding armies of empires in conflict!

This is the best time to be Irish, when our rapid economic progress has catapulted us from the role of poor laggard to successful Tiger. During the 1980s, we huddled in our wet and windy island and dreamed of being Dutch or Danes or Finns or Norwegians; anything but facing into the abject failure of being Irish! Today we have become a development role model for the smaller states of Eastern Europe, and the object of much international study and admiration. We would be less than human if we did not enjoy this role, but we know in our hearts that success surprised nobody more than ourselves.

There remains one area of my professional life where my sense of being Irish has failed to be an aid to communication. From the early 1990s, I have carried out research on North–South business opportunities, initially in collaboration with Northern economists. Very quickly I came to realise that this research meant much more to me than merely exploring opportunities for greater trade, growth and profit. It was also about being a tiny part of the process of rebuilding the shattered community of common interests on the island and improving the quality and security of our lives.

With the benefit of hindsight, I should have known that the emergence of more trusting North–South Irish relations from the permafrost of almost 50 years of barely concealed hostility and 25 years of Northern civil unrest was never going to be simple or easy. I came to realise, with increasing dismay, that North–South economic discourse was either kept at a well-intentioned ano-dyne level or risked being misunderstood. At best, suggestions of greater North–South Irish co-operation were regarded by many as unwelcome, un-necessary and unhelpful interference. At worst, they were potentially hostile and threatening acts that struck at the heart of what many thought of as the separate identity of the Northern Irish.

The paradox was that the fossilisation of North–South social and commer-cial relations during most of this century had become so deep and pervasive that — like the air we breathe — it went almost unnoticed. Both regions of Ire-land seemed to have gone their different ways and lost the ability to find a common purpose. Reconciliation of our different Irish identities remains our greatest challenge.

John Bruton

John Bruton TD is the leader of the Fine Gael party in Ireland. He was Taoiseach from 1994 to 1997.

It is important that people who live in Ireland who come from the two main traditions on the island — Unionist and Nationalist — should be reconciled with one another. I do not believe that that can be done other than by accepting legitimacy of any allegiance that may be held by any person who lives on the island, once they live here. If one starts to use heritage as the means of defining Irishness, one then proceeds to exclude from the definition of "true Irish" some people who have every right to be in Ireland.

For me, the idea of "being Irish" means living and working on the island of Ireland. I have difficulty with any other concept of "being Irish", because it might exclude some group that is living on the island of Ireland.

I consider an Orangeman living in North Down, a Pakistani-born person living in Ballyhaunis, County Mayo or a Gaelic-speaking resident of Connemara all to be equally Irish, because all are living in Ireland.

I do not believe that to be Irish one has to call oneself exclusively Irish. There are people who live and work in, and contribute to Ireland, who might consider themselves to be British as well as Irish. I do not believe that having a British allegiance makes them any less Irish. Nor do I believe that someone who lives in Ireland can assert that they are not Irish. Once they live and work here they are, to my mind at least, Irish by definition.

I do not believe that it is essential to have a particular political allegiance to be Irish. One can be Irish and believe in the separation of Ireland from all other political entities, whether from the European Union or from the United Kingdom. But one can also be Irish and accept the association of Ireland with either the European Union or the United Kingdom.

One does not have to belong to a particular linguistic, ethnic or religious tradition to be truly Irish. People of the Gaelic linguistic and ethnic tradition have been moving to and fro between Ireland and Scotland over the last 2,000 years. Scotland did not become part of Ireland just because a large part of it was settled by Gaelic speakers from Ireland in the first millennium. North Eastern Ireland did not become Scotland just because a large part of it was settled by people originating from Scotland and the borders in the seventeenth century. Scotland and Ireland are both separate and together.

There is, of course, a distinction between "being Irish" and "being of Irish heritage". There are many people, all over the world, who are proud of their Irish heritage. But many people in Ireland have heritage that originates in other countries too. Many Irish surnames originated in France or Britain.

Irishness is comprehensive and inclusive, ancient and ever-changing. Irishness is a growing thing. It does not stand still.

Pat Buckley

Bishop Pat Buckley is a dissident Catholic bishop. He was removed from his parish by Cardinal Cathal Daly for being overly involved in community work and for criticising the Catholic Church in the media. Since 1986 he has had an independent ministry based at Larne and is the unofficial chaplain to Ireland's increasing number of alienated Catholics.

When Cardinal Cathal Daly offered me a parish in California in 1986 and thousands of pounds to get there, he was not allowing for the fact that, psychologically speaking, I would be incapable of living happily anywhere except in Ireland! I am absolutely Irish — totally and even compulsively in love with the country, its people, its history, its heritage. During a brief sojourn as a priest in Wales during 1976 and 1977, I was emotional and broken-hearted for my homeland, which was only three hours away by boat and 30 minutes away by air. I want to live and die in Ireland and be buried in Irish soil and I will regard my life as having being worthwhile if it has made some aspect of Ireland a little better.

As I write this piece in May 2000, what are my feelings about being Irish? As I look backwards from here, I have a sense of pride and shame. As I look to the future, I have a sense of determined hope.

Pride and Shame

I am first of all proud of my Ireland. I am proud of the beautiful island on which I live. I love its mountains and valleys and bogs. I love its powerful skies with their mixture of calming blue and stormy cloud. I love the rare summer sun that fills me with hope and joy but I equally love those winter nights when

I lie in bed in my Donegal cottage listening to roof-raising winds and driving rain.

I love the thoughts and memories of the ancient people of my island — the Firbolgs, the Tuatha Dé Danann, the Milesians and the Celts — with their own cultures and religions. My Irish spirituality, thank God, is as much pre-Catholic as it is Catholic and therefore as much anti-Rome as it is pro-Rome! When I stand alone in the middle of the old circular fort and place of druidic worship — Grianán of Aileach at Burt in Donegal — I can almost see the old cowled druids with their staffs and I can almost hear their ancient prayers and I feel as much in touch with my spiritual roots there as I do a few minutes later sitting before the tabernacle in the fine award-winning modern church at the foot of the hill leading to the more ancient spiritual site. I love not only the spirituality of my earliest ancestors, but their battle with the elements, climate and terrain of our island and their part in passing on the beauty that we have.

I am proud of the generations of Irish who resisted invasion and persecution and hardship and famine. I'm proud of Patrick, my namesake, and Brigid — Brigid, who was ordained priest and bishop by St Mel of Longford! I'm proud of the Irish monks for their legacy of learning and art and literature and I'm proud of the Irish missionaries — the early ones who went out to light the lights of learning in dark times and places and the later ones who brought and still bring education and practical help to far-flung places in the globe. I'm proud of the lovely architecture and artefacts our secular and religious forefathers have left us. I'm proud of the radical people in Irish history — the Dean Swifts, the Noel Brownes and latterly the Garrett Fitzgeralds and David Norris.

But I have a strong sense of shame too as I reflect on being Irish. I recognise that we have often been famous or infamous for fighting with each other and more seriously for hurting and killing each other. I feel a sense of shame for all the blood that has been spilled by us Irish during our 800-year-old resistance of "the British" and especially for all the blood we Irish have spilled during the past 30 years in Northern Ireland. I am ashamed of the small-minded Catholicism of the Irish Republic (1922–c.1970) that caused the Republic's Protestant population to shrink from 12 per cent to 3 per cent in too politicians who allowed John Charles McQuaid and the Catholic Hierarchy to govern on their behalf and latterly I am ashamed of all the corruption and brown envelopes in Irish political life.

I am most ashamed of the physical, mental and sexual abuse that went on in our schools and institutions presided over by priests, brothers and nuns and of the cover-up of that abuse at the very highest levels of church and state life. And in the North, I am deeply ashamed of my Protestant and unionist brothers and sisters who presided over 50 years of misrule, injustice and discrimination from 1922 to c.1970. I am ashamed of the Protestant church leaders in the North who did not condemn, from the Gospel perspective, all that injustice. And I am still deeply shamed when I see military trappings hang in Church of Ireland cathedrals and churches and see Anglican and Presbyterian church-men walk with clerical collar and Orange sash. I wonder if they will ever learn to give to God what is God's and to Caesar what is Caesar's.

A Determined Hope

However, as I stand here in May 2000, I am filled with a determined hope. I never thought that I would see Ireland, North and South, change as much as it has in my lifetime. The Republic of Ireland is fast becoming a modern, secular and pluralist state. Old corruptions in politics, judiciary, police, church, etc., are being exposed and eradicated. We are being helped as much culturally as financially by our membership of the European Community. There are big battles ahead — with poverty, with ethnicity, with crime, with drugs — but these are the battles facing every nation in the world.

Northern Ireland has changed unbelievably. Stormont is gone. The B-Specials are gone. The UDR is gone. The RUC is going. Discrimination in housing and employment is becoming a bad memory. Ulster Unionists are sitting down and governing with Sinn Fein. The IRA is involved in a process whose logical outcome is decommissioning. We have cross-border bodies and British/Irish bodies. We have huge investment from Europe, the US and the international community. At last, at long last, the British Lion and the Irish Lamb are lying down together. I believe that we are on the threshold of a new and never-before-seen era of peace, justice and unity.

There has never been a more exciting time to be alive in Ireland. There has never been a more appropriate time for celebrating Irish identity with pride. I am thrilled and feel truly privileged to be a minor oarsman on the ship — *The New Ireland* — that has voyaged through many past storms and is now bearing down on the port of all our dreams. Of course, there are the difficulties of the home straits. Of course, there will be the complex berthing challenge. But like old Simeon of the Gospels I can almost pray:

"Now master, You can let Your servant go in peace."

Anne Cadwallader

Anne Cadwallader was born in London and has lived in Ireland for 19 years. She is a journalist who works in the North for Independent Network News, in Dublin for Ireland on Sunday, and the Irish Echo in New York.

My mother once told me that her father had commissioned a genealogist to investigate our family tree. When he asked for travelling expenses to visit Ireland for further inquiries, he was told not to bother. If our family had any Irish ancestry, then my grandfather decided he would rather not know about it. The implication that I, fairly reasonably, took from this story as a child was that being Irish wasn't something to be terribly proud of.

When I came to History "A" level at school, we had the option of specialising in Irish history. Only one girl in the class did. The rest of us opted out of learning about Cromwell, Drogheda and the potato famine to concentrate on the far more interesting life stories of the Tudors and Stuarts.

So it was hardly surprising that, until my 20s, like many young English people, I never realised that Ireland was different from Scotland and Wales, that it had had its own rebellion and was now independent with its own coinage, stamps and government.

Since then, I have discovered that one branch of the Cadwallader family were particularly bad landlords around Castleblaney, County Monaghan, and that there was once a Cadwallader who served as a Church of Ireland minister in County Wicklow. There were also, of course, the despised maternal ancestors, the Dawsons, of whom I still know next to nothing. So it could be said, although I am indubitably and unashamedly a thoroughgoing cultural product of the British home counties, I do have some Irish blood running in my veins.

I came to Ireland as a tourist in the mid-1970s and, like many Brits before me, fell in love with the countryside, the Murphy's stout, the villages with their quaint pubs that doubled as funeral parlours and the fuchsia hedges of Cork and Kerry.

Five years later, out of sheer curiosity, I visited Belfast at the height of the 1981 hunger strikes. I was horrified and yet fascinated (the classic Aristotelian reaction to tragedy) with this country whose history I had wilfully ignored and whose people were a complete mystery to me. Standing at the memorial to the Bloody Sunday dead in Derry, reading Thomas Kinsella's "Butcher's Dozen", watching a black flag protest in Dublin the day Bobby Sands died and listening to the "Derry Air", I began to realise the enormity of the tragedy that had been visited on these people. I was hooked and six months later, in November 1981, left Bradford in Yorkshire, where I was a trainee journalist, packed all my belongings into the back of the car, drove to Liverpool and onto the ferry to Dublin. I have never looked back or regretted making that journey once.

What I instantly loved about the Irish people I came across in Belfast and Dublin was their intense interest in each other, their warmth, humanity and willingness to take me at face value. The old cliché about the friendliness of Belfast people, even when you ask directions, is actually true.

I came from a somewhat sterile middle-class British environment, where families didn't matter terribly and where the main function of one's life was to amass material acquisitions and make a "good" marriage. My background was dominated by a sense of class and materialism. Ireland seemed a much healthier meritocracy, where your name and money didn't matter nearly as much as if you could tell stories and sing songs and make people laugh.

I was enchanted by the informality, the spontaneity of the people I met in Belfast. Also by their consuming interest in the world around them, by their devotion to causes other than the purely materialistic and their holding tight to principles, not crass pragmatism.

Something in Irish music struck a chord deep down. I liked it that working class people had a cultural life and positive pride in their national identity, so totally lacking in the working class estates of England where lager-lout Britishness is violent and unattractive.

In the nearly 20 years I have lived in Ireland, I have only extremely rarely experienced anything remotely anti-British or racist. On the one or, at most, two occasions it has happened, other Irish people have been mortified with embarrassment on my behalf. My husband's family, his children by a previous marriage and even his ex-wife and her parents, have welcomed me into their lives with open arms and I count them amongst my best friends with whom I look forward to spending the rest of my days. My own brother and sisters have similarly felt at home in both Belfast and Dublin. When you look at our experience, it makes you wonder about those tragic generations when our peoples have been at war with each other.

Of course, it's unrealistic to look at an entire people with rose-tinted spectacles. With increasing wealth has come an increase in materialism and the anti-foreigner racism which is so disturbing as some Irish people reject the kind of "economic refugees" they have themselves been for the past four centuries.

It's also impossible to look at the North without criticising the dreadful sectarianism that has blighted community relations for so long. I find the Orange Order, as an institution, very hard to take. The concept of dismissing Catholicism as blasphemy is abhorrent to me. I will probably get into trouble for saying this, but when unionists come to terms with the Irishness in their identity, while retaining a loyalty to the past and to Britain, they may find a security and comfort they currently lack.

I see neither unionists nor nationalists as "victim" communities. Both have been shamefully treated by the colonial power, much blood has been spilled and agonies endured unnecessarily, but both can survive and flourish as equally valid expressions of their different traditions. If there is any self-indulgent "victimhood" arising out of the miserable past centuries of ignorance, fear and violence, then the British seem to me to fit the bill best with their arrogant assumptions, racism and patronising wailings about having to "endure the ghastly Irish".

They will never know what they've missed, will they?

Gregory Campbell

Alderman Gregory Campbell, a member of the Democratic Unionist Party, represents East London-derry. He is the security spokesman for the DUP and has written a number of booklets on the question of discrimination against the Protestant community in Northern Ireland.

Who Are the Irish?

The problem with Irishness is not that it is traditionally viewed as being Roman Catholic, Nationalist and Gaelic and therefore those of us who are none of these feel left out. The problem is that Irishness is something that is celebrated by IRISH PEOPLE, and Irish people are, by definition, part of the Irish Nation. There are many of us who, although we live on the Island, are not part of that Irish Nation. Quite often, commentators (and some politicos) say Unionists are Irish but have been prevented from celebrating their Irishness by the exclusive nature of that Irish tradition. Put another way, they say that if the factors that they believe Protestants object to in the Irish tradition can be addressed and alleviated then there will be no barrier to those Protestants joining in the newly INCLUSIVE sense of Irishness.

Recent Changes

This ill-judged and completely incorrect notion has permeated a lot of thinking behind the entire development of politics in Northern Ireland. The idea that there is something that inhibits Protestants from wholeheartedly endorsing Ireland and all things Irish has been propagated for decades. This is why in recent years there have been moves to broaden the scope of celebrations on St

Patrick's day, to make the Irish language less of a political tool and to make the Republic of Ireland a more secular country.

Rediscovering "Lost" Roots

All of this is part of a wider political notion whereby Unionists in Northern Ireland need to be persuaded that there is little encouragement for them in the future of the United Kingdom. At the same time, if there are "significant" changes going on in the Republic which make it less offensive to those Protestants, then there is much more likelihood of some of those same Protestants "rediscovering" their lost Irishness as they find out that perhaps life in the new Ireland isn't so bad after all.

Living in Hope

This is absolute poppycock and has been and still is peddled as a realistic long-term hope by many who should know better. These people believe that in the early part of the twentieth century, the Protestant fear of Home Rule being Rome Rule in Ireland was the only factor in the political equation. They also believe that if the unacceptable and antiquated versions of Irishness can be jettisoned, then Protestants will accept this new identity.

Ulster is as Irish as Canada is American

The reality of course is so radically different. The sense of Ulster's place within the United Kingdom is much stronger than just a religious or political choice. Put another way, if the Irish Republic were to declare itself a Protestant Nation, we still would not advocate joining it. If the green shamrocks were all to be painted Orange it would not change anything and if King William's portrait were to be hung on every Town Hall in the Republic, WE STILL WOULD NOT WANT TO BE PART OF IT. Irishness comes from being part of the Irish Nation. Just as being American is derived from being a citizen of the United States of America. Most Canadians take exception to being called Americans, not because they are not from the land mass of North America but because they are from a different country to the USA. Unionists feel the same way about Irishness. Of course we are Irish in the sense of being born and living on the Island of Ireland, but we are part of a separate country, the United Kingdom.

End the Cold War

Any attempt (and there have been numerous) to remove our citizenship, our nationality, our unique British cultural outlook and identity will be resisted. This is why the makeover of Irishness is totally meaningless in the context of trying to attract people who belong to a different nation. When this is understood Irish people should be able to comprehend why Unionists view with so much suspicion the cross-border bodies which have been set up under the Belfast Agreement as they seek to draw our two countries together as one. The cold war between our two countries should have ended a long time ago. Any international co-operation would of course be welcome, but the problem that many of those who declare themselves to be Irish have with that is that in almost every instance there is mutual co-operation with no long-term aim of absorption or amalgamation in mind. Now there's a radical idea for Irish people to give consideration to!

Norah Casey

Norah Casey is Editor in Chief of The Irish Post *in London. She lectures internationally on the media and communication skills, does weekly radio and regular television slots on Northern Irish affairs and has published widely in national newspapers and publications.*

I left Ireland at the tender age of 17 swearing I would be back by the end of the year. I remember this friend of the family picking me up from the airport. I knew she had been brought up in Dublin but she spoke with a strong Scottish brogue. I asked her how long she had been away from home. To my shock, she replied 15 years, adding with a laugh that she only intended staying for a year or so. Funnily enough no warning bells sounded; I just thought how sad it was that she was exiled for such a long time. So here I am having lived more years in Britain than in Ireland. I've clocked up 22 years now and still say on 31 December each year that it will be my last. It's not that I don't enjoy my life here; in many ways it's far better than it might have been back home. Its just that unsettled feeling of living in a country that's not your own; worse in fact, a country that for most of my life has been in conflict with my own.

I was a '60s baby, brought up in an Ireland that was almost exclusively Irish. I remember my best friend's cousins would arrive from England speaking in a strange manner yet calling themselves Irish. We used to laugh at their posh English accents and claims of Irish roots. But I also remember a feeling of inferiority to these well-dressed and well-spoken boys who lived across the water. Apart from their infrequent visits, my early years were spent in the company of Irish people. My infrequent trips home from Scotland as an impoverished student were strange and unsettling. Conversations were stilted and limited. After five years in Scotland, I was probably the most exotic visitor to my little corner of Dublin.

Now I find myself at the helm of a "little Ireland" in London. *The Irish Post* is the flagship publication in Smurfit Media's stable — a wonderful community newspaper that has been around for 30 years. We employ predominantly Irish people, write about Irish events, review Irish plays and attend most of the many Irish social events in Britain. It's a wonderful home from home. When I came here as Editor, my father and I had something to talk about for the first time in 18 years. I could relate to my brothers and sisters (all but one of whom live in Ireland). I knew the latest gossip, the tribunal trivia, when Charlie Haughey sneezed. I rediscovered my Irishness through *The Irish Post* and found opinions I didn't even know I had. Since then, I have seen the same transformation happen to our unsuspecting new recruits — usually second generation Irish people with vague memories of childhood holidays on an uncle's farm. The extraordinary thing is that many of our staff speak with English accents, but not only do they have an enormous knowledge base about Irish history and politics, they are usually more up to date on the Irish music scene than the average Irish man or woman.

Its amazing that a whole generation of young Irish here in Britain are more Irish than the Irish themselves, yet were neither born nor brought up in Ireland. To them the jibes about "plastic paddies" are demeaning and hurtful. Why should where you were born dictate who you are? They were born of Irish parents and have retained a strong cultural link with the Ireland of their parent's generation. In a way, I have a stronger affinity with them than I do with the new generation of Irish people who I meet in my frequent business trips back home.

I receive no end of comments about how the Irish are taking over Britain; but in reality, given the numbers of Irish people here, it is hardly surprising. Britain is home to nearly five million people of Irish descent with around one million first generation (the largest number outside of Ireland). My non-Irish friends find the whole notion of Irishness amusing when it comes to actors like Pierce Brosnan and accuse us of laying claim to anyone with even the vaguest of Irish roots. But many famous and influential Irish people haven't always found it beneficial to boast of their heritage as they climbed to the top. Indeed it is only in recent years that Irish people in business here in Britain have felt comfortable in proclaiming their Irishness. Each year, *The Irish Post* awards seek to honour Irish men and women who have excelled here in Britain. Previous winners read like a who's who of the arts and entertainment industry. Recent award recipients include Kathy Burke, Patrick Bergin, Ralph Fiennes (and his entire family), Caroline Aherne, Niamh Cusack, Fiona Shaw, David O'Leary, Roy Keane, Steve Collins, Eamonn Holmes, Dermot O'Leary, Shauna Lowry, Fergus Sweeny, Fergal Keane, Craig Doyle and Terry Wogan.

Ireland's phenomenal economic growth has brought a new confidence to Irish people at home and abroad. For the past six years, Ireland has been the fastest growing economy in the OECD. Decades of mass emigration have been replaced by net immigration and unemployment by virtually full employment. As evidence of its success at the leading edge of technological development, the OECD recently declared Ireland as the world's number one exporter of software products — a tremendous achievement for a country of its size and history. The effects of the Celtic Tiger have been felt the world over, but particularly here in Britain, where so many Irish people have made their home.

Ireland's booming economy has been matched by an impressive growth in the scale and influence of Irish business people in Britain. Companies House can provide a database of some 11,000 Irish directors of British-based companies. Research conducted by Smurfit Media two years ago showed Irish high-fliers were disproportionately represented at the top of British businesses. This highly skilled and well-educated group of Irish people have bucked the trend and overturned many of the stereotypical images of Irish people as all brawn and no brains. I don't believe we need make any apology for claiming some of the best of Britain's business brains and artistic talent as our own; Ireland needs its heroes and heroines here in Britain. Young Irish people growing up in Britain need role models to emulate. They need to be reassured that today's Irish expat is a far cry from the stereotypical images suffered by their parents and grandparents.

It's a far cry from those days when those infamous "No Blacks, No Dogs, No Irish" signs graced the doors of British pubs. For one thing, the pub is more likely to be managed by an Irish landlord. It's cool to be green at last, even if it's only in the minds of the marketing moguls in the drinks industry. Being Irish in Britain has become easier over time, especially for my generation. There are those who live here who will never integrate into the community or feel they are part of British society. It comes from living in a country you believe to be not only foreign but the enemy. And in turn, Britain hasn't treated them well. Many older Irish people suffer appalling health and social problems — the worst of all other ethnic minority groups and the host population. It is a hard legacy for the generation who lived here during the worst of the bombings. They learned to stay with their own, keep their heads down and to distrust officials of any kind (which is why they have the lowest take-up of GP services and social benefits). The tragedy is that many of that generation also feel let down by the new, improved Ireland. They got left behind over the decades, and no longer harbour a dream of returning home because today's Ireland is as foreign to them as Britain was all those years ago. It's not surprising that Arlington House in Camden, home to 130 men with an average stay of 35 years, is the biggest group of homeless Irishmen in Europe.

So being Irish is all of those things to me — the rich and famous who give us our heroes and heroines, the business brains who pave the way for the next generation and the residents of Arlington House, long forgotten heroes in their own way. I had a secretary once who was Afro-Caribbean; she lived in Peckham in South East London, an area rich in multicultural inhabitants. She told me once that she rarely ventured into the more affluent areas of London because she felt so exposed, being the only black face walking down the street. I have never felt that sense of difference where the colour of your skin immediately sets you apart from those around you. For me, it is the moment I open my mouth that my difference is exposed. In Britain it sets me apart as being Irish and all that brings with it, yet in Ireland I am deemed to have a British hint to my brogue, which brings with it a whole different set of negative perceptions. I no longer live in that twilight zone between Britain and Ireland. I still promise myself that I will once again live on Irish soil, but for now I am an Irishwoman who lives in London, comfortable and confident in that label. It has taken nearly two decades, however, for me to come to terms with that.

Mary Boylan Clarke

Mary Boylan Clarke lives in County Donegal. She is a mother of four, a schoolteacher, loves gardening and is a member of An Taisce.

There is a landscape in which I function. It is where I was born and into which I will finally be laid. Within this landscape there are many paths. These paths are my personal maps. Some I will never walk again. Some I will revisit and hopefully some are yet to be explored. For me, this landscape has been nurturing. It forms the backdrop to my Irishness. It is Donegal. Maybe I am Donegal first and Irish after that.

Had I been born in any other part of Ireland, I am certain that the person I am today would be different. Having a father in the Garda, there were a few short moves for our family, but always within Donegal. I remember clearly my first day at school in the Falcarragh Gaeltacht. The Irish language became second nature to me. When I was nine years old, we as a family had to transfer to East Donegal to Newtowncunningham in the Lagan area. There the culture was noticeably different. There was no use of Irish and at school they said we were from "the back country". But there was for us an excitement about having Derry on our doorstep. There was the fear and excitement of going through customs. You could buy Mars Bars there and Derry was always full of sailors.

Near where we lived was the local Orange Hall. From there we could hear the beating of the drums and the swirl of the pipes coming up to the Twelfth. We even stepped along in the Parade because our neighbour Tommy Logan was in the march. We children of "the back country" saw nothing sinister in any of these events. Later when in 1969 I met my first convoy of armoured cars outside Omagh, I cried all the way to Dublin.

Our stay in the Lagan was short. When we left, our neighbours told us we were going to "the back country". And happily we did come back to the Gaeltacht, to Carrigart in the beautiful Parish of Meevagh. This is the landscape which has been and is my source. The sea, the sky, the contours and the light comfort and nourish my spirit and my mind.

Australia gave me space to contemplate my Irishness. The state of being Irish bestowed on me a special mantle. It gave me a status. Sometimes that very acceptance of me and the inclusiveness it generated made me feel ashamed. Because it was living there that gave me my close encounters with racism. Ironically in our own newly found prosperity that same brand of racism is alive and well and thriving here in Ireland. This strikes me as our greatest new challenge. It is now our time to embrace change and celebrate difference. I am optimistic enough to believe we can do it. Clearly there is no acceptable set of excuses for not tackling this problem and tackling mindsets where they exist.

The most jubilant moment for me as a teacher came when access to second level education became the norm in 1969. Of course it was a difficult birth and there are still many gaps to fill, but ignorance can no longer be the excuse for injustice. We now need our migrants and asylum-seekers. We of all people should know better.

Yet for many being Irish has not been so good. In moments of quiet reflection come thoughts of my people who were forced to leave their own places, our emigrant population transplanted to so many alien soils, those who left school before they reached their teens and for whom survival meant being torn from roots, family and friends. What tortured thoughts these families lived with in realisation that they might never meet again. I am confident that our present generation never need suffer those cruel wrenches of our past.

My special wish is for our language to survive. For me, it is the key to who we are. It is where we find our laughter and our tears, our hopes and our fears. Perhaps I, like many others, had to leave Ireland to come to this realisation.

Our language is our uniqueness; it is at the core for me of what being Irish is all about.

There is a perversity in Irishness too! Recently, when trying to find my way to Donegal Airport, I cursed the roads, the signage and the traffic all the way. My modern daughter reminded me that this is part of our special charm — putting an airport where it is hard to find.

To me, being Irish and Donegal Irish is about shared experiences, invisible connections and having the *craic*. It is about being able to feel a laugh or a song coming on and going with it. It is about sometimes making a fool of yourself. It is about feeling the bile in your throat when you know that something is just "not fair". It is about going to wakes and standing at graves. It is about tears streaming down your cheeks when Donegal won the Sam Maguire. It is about sunsets and indescribable skyscapes, it is about bogs, mountains and holy places. No one should get too big for their boots in this landscape.

Martin Collins

Photo: Derek Speirs/Report

Martin Collins is a 34-year-old Irish Traveller, work-ing with Pavee Point Travellers Centre. He was a member of the Taskforce on the Traveller Community and has spent 15 years campaigning to improve the quality of life for the Traveller Community.

The very first time I became conscious of my Traveller identity was when I started attending primary school in the mid-seventies. My brother and I were the only two Travellers in the whole school and it was also the first time I had any real contact with the majority population.

When I say this was the first time I became conscious of my Traveller iden-tity, it was not because there was an intercultural curriculum in the school which valued and respected different cultures. In fact and unfortunately we did not and never had an intercultural curriculum, but rather I was reminded I was different in negative ways — by way of discrimination, prejudice and har-assment, not just from other pupils but also from members of staff. Unfortu-nately, discrimination and prejudice is still a big issue for Travellers, both in school and in the wider society.

We Travellers are an indigenous ethnic minority group who have been part of Irish society for centuries. We have our own value system, language, cus-toms and traditions, which makes us identifiable to both ourselves and others. It saddens me to say that the approach this society has taken to Travellers is one of assimilation and rehabilitation. We are perceived as a problem; our cultural identity has been and continues to be rejected and devalued. As a Traveller myself, I feel offended when I am labelled as a problem or someone in need of rehabilitation.

It is important to recognise that Irish society is not mono-cultural; in other words it is not only composed of white settled Catholic people. In fact, this was never the situation. We have always had other distinct cultural, religious and linguistic groups and now we have even more with the arrival of refugees and asylum-seekers and this poses a challenge to us. How do we create a more inclusive anti-racist society, where all cultures and identities are respected and protected?

When asked to introduce myself or describe myself I would always respond by saying I'm an Irish Traveller, because being Irish is also important to me as this is the place where I was born, grew up and now live. It's part of my lived experience. I, like other Travellers, take immense pride in being Irish and this manifests itself in many ways, particularly when other Irish people achieve and have success, whether it's in sport, singing and music, acting, politics, the corporate world and so on. Travellers do rejoice and celebrate in their success. One example that comes to mind was when Ireland played in the 1990 and 1994 World Cups. Every Traveller trailer and house had Irish flags and bunting on it, despite the fact that Travellers could not get into the pubs to watch the matches because of the discrimination and prejudice we have to endure. But this did not discourage us from supporting and celebrating in our country's success.

I am of the opinion that you can have dual or multiple identities; for example, you have Irish Jews, Irish Travellers, Irish Catholics and Irish Protestants and there are many more. It's for the groups themselves to decide what is their primary identity, but for me, first and foremost is being a Traveller. That is my primary identity and while I felt immense pride when Ireland competed in the World Cup and Steve Collins won his world boxing title, it did not come close to how I felt when Francie Barrett led out the Irish Olympic team in Atlanta or when the first Traveller was awarded her degree from Trinity College Dublin. These were very special moments for me, moments I will never forget. I would hope and like to believe that the majority population can celebrate in our success and achievements, just like we do in theirs.

So it is my view there are many ways of being Irish; there is no one way and the sooner people learn that, the better off we all would be. Culture and identity is always difficult to define and pin down but in doing so we must be careful not to look at it through rose-tinted glasses. Rather we must take an honest look at what is positive and negative about our cultural identities, because not everything in our cultural identity is positive and this applies to all nationalities and ethnic groups universally.

It is also important in my view to recognise that cultures and identities are fluid; they change and evolve and adapt, and rightly so. As a Traveller, when I meet settled people they have the preconceived notion that to be Traveller you must be living in a colourful barrel-top wagon and be a great singer or musician and storyteller. This is dangerous because it is stereotyping and we must avoid this. Travellers don't live in barrel-top wagons and sing songs at the campfire any more, just as settled people no longer live in thatched cottages with turf fires or dance at the crossroads.

In the Ireland of today we have a lot more people from different cultures and ethnic groups and this should be welcomed as a positive development rather than seen as a threat. The Irish are perceived worldwide as friendly, hospitable and welcoming people. But it is only a myth, because I have not seen this friendliness or hospitality extended to minority groups in this society

It's very much like the song: if your name is Timothy or Pat, then there is a welcome on the mat, but if your name is Demeter or Stankiewicz, there is no welcome on the mat for you.

Of course, this is not true of all Irish but it is true of a significant number of us. I do believe that all cultures and identities can peacefully co-exist. What other options do we have? Domination? Conflict? Genocide? It doesn't bear thinking about.

Peter Cosgrove

Peter Cosgrove lives in Leitrim.

"O'm sceol o'n ard-mhaigh fail ni chodlaim oiche"*
(Geoffrey Keating)

Ireland is a great big iron pot bubbling and hissing over a blazing turf fire. The pot is full of lumps of gristle and bone. Lift the lid off and look but do be careful. Keep breathing out because one whiff of the steam could make you drunk forever.

For me, it all began in the hills above Roslea where I come from. We grew up in a three-roomed thatched cottage with a huge turf fire. There was no running water or electricity. We walked five miles to and from primary school getting regular soakings from the unceasing rain.

I passed the eleven-plus qualifying exam and was sentenced to six years in St Columb's College which loomed over and sneered down at Derry's Bogside. I did my time at St Columb's, my first tasting of the bitter bread of exile. I moved, on my release, to the Queen's University of Belfast where the Oxbridge rejects who controlled the History department tried their best to make history boring.

For me, Ireland has a history which remains largely unexplored. It is Sean a'Diomais telling the Viceroy: *"Ni cheasfainn mo bhéal leis an bhearla"*.** It is William Drennann and the young Wolfe Tone. It is Henry Joy McCracken's immortal order to one of his commanders: "Haste ye to Antrim driving Ran-

---

* "From the news that I hear from Ireland, I do not sleep at night."
** "I would not twist my mouth with the English language."

dalstown afore ye." It is Mitchell and Lalor, Devoy and Connolly, Jo McKelvey and Charlie Daly, Mickey Coll and Patrick Tymon, Frank Ryan and Kit Conway. It is Keenan's barn where they found the bodies of young Fergal O'Hanlon and brave Sean South. It is wondering at the calmness and courage of Michael Farrell and Eamonn McCann as they marched on towards Derry after the ambush at Burntollet.

For me, Ireland is people and places. Derrygannon where I met Pat and Stevie and wee Luke. Derry where I met Paddy and Eamonn. Dirty dark Belfast where I met Bowes and Michael, Nixon and Raymond, Maggie and Joyce.

Lumps of Ireland are also to be found in Camden and Kilburn, Shepherd's Bush and Willesden where I heard a man sing "Pat O'Donnell" in the summer of 1961. Many of you may have had the experience of meeting a friend in the Euston Tavern and then running like hell for the train to the cattle boat and home.

I could go on.

It is the only Ireland we have got. We are no mean people and we are starting to get ourselves together. With a bit of luck, the best is yet to come.

Polly Devlin

Polly Devlin, OBE, is a writer, broadcaster and conservationist. Her account of an Ulster childhood, All of Us There, *was highly acclaimed for its lyricism and fine writing.*

Something extraordinary happened to me at the age of 19. An accident of emigration. I never actually used the word since it didn't occur to me that that was what I had done.

I went to London at age 19 because I'd won the *Vogue* talent contest and the prize was a job at the magazine. So I just went there. And whenever I could afford to — which wasn't often as *Vogue* was as mean as they get — I flew home to Belfast on BEA and then wriggled my way towards the Lough shore like an eel, albeit on an Ulsterbus. The whole thing of going to work in London was accidental and arbitrary. I had no idea at all I was leaving home for good. And home was such a specific place. To leave it was unthinkable, though of course I couldn't wait to get out. If I was asked where I was from, I answered Tyrone or Ardboe, and I'd be identified as somebody's daughter or someone's sister. I was as tied to it as a tree to the ground.

Emigration was a big sad Irish word in every sense and my Irishness gave me no sense of size except an ability to feel vanished and the sadness seems to come with the territory. All our Irish prayers and songs daily delivered the same lesson; that we lived in a vale of tears, a stepping point on the hasty road to eternity. We were all poised on the point of eternal emigration.

I thought that when you emigrated you left Ireland behind you weeping and wailing and waving from a boat; you were sent into exile; you felt banished;

and that certainly you left home because you had little choice. Then too there was the sub-text of helplessness. It didn't mean going to work for *Vogue*. But all the same, I had emigrated.

When I went to *Vogue*, my Irishness became something new in my life — something much less local but not quite real. Being Irish was both special and a factor to be used for forgiveness for that very specialness. My being Irish was used as an explanatory sort of fond shorthand among my English peers on the magazine. The way "she's Irish" or "that's very Irish" was said seemed different from how "she's French" was said. It seemed to me that there was a lot less baggage to being French in England. My nationality seemed more of a personal matter, as though it would account for any unpredictability in my nature. Sometimes I felt I wore a kind of green integument. I was both flattered and resentful and, perhaps, being young and isolated, played up to it.

Soon after I arrived, I began writing a column for the *Evening Standard*. My efforts were given a full page and my nationality was spread all over the lead-in. I wrote:

> *"When I first came to England I fed a sixpence into the machine in the underground to console myself with a bar of chocolate, the machine gobbled the sixpence, gave nothing in return and I kicked it. But I learnt the lesson the English teach well and the next time it took my money and bit my finger I apologised to it."*

It went down a treat. The following week I wrote:

> *"The Irish and the Jews are alike in so many ways. Both are romantic, clever, musical. The big difference is that Jews are sexy. Irish don't care to know about sex."*

I was 19. I knew nothing. My lover was Jewish. I was Irish. But I already knew enough to play up to my Irishness. That was the lesson the English had taught me well. Irishness was, I thought by now, my only and unique selling point and I cashed in, as both victim and special. And so my Irishness for a long period was a nervous, unsettled kind of a thing. And another thing: when I'm talking to an Italian, say, or a Parisian, who has permanently left home and lived in England, I never get this sense that their native country has such a hold in their mind. The scattered Irish all seem to love and cling to a memory of their lost land, etiolated and vivid as though a living part had been wrenched away. Ireland shivers at their extremities like a phantom limb, whereas an Italian or a Frenchman will speak of the sensual and aesthetic pleasures of the country they have left behind. (Chance would be a fine thing.)

Growing up in Northern Ireland made the whole concept of my Irishness complex. The idea of Englishness (but never ever Britishness) became mixed with the idea of superiority. Englishness became almost the authentic moral condition. And then there was that too-often-rehearsed ambiguity — in the same way that many Protestants emphasised their Britishness, we unprotected Catholics felt more Irish than the Irish. Because our Irishness was under threat, it became more valuable.

I think all this has gone from my psyche — a change brought on by age and confidence; and although my Irishness has become if anything a more valuable and vivid part of my life, I don't use it. When I'm with my Irish friends, we share a shorthand, a sense of humour; and something else — an acknowledgement of the history that lies within us, a recognition of the journey we've made — out of Ireland in every sense — to get to where we are. My nature is fixed on Irishness, the condition of being Irish. It is a condition I am happy to live in. I cannot imagine being anything else.

Ken Doherty

Ken Doherty was the Embassy World Professional Snooker Champion in 1997. From Ranelagh in Dublin, he was the youngest winner of the World Amateur Championships in 1989. He is currently ranked seventh in the world.

Many things can be taken for granted and I suppose being brought up in Dublin and being Irish perhaps falls into that category.

Travelling the world as I do in my profession, you meet people from Ireland or with Irish roots in all corners of the globe and perhaps the most significant incident in my life was winning the World Professional Snooker Championship in 1997 and becoming the first player in history to win both the World Amateur Championship and the Professional Title — that was special.

However, returning from Sheffield to Dublin Airport and being honoured with an open-top bus from the airport to the city was something I will never forget and probably at that point, whilst I was always proud to be Irish, I think that experience made me realise there was more to it than just personal pride. It was the pride for a whole nation. The pleasure that my win gave not just to family and friends, but to people all over Ireland, north and south, was very special. As a nation, Irish hospitality is legendary; wherever you go, the normality of Irish people who live in the public eye is testament not only to the friendliness of the Irish people worldwide but to their upbringing — the respect of family, the respect of others.

Every time I pick up my cue to play in an event, I am conscious that the whole of Ireland is rooting for me to win. Ireland, perhaps more than any other country in the world, respects and acknowledges achievers from whatever field in life.

Snooker has one major tournament in Ireland each year, the Benson and Hedges Masters at Goffs, County Kildare, featuring the top eight players in the world and four wild cards. The event is held in the highest esteem by every player round the world and the scramble to be chosen as one of the four wild cards is enormous. To have an event that means so much to professionals around the world is testament to all that goes on surrounding this event.

For me and my Irish colleagues, to walk out into an arena in front of the Irish public is indescribable. The hairs stand on the back of your neck and at times it is difficult to perform to your best, knowing that a win means so much to them. The feeling reflects the warmth of the Irish people.

In my travels, I find that sportsmen in certain countries are looked upon with jealousy by their fellow countrymen but certainly Ireland is very different. Even with the press in Ireland — who can be extremely critical in relation to a bad day at the office — you get the feeling that they support you all the way.

The Irish identity is one of friendliness throughout the world; as a result of that friendliness, people round the globe find it difficult to come to terms with the problems that we have had on our island over the years.

Incredibly, the support that my colleague Dennis Taylor has had from people in the south, and that I have had from people in the north, is contrary to some people's understanding. When Taylor won the World Championship in 1985 and I in 1997, there was reputedly not one solitary emergency call in the last hour of our matches. To believe that people postponed their heart attacks for an hour, postponed burglaries for an hour and all other emergency calls for an hour, seems incredible. It is a wonderful Irish story — perhaps only an Irishman could tell it and be believed.

Brian Dooley *

Brian Dooley is the author of Black and Green: The Fight for Civil Rights in Northern Ireland and Black America. *He was born in London and now lives in Dublin, where he works for Amnesty International's Irish Section.*

My south London schoolmates and I struggled with our Irishness during the 1970s. Nearly all of us had Irish parents who had settled in England in the 1940s and 1950s, but we had been born and raised in London. Did that make us English or Irish? Most of us made regular summer trips to Ireland, looked Irish, even knew a few Irish words. Some of us just felt Irish — all our relations were Irish, as were most of our parents' friends, our priests and our teachers.

But identifying yourself as Irish was problematic. The IRA was attacking London; in the twelve months starting October 1974, the British capital was bombed, on average, once a week. The explosions forced us to choose whose side we were on. To many of our teenage minds, being Irish meant being experts on Ireland and supporting the IRA.

We tested each other on Irish trivia. What number plates do they have in Wexford? How do you say the Hail Mary in Irish? Is Bomber Liston a Kerry footballer or an IRA man? (One kid impressed the playground by brandishing the leather bracelet his uncle, a prisoner in Long Kesh, had made for him.)

---

* This essay originally appeared in the October/November 2000 (15th Anniversary) issue of *Irish America* magazine. Reprinted with permission.

We learned the words to rebel songs and read books about Easter 1916, thinking it made us more Irish. Our special hero was IRA leader Seán Mac Stiofáin, a London Irish boy who'd been imprisoned for stealing weapons in England. In the early 1970s, he was the head of the Provisional IRA, one of us, Cockney Irish.

On a school trip to Ireland in 1976, some of us made the pilgrimage to Dublin's GPO, genuflected at Wolfe Tone's grave, and stood to attention for the Irish national anthem in a Limerick cinema after all the locals had bolted out the door. We insisted to kids in Laois that we really were Irish, despite our accents. "Look at the heroes of 1916," we said smugly. "James Connolly, Tom Clarke, Eamon De Valera — none of them born in Ireland." The Irish kids laughed at our pretensions.

Some of us joined under-age Gaelic football teams in London. In 1979, I captained the "county" of London against New York in an early round of the All-Ireland Championship (our team barely touched the ball).

We were Irish wannabes, derided by Irish relations as "Plastic Paddies" for not being the genuine article. And London Irishness was different from Irish Irishness. Cousins in Dublin or Boston weren't surrounded by English people, and couldn't understand why it was difficult — even dangerous — for us to wear shamrock on St Patrick's Day. For our parents' generation, the bombings made things even more complicated.

Their accents immediately identified them as Irish in a city where Irish people were killing civilians. They were keen to show suspicious Londoners that the IRA didn't represent them, and missed few chances to denounce the bombings. "We don't bite the hand that feeds us," said many Irish people who had earned livelihoods in England for 30 years. Irish clubs across London banned IRA songs — modern or ancient — from their dances lest there be any doubt about their loyalties.

On weekdays, my dad worked as a postman, and when one of his work mates had his fingers blown off by an IRA letter bomb, we were scared he would be next. At weekends, he moonlighted as a cabbie, and we waited in silence for his safe return every time a news flash interrupted evening television to report another random bombing in central London.

When we reached our late teens, most of my schoolmates were faced with the Great Passport Decision. Those of us with Irish parents had the choice to be British subjects or Irish citizens. It was an official, legal choice. You could be one or the other. Some opted for an Irish passport because it was a few pounds cheaper, but for others it was a decision loaded with political significance. The weekend of my 18th birthday, Bobby Sands began his hunger strike, and I chose an Irish passport.

The arrival of an Irish passport was the ultimate validation of our claims — there it was, in green and white, our national status legally declared. True, we had not been born in Ireland, but we had chosen Ireland in a way our Kerry cousins had never done, and surely that made us even more Irish?

A decade later, things became easier for London Irish teenagers. Random bombings in the city were rare, and while militant Republicanism still has its pull for some youngsters (Londoner Diarmuid O'Neill joined the IRA, and was shot dead by police in Hammersmith in 1997), modern Irish London offers more than a miserable anti-Englishness.

The success of The Pogues helped legitimise being Irish in London, and even made it trendy, while soccer stars like Tony Cascarino and Andy Townsend replaced Mac Stiofáin as the new Cockney Irish heroes. Today's London kids with Irish parents are free from the edginess of the 1970s, and now the Irish or English dilemma is far more likely to be argued in the context of sport or music than political violence.

I left London many years ago, and now live in Ireland, more at home than I've ever felt in my life. Living in Ireland is all I hoped it would be when I used to dream of it 25 years ago. I play soccer in the local sports club, where I'm known, inevitably, as "the English fella".

Sammy Douglas

Sammy Douglas is an active community development worker and is currently involved in a wide range of voluntary activity, including chairing The Greater East Belfast Partnership and a trustee of the Northern Ireland Voluntary Trust. He is former chair of the Belfast European Partnership Board.

Shades of Irishness

I have fond memories of my late grandmother who grew up in the Grosvenor Road area of West Belfast. I remember her as a staunch Protestant and active unionist. Born in pre-partition Ireland, she was also proud of her Irish identity and she knew many Irish ballads off by heart.

When it came to my generation, I had absolutely no sense of Irishness. Growing up in the loyalist and unionist Sandy Row area of Belfast, everything around me affirmed a sense of being British. Red, white and blue painted kerbstones, royal photographs hung up on kitchen house walls and family links with the British forces going back decades, epitomised a proud British association and belonging. These "traditions" helped to copper-fasten a passionate and emotional attachment to mainland Britain.

On the other hand, all things Irish were alien to me. I had learned from a very early age that their forces were always waiting along the border for an opportune time to take over Ulster and turn it into a Gaelic-speaking, priest-ridden, Roman Catholic republic. Irish "neutrality" during the Second World War fuelled these anti-Irish attitudes and led to further alienation within the unionist community that I belonged to.

The negative feelings and hostility that I had harboured towards all things Irish were reinforced on my first day-trip across the border. As I arrived in the capital, tricolours, nuns and priests, huge chapels, an alien language and "lep-rechaun pubs" confronted me. I felt like a stranger in a foreign country as I walked through the streets of "dirty Dublin". My sense of detachment from the Irish nation was compounded even more.

A traumatic experience a few years later was to challenge my long-held prejudices and enable me to examine an identity which had afforded me cultural and political security. In the 1970s, my sister was nearly killed after the IRA bombed the pub she was frequenting in Sandy Row. As I clawed through the demolished building looking for her, I was filled with raging anger and a sense of revenge. As an angry young man, I made a decision that had a major bearing on the direction of my life. I went to live in England.

When I arrived in Derby, East Midlands, any notion that I had of living in some sort of British Utopian state was soon dispelled. The people that I met didn't accept that I was from British Ulster. I was from Ireland and I was "Paddy" to them. And I was no different from the "Paddies" from the Falls Road, South Armagh, Dublin or Cork.

Like some of the ethnic minorities where I lived, I was racially abused at times. It was particularly bad after British soldiers were shot in Northern Ireland or when bombing atrocities were committed. It was hard to take and it began to shake my sense of identity to the core. It left me confused and bewildered.

As a result of these experiences, I made friends with Irish people from the Republic of Ireland. I came to realise that I had much in common with those, who, previously, I had perceived as foreigners. Although it was uncomfortable at first, I began to enjoy some aspects of Irish culture for the first time in my life. This included Irish literature, traditional music, dancing and songs. In cultural terms, this was a seismic shift for me. While I still considered myself an Ulsterman loyal to Britain, I gradually became more aware of my Irishness during my two-year stay.

Over the years I have retained the Irish angle to my identity, which I discovered during my time in England. The present peace process has created the conditions where unionists like myself can explore the Irish aspects of our identity in a relatively safe environment and in a way that does not threaten our Britishness. This is happening on a much wider scale than is generally recognised.

One only has to look at East Belfast where the "writing is on the wall". Murals such as St Patrick and Cuchullain are examples of an openness within our community to examine political "hot potatoes". And there are others. Irish and Ulster Scots dancing survive alongside one another in some community centres while Irish jigs and songs are often played by loyalist flute bands.

But these changes are not just happening within the shadow of the giant cranes of Harland and Wolff shipyard. Through East Belfast Community Focus (funded by Co-operation Ireland), over 60 community organisations from East Belfast have travelled across the border to meet their counterparts. These exchange visits have taken place within this last year and have included organisations such as the British Legion, Ulster Scots, loyalist prisoners' support groups and unionist politicians.

In conclusion, I am not trying to infer that many unionists have suddenly become Irish overnight or that there is a wee Irish person within us ready to jump out. Rather, there is a growing recognition within our community that an Ulsterman like myself, living in East Belfast, can be staunchly loyal and British but peculiarly Irish.

Jill Fergus *

Jill Fergus, a New York-based freelance writer, was formerly an editor at Travel & Leisure *magazine. She has written for* In Style, Marie Claire, Travel Holiday, Irish America *and the* New York Daily News *and has completed a screenplay. She has also appeared on CNN and MSNBC discussing travel trends.*

What it Means to Be an Irish American

When I was 13 years old, my mother took me and my siblings to Rockaway Beach for the day. After we romped in the ocean and got sufficiently sunburned, we ended up at a rather run-down Irish tavern that was sponsoring a singing contest. Since I can carry a tune, my mother made me enter. All the entrants, adults and kids alike, sang well-known Irish songs. I sang "Do Re Mi" because I didn't know any Irish songs (other than "Danny Boy" and that was already taken). The crowd gazed at me with mild puzzlement as I nervously made my way through the simple *Sound of Music* tune. I received tepid applause and my brothers laughed their heads off. I knew I was better than the girl who won first prize and the blue ribbon with her who-killed-the-cat version of "Four Green Fields", but that didn't matter — her song connected with the crowd and mine didn't.

It was that episode that kept returning to me as I thought about what it means to be an Irish American. I couldn't pinpoint why exactly, but as I sat down to write this essay, the reason gradually came to me. Growing up, there was always something to remind me and my siblings of where we came from —

* This essay originally appeared in the October/November 2000 (15th Anniversary) issue of *Irish America* magazine. Reprinted with permission.

whether it was the stories of Cuchulainn or the leprechauns my Mayo-born father would enthral us with or the delicious soda bread my mother baked. Of course, each March, there were lively St Patrick's Day celebrations. And there was always music. My father would play John McCormack or listen to Irish radio stations on a Sunday morning. To be honest, I never gave those songs much thought. I had no idea that the "Four Green Fields" was a reference to Ireland's four provinces. Perhaps the image I had of Irish music was tied to those cheesy songs like "When Irish Eyes are Smiling" or "McNamara's Band" and, secretly, I was embarrassed to know them.

In my late teens, my parents took my two younger brothers to Ireland. At the time, I had no interest in going back (I was there once when I was just a child). All I could think about was three weeks with no parents around. When my brothers came back saying they had the best time ever, I was surprised and more than a bit jealous. They really got in touch with their roots, reading up on the country's history and getting into the music, past (The Chieftains, The Wolfe Tones) and present (Black 47, Saw Doctors). It rankled me that they knew so much more about Ireland than I did — wasn't I just as Irish as they were? I began to look at old photos of my father's family and asked him questions about what it was like growing up and why exactly he had to leave to come to America. I soon realised that I would never truly understand and embrace my heritage until I went back to Ireland and experienced it for myself.

And so I did. I visited my mother's relatives in Cork and my father's in Mayo. People that hadn't seen me in 20 years or never at all welcomed me into their homes for tea and sandwiches as if I were a long-lost daughter. I immediately sensed that I belonged there. To visit the graves of my grandparents filled me with an emotion I never expected to feel. At one get-together, someone produced a guitar and the singing began. They were singing the classics like "The Town I Loved So Well", "Fields of Athenry", "Spancil Hill", "The Flower of Sweet Strabane", "Only Our Rivers Run Free" and "Flight of the Earls" — though I didn't know all of the names at that point. Sure, I felt foolish for not knowing the words, but more than that, I felt incredibly left out. For to understand those songs is to understand not just what your own ancestors have gone through, but the ancestors of practically every Irish family.

As I knew I would, I returned to Ireland soon after that amazing two-week trip. Late one evening in Mayo, as I sipped a Guinness by the turf fire of a local pub — a pub that my father and uncles frequented years ago — a singalong was inevitably started. As people belted out heartfelt versions of the old standbys, I gathered up my courage. Yes, this time I was prepared. I sang "Carrickfergus" (with my last name, I thought it was entirely appropriate). The crowd looked on appreciatively, some even mouthing the words. For each person, it meant something different, but it meant *something*. It was a magical night for me and I plan on having many more like it in the future. I fully embrace my Irish heritage and am proud to call myself an Irish American. And someday soon, I am sure I will get over not winning that blue ribbon.

Aengus Finucane

Aengus Finucane joined the Holy Ghost Fathers in 1949. Ordained in 1958, he was posted to Nigeria. He has worked with Concern, the non-governmental humanitarian relief organisation, since it was formed in 1968. After serving with Concern in Gabon, Bangladesh, Thailand and Uganda, he became Chief Executive in 1981. Since his retirement in 1997, he has been honorary president of Concern Worldwide US.

My sense of being Irish matured when I went to work overseas 40 years ago. Prior to that, my "being Irish" contained a negative anti-English component. I had a pride of race which had been nurtured on Irish history, literature and language. But those same sources, so often dwelling on past wrongs, had nurtured a sense of hurt. Added to that, my father had been jailed for his active role in the Troubles and my mother could recall the fear engendered by the Black and Tans. Being Irish for me in my growing-up years was a mixture of being romantic and belligerent. Before I left Ireland I had met no more than an occasional foreigner. In my milieu they were all Irish. Any "special something" that made us Irish wasn't particularly relevant.

Once outside Ireland, I learned that it is our Irishness that defines us. The sum of our differences adds up to our not being English, French, German or anything but Irish. It is the "sum" of our qualities that constitutes that "something special". Inevitably, some of "our" characteristics will overlap with those of other peoples, but the sum will be different.

Irishness is a changing commodity. Being Irish in 2000 is not quite the same thing as it was in 1900. What we are is basically determined by "nature" and by "nurture". The genes we inherit determine much of our physical make-up; it is our environment and upbringing that most influence and shape us.

The genes which the Irish inherit today may remain the same, but there are scarcely words to describe the changes in environment and upbringing that have occurred in Ireland over the last century and especially in the last 50 years.

The majority of the Irish of today have no memory of the scarcities of the war years of the 1940s or the unemployment and mass emigration of the 1950s. Many of that majority, though inheriting the values and certainties of the 1950s and earlier decades, grew up in the more buoyant and forward-looking later decades. On the crest of the wave of increasing affluence, of more questioning, of the ever-broadening horizons explored by television, and of the expansion of communication and travel, they very often "outgrew" the value system and certainties in which their very stability was anchored. Most of the Irish parents of the period of the late 1970s onwards were more self-assured, better educated and better off than those of earlier decades. They sought to ensure that their children were not deprived. Unfortunately, "not deprived" too often translated into "indulged".

The teenager of the 1990s did not have the advantage of knowing any real measure of want. Amid the more widespread wealth of the Celtic Tiger years and freed from the constraints of what had been a supportive but somewhat restrictive value system, they could indulge their whims and merge with the ever-widening world of their TV sets and computer screens. The Irishness of the young person moving into adulthood today is being shaped in a very different environment from what our over-fifties knew. Staying in tune with the changes and adapting to them is a daily challenge for us older Irish, even if we have contributed to bringing about those changes.

Abroad, attitudes to the Irish became progressively more positive during the last 30 years. Our strong "social" qualities have won friendship and esteem around the globe. We are seen to be fun-loving, hospitable, friendly, gifted talkers and storytellers, music and dance loving. To these, as attractive Irish qualities, you may add flexibility, a readiness to work hard, family and home loyalty, a predisposition toward caring and sharing with the less fortunate. These are traits that give the lie to the old stereotype of *Punch* and the music hall where the less attractive qualities and behaviour of a subject people were parodied and made fun of. The attractive qualities I have enumerated belong to the self-confident and prospering people of recent decades. Irishness will undoubtedly continue to evolve and further radical changes will take place in Ireland as global thinking gains ground. It is to be hoped that the more evolved Irish will continue to be recognisable and cherished for being just that — Irish.

Young or old, living at home or living abroad, we share that something that makes us proud of being Irish. That "something", like so many things Irish, can be talked about for hours but cannot be analysed adequately or defined. We experience a surge of this Irishness when "one of our own" does well. It may be as we watch an Irish athlete gain victory in an international arena; as we cheer an Irish soccer or rugby team on the playing fields of Europe; as we identify with any compatriot doing well in any discipline on the world stage. We can even experience a surge of Irishness as an Irish horse (or even a horse trained in Ireland) goes first past the post in an international contest. All these things reaffirm us and help erase any nagging traces of a national inferiority complex that, happily, belongs to the dim and distant past.

Hugh Frazer

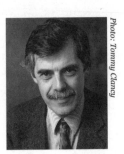

Hugh Frazer has been Director of the Combat Poverty Agency, an Irish government agency, for the past 12 years. A native of Cullybackey, County Antrim, he is also a painter of the urban landscape.

Dear Paddy, Did you realise what a difficult task you were setting? It is hard enough just surviving all the manifest contradictions and tensions of being Irish without actually being expected to face up to, resolve and explain them in print. It is one thing to say what I would like being Irish to be and to sit down and write a manifesto. That would be relatively easy. Such clarity would be comforting but it would not be the truth. It would in no way mirror reality. For me at least, being Irish today is a complex matter, an ongoing struggle. It is no cosy place.

I should of course have taken the easy option. I should have just sat down and penned the first thoughts that came into my head when I got your letter. The longer I have left it, the more difficult it has become and the less sure I am of what I want to say. I keep finding myself suspended in some limbo of uncertainty.

I have taken to staring long and hard into my mirror each morning to see if I can find there a clear identity staring back at me. But there is no easy answer. Some mornings I seem to detect images that hint at my British identity; on others my sense of being Northern Irish is captured. On another morning elements of my Welsh ancestors peer suspiciously back at me. Sometimes I think I can see the orange sash of unionism and the sturdy individualism and integrity of the Protestant community that was so prevalent where I grew up in Cullybackey. On others I get hints of the nationalist and republican idealists that I have admired. But more often than not, I appear to be staring into a cracked and fragmented mirror reflecting a jumbled mix of different identities and traditions waiting tentatively and not very confidently to be resolved into some new, all-encompassing identity.

Of course, there are those mornings when I look into my mirror and feel alienated from everything I see there. Usually these are the mornings when the radio in the background is relaying the latest tribunal story of corruption and political chicanery or the latest stand-off at Drumcree or attack on an Orange Hall or Catholic Church. Perhaps it is also documenting the previous night's racist attack on a Travelling family, refugee or asylum-seeker. Maybe it is reporting on the growing gap between the rich and poor in our society while regaling us with the exhortations of arrogant politicians who want us to celebrate our conspicuous affluence and who accuse those who argue against widening inequalities and for the marginalised and excluded of being begrudgers or left-wing pinkos. Then I feel anger. Dear God, this is none of what I want for my identity. If this is what being Irish is about, then perhaps I do not want to be Irish. Maybe I am better off being an outsider or a citizen of Europe or the world. But then again, these images of sleaze, abuse of power and racism are part of current Irish identity and so I cannot escape them.

So perhaps increasingly for me, being Irish means being different from but also part of all of the above. So can I at last feel free to celebrate and be enriched and not burdened by these many contradictions? Maybe the only certainty is that in a rapidly changing society, being Irish means being uncertain and accepting and living with difference and diversity and with multiple identities.

Contradictory though it may seem at times, I can identify with the hurts, the fears, the hopes and the aspirations of both major traditions on this island. However, at other moments I can be frustrated and angered by the arrogant assertiveness, the righteousness and the often unthinking and unwitting intolerance of many of the spokespersons of both traditions. There is some perversity in me that means that when living and working in a nationalist and Catholic environment, I feel the need to assert my unionist and British background. However, conversely, when in a more unionist and British setting, then I miss many of the aspects of nationalist culture and identity that I find so attractive. In general, I feel the need to challenge the tendency to exclusiveness in both traditions and to appeal for greater generosity, tolerance and understanding.

At the end of the day, this anguishing over the issue of identity has led me to conclude that there is no room for complacency or certainty about our Irish identity. That way lies the scrap heap of history. We are facing an enormous challenge, both those of us living in Ireland, and all our friends and relations in the wider world, to redefine an Irish identity. We need to discover an identity that is forward-looking and inclusive, that accommodates and builds on all our different traditions and that celebrates and encompasses those from other cultures and traditions who are increasingly arriving on and enriching our island.

Irish identity is at a crossroads. We will need all the help of our artists and writers, philosophers and political scientists, idealists and environmentalists to help us to move on from the past and to imagine and envisage a new and a rich identity. At present, we seem to lack a vision of what our future should be, of how we can use our new wealth to be a rich and inclusive society and not just a collection of rich and selfish individuals and alienated minorities.

The current tide of change could well swamp our old squabbles. However, at the same time, the best, as well as the worst, of what all our traditions have struggled for for centuries could be lost. We could find ourselves subsumed into some bland mid-Atlantic global culture and economy. In our blind rush to globalisation, in our valuing of private profit over principle, of individual gain over collective solidarity, we could destroy all that is valuable in being Irish. If that happens, I will be found staring into my mirror and there will be nothing left to be reflected back. Where once there was at least the confused elements of an Irish identity, there will be just a blank glass. Being Irish will have ceased to have a meaning and maybe I will have ceased to exist.

However, it needn't be like this. The cosy complacency of affluence need not prevail. In a more positive scenario, I will look into my mirror and see a constantly changing mosaic of colours and identities enriching and giving value to each other. That is a vision of Irishness worth continuing to strive for. It can transcend yesterday's arguments and today's corruption. It can challenge injustice and inequality, greed and intolerance. It can be a positive influence in the world in support of human dignity and decency. It can liberate imagination and creativity. It can foster and celebrate difference and diversity. Then and only then can one be proud to be Irish.

Anthony Gifford

Lord Anthony Gifford practises as a barrister in London and as an attorney-at-law in Kingston, Jamaica. He has been involved in human rights issues in Britain, Northern Ireland, Southern Africa and the Caribbean. He is currently acting for the family of James Wray at the Bloody Sunday Inquiry. He was a Labour member of the House of Lords before the abolition of hereditary peers, which he supported.

A Letter to the Irish from a Friend

Dear People of Ireland: After visiting you for over 30 years, I have come to admire some of the ways in which you are, most assuredly, not British. You do not want to rule the world. You have never been conquerors. You do not try to beat up the opposing fans when you go to a football match. You do not sit on a train looking miserable and avoid talking to your neighbour. Your weather is just as rotten as ours, but you somehow keep more cheerful about it.

You have a patriotism which is like a bottomless well, a patriotism which burns for the dignity and honour of your people, rather than the "Rule Britannia" patriotism which seeks rather to heap indignity upon others. Ten of you, including a Member of Parliament, died in 1981 by refusing to eat food, all for the cause of dignity and honour. To me, that shows a courage which is unimaginable.

In the North you have sectarianism, a fault bequeathed by history. It has brought out a streak of cruelty which can affect any people under great stress. But you are trying to deal with this in a spirit of love and co-operation. It cannot be easy. I do not know your Orangemen and your Ulster Unionists, so I cannot speak of them. I only know that when I did a study of the "supergrass" trials, and had meetings with the Catholic "Relatives for Justice" and the Protestant "Families for Legal Rights", I saw working class women who were all suffering the same anguish for the same reasons. Whatever the provocation, you must avoid any return to those days of blood and bereavement, and find other ways for justice to prevail.

You mix easily with other peoples. You are not, on the whole, racist. Because you did not go around enslaving other people, and indeed were made to live in a state of semi-slavery yourselves, you did not grow up thinking that you were superior to other races. Your prisoners in the English jails made common cause with black prisoners. Only when you migrated to the US did you start to join the "us against them", white against black ideology. You got corrupted and stopped being truly Irish. I remember a day spent in Washington with Gerry Conlon of the Guildford Four. He was determined to persuade Jesse Jackson and other black leaders to support the Birmingham Six, who were still in jail. He showed a true Irish spirit.

Your church has both pressed you down and lifted you up. Behind those hierarchies of priestly power, which have done a lot of wrong, there is a force for good which shines through. I think of Bishop Daly and his leadership over the Bloody Sunday massacre. He was there on the ground when the bullets were flying, and he never stopped witnessing to the horror of what he had seen. Also there were the Knights of Malta, paramedics of the Church who saved lives by stepping in front of British paratroopers when they were about to shoot. In them you can see the best of the Catholic Church. England, apart from its non-white communities, has become largely de-Christianised. Is it not better for a people to have a contradictory religion, one which they sometimes have to rebel against, than no religion at all?

At the core of Ireland is its beauty. Not just those incredible hills and sea-coasts, but the beauty of the people. Your women bloom like fresh flowers long after their English contemporaries have faded. Your music is lyrical, and your writers have turned the invaders' language into pure poetry. Your beauty is not accidental; it reflects a sense of inner well-being which many in England would pay thousands to their therapists to achieve.

You deserve your economic boom. You have suffered enough for it. But please, if you become rich and successful, do not stop being Irish. Continue to be the human face of English-speaking Europe. Be welcoming to those who seek asylum, because you know what it means to be forced to migrate. Send your best leaders into the international arena as messengers for justice, as Sean McBride and Mary Robinson have been. And if you stand up for peace and love in the world, then of necessity you have to put an end to war and hate at home.

Yours affectionately,

Anthony Gifford.

Andrew Greeley[*]

Father Andrew Greeley is a Chicago priest who teaches at the University of Chicago and the University of Arizona. His most recent novel is Irish Eyes.

On Being Irish in America

There are many advantages to being Irish in America. One of the least of them is that despite our own blustering self-hatred and despite the contempt the elite media and academy have for us, we are strictly a high prestige group. The research my colleague Michael Hout has carried out shows that there are a lot more Americans claiming to be Irish than one might expect from the immigration figures because the children of ethnically mixed marriages tend to identify with their Irish ancestors. The old St Patrick's Day quip about there being two kinds of people — those that are Irish and those that wish they were — turns out to be not so far from wrong.

Moreover, it is permitted for us to be playful, perhaps the most characteristic quality of those who live in our land of origins. The Irish love play. They even invent new sports on which to gamble. They play with their kids on every possible occasion. They play in their conversations. They play in their pub chatter. They see politics as a form of play. Their incredible skill with words in poetry, drama and fiction is the result of the play that infects their culture at every level. So other Americans are not surprised when we talk funny and en-

---

[*] This essay originally appeared in the October/November 2000 (15th Anniversary) issue of *Irish America* magazine. Reprinted with permission.

joy verbal contests and put together compromises in politics because we know that really politics are only a game and that hardline ideology spoils the fun of the games.

There are of course some Irish and Irish Americans who are dull and sombre and nasty and mean, God forgive them for it. The broad culture, however, exults play, legitimises and reinforces it.

The mystical dimension of the Irish heritage — simple nature mysticism elaborately, even convolutedly described as in the Book of Kells and James Joyce for example — permits Irish Americans to indulge the dreamy, meditative dimensions of their personalities, to understand what John O'Donohue means when he says that the body doesn't have a soul, the soul has a body. The soul he means is the human person reaching out to embrace others, the world and God. My own research suggests that, while many of us (in both countries) repress our mystical possibilities, they still lurk within us. Perhaps this is why the revival of Celtic spirituality is so popular in both countries.

Our Irish heritage also permits us to remain Catholic despite the idiots who so often run our church. We can laugh at them behind their backs when we think that for all their pomposity and ignorance they are still the successors of the apostles and that the latter were a pretty disreputable and undependable lot of traitors and cowards and thieves. In Ireland, since the memory of humankind runs not the contrary, we laughed at the clergy behind their backs. The only difference now is that we tell them what we think about them to their faces, which is good for them and good for us too. Some of them even seem to be learning from the experiences. Thus the late Cardinal O'Connor, God be good to him, admitted in his later years that he had probably talked too much in his early years in New York. Not all of them have learned this, however.

Being Irish also provides justification for being recklessly generous. Just as the monks went off to Europe in huge numbers and converted much of it, and in more recent generations Irish priests and nuns went to every nation under heaven (including this one), so too do Irish and Irish American young men and women show up on television in all the places of the world where bravery and energy and compassion are needed to take care of the suffering brothers and sisters.

None of these characteristics I celebrate are qualities of which to be proud. They are rather obligations, challenges, opportunities. We do not use them as standards on which to compare ourselves with others, but rather as criteria against which to judge ourselves in comparison with the norms of our heritage. To be playful, mystical, Catholic and generous are provocations and indeed vocations.

How are we doing? A question which always troubles us, especially when we consider that there are still those in our society who do not like us or accept us, who think we are corrupt, superstitious, rigid, puritanical.

There's no way one can really answer that question. God knows and She hasn't issued any reports lately. Not as well, certainly, as we might. Better, perhaps, than we sometimes think. Still impelled and compelled by the place and the people and the heritage from which we come?

I think so. Moreover, I think we will be that way, that is, we will be Irish, for a long time to come.

Desmond Guinness

The Hon. Desmond Guinness founded the Irish Georgian Society in 1958 and has lectured all over the world. His publications include Georgian Dublin, Irish Houses and Castles, The White House: An Architectural History, Dublin — a Grand Tour *and* Great Irish Houses and Castles. *He lives at Leixlip Castle, County Kildare.*

The Guinness family is Irish. We very likely dropped the Mc when Richard Guinness "took the soup" and conformed to the Protestant faith. The telephone directory has pages of McGuinness but only a few Guinness entries; all of these are related and descend from Richard, father of Arthur, the founder of the St James's Gate Brewery.

My great-great-grandfather, Sir Benjamin Guinness, was Lord Mayor of Dublin and sole owner of the Brewery. He was made a Baronet, a "Sir" that can be inherited (one better than a Knighthood, which only lasts for the lifetime of the recipient). The honour came to him for saving and restoring St Patrick's Cathedral in Dublin at his own expense.

Guinness was one of 300 Dublin breweries when it started life, because beer did not last long or travel well, so country pubs had to make their own. My forebears must have been good businessmen to have made "our" brewery for a time the largest in the world. It is a strange paradox that Fr Mathew's Temperance campaign should have helped to get our export trade going fortunately for "our" brewery, his preachings against drink were soon drowned by the horrors of the Famine.

The first Lord Moyne was my grandfather, grandson of Sir Benjamin. Lord Moyne was the youngest of three sons and more interested in British politics than Irish brewing. He was born on the steps of his father's house, 80 St Stephen's Green, Dublin in 1880, having decided to take his place in the world when his mother was attending a reception. He made his life in England where both my father and I were born, raised and educated.

My parents divorced almost as soon as they set eyes on me, but by 1950 both were happily remarried, with younger children, and both happened to be living in Ireland for part of the year, my mother in County Galway and my father in County Dublin. This was one of the reasons I decided to live in Ireland; I bought a farm in County Kildare in 1958, four years after getting married.

Neither my first wife or I felt in the least Irish. She was German and I was English by both birth and upbringing, but while looking for a farm we had the luck to live at Carton, County Kildare, a magnificent Palladian house, standing empty, belonging to Lord Brocket, a kind English peer who lived in an equally magnificent house in Hertfordshire. We spent two happy years at Carton, where both our children were born, and we had the time to became immersed in eighteenth-century Dublin and the amazing beauty and variety of the interiors of the town houses, then being decimated in huge slum clearance schemes. In this way, the Irish Georgian Society was born, and a campaign to preserve from destruction the wonders of the eighteenth century in both town and country was started.

This lengthy preamble is necessary to see where I personally stand in regards to being, or feeling, Irish. Having been born and educated in England, I was forced to join the army as a conscript at the age of 19 and eventually served in the Seventh Hussars in Germany. I was "released" after 18 months, or else Oxford, where I spent three years, would have had to wait yet one more year before it embraced me.

When I came to live here, I knew nothing of the language, and not enough of the history of Ireland, my adoptive country. For about 30 years I edited a slim journal devoted to Irish eighteenth-century art and architecture for the Irish Georgian Society to awaken interest in the period. At one of our meetings, it was suggested that the Society should change its name, as "Irish Georgian" would perhaps alienate people who felt as we did about the destruction going on all around, the loss, the waste. I remember saying "perhaps I should change my name to George". Over the years, I've written three books on Dublin architecture and collaborated on two devoted to country houses in Ireland. I am passionate about Ireland, but my formative years were in England.

Our aim was to preserve and record, to help researchers and to save what could be saved of the best buildings of the period. We saw ourselves (in the way young people do) as crusaders against the determined Philistinism of the elders who made decisions. Ours was a youthful and enthusiastic campaign, and it is good to see that some of the work we began is now being carried on by the State, 40 years later. Attitudes have changed!

Fred Halliday

Fred Halliday is Professor of International Relations at the London School of Economics. He was born in Dublin and educated at the Marist School, Dundalk, and Ampleforth College, Yorkshire. He is the author of a dozen books, including studies of the Cold War and of the Middle East.

Sentiment and Scepticism

Most, if not all, the questions I work on have their origins in Ireland. I have spent much of my life analysing and writing about the third world and international conflict, most particularly with regard to the Middle East. For the past two decades, as a university teacher, I have taught international relations, a subject that includes both analysis of how the world works, and of the moral issues involved. Yet my views on these topics have been shaped, in a way that I have found fruitful, by my own background in Ireland and in the particular place where I grew up, just south of the border, Dundalk. The whole agenda of international relations is there: state formation, frontiers, colonialism, revolutionary struggle, nationalism, industrial rise and decline, illegal transnational flows, environmental damage, perhaps now a bit of international co-operation.

One of three sons of an Irish Catholic mother, Rita Finigan, from families of civil servants and farmers long established in County Louth, and of an English Methodist father, Arthur Halliday, who had moved his shoe business from Leeds to Dundalk in 1930 to gain access to a protected Irish market, I have always felt personally and morally involved in the story of Ireland, but in an unresolved way. My own parents were, in their distinct ways, part of what one may term the dissident middle classes, indigenous but contentious. My mother's family were staunch nationalists. My grandmother was always proud of having, as a schoolgirl in Balbriggan, been presented to Parnell. One of my great aunts had been taken off to the Crumlin Road after Easter 1916 as a suspected nationalist supporter. One of the reasons my father got on well in Ireland was that, although a very English Englishman, he was, by dint of his nonconformist Yorkshire background, a republican in sentiment. In 1935, my parents crossed the religious divide in a mixed marriage in a country church in County Wicklow. In keeping with the traditions of this island, no relative came to the wedding: the witnesses were the gravediggers.

After some time at the Marist School in Dundalk I was sent to boarding school, Ampleforth College, in England and have, since the age of 16, had my home outside Ireland. The involvement is, therefore, very much one of being part of the imagined community and of sharing in historical moments: I can well remember the first IRA bombing campaign of 1956, organised in part from Dundalk and the Cooley mountains across the bay, the role of Irish peacekeeping forces in the Congo in 1960–1961, which so enraged my English teachers and fellow pupils; as I can recall where I was in February 1996 when news of the Canary Wharf bombing came through. My hopes have risen and fallen with events surrounding the Good Friday Agreement.

Yet I must also be considered as not really part of the major groups involved in the Irish conflict; indeed, while a loathing of the complacency of power, not least in its English Home Counties variety, is one abiding legacy of my Irish formation, a suspicion of nationalist and religious claims, on land or people, is another. It is those who, in Ireland as elsewhere, have criticised and rejected the claims of identity and history that I most esteem. When I hear the word "community", much used by well-intentioned political theorists in recent years, I reach for my exit visa.

Being brought up in Dundalk, one could not be unaware of the conflicts in the "north". I shared in the optimism of the Lemass–Chichester Clark talks of the mid-1960s and in the horror at what followed. In keeping with similar scepticism about nationalist claims in other parts of the world, such as Palestine/Israel, I was an early, if none too optimistic, convert to what became known as the "two nations" theory. I doubted, and doubt, if any community is all virtuous, or all fascist, or something. In analysing nationalism, I am very much a modernist.

While brought up as a Catholic, I was later to acquire a Loyalist mother-in-law, Sarah Molyneux, née Jamison, from a Presbyterian family in Ballymena. Her firmness of vision, and sharpness of tongue, kept me sensitive to her views. Having a Catholic mother and Protestant mother-in-law is a fascinating opportunity for comparison. Some things differ, such as attitudes to money, but others do not: the word "eejit" seems to know no confessional boundaries. In the matter of dealing with inflated male egos, I can detect, on the basis of some half century of observation, no difference at all. Some years ago I was invited to Dublin by the Irish School of Ecumenics to address a conference on "Morality in International Relations". I happened to mention this to my mother-in-law; going to Dublin was bad enough, but the topic did not impress either. "Morality and international relations, is it," she replied, "I suppose you have an A-level in that too, do you?"

"Being Irish" is a title that repels but also invites. It repels, in that it suggests what so many inside and outside the island too easily engage in — stereotyping, atavism, maudlin nonsense of multifarious kinds. If I were to re-design Dante's hell, I would include in it a room where Americans were permanently celebrating "St Paddy's Day". Yet "Being Irish" invites, to value the ties of family, friendship, experience that Ireland has given and gives. Beyond these links of family, memory, political concern, Ireland has therefore taught me, and continues to teach me, much of what I know about the broader world. As to how much Ireland itself has learnt from the lessons of its own history, I remain fascinated and concerned. A certain creative unease may also be part of that legacy.

Patricia Harty

Patricia Harty, a native of Tipperary, is Co-Founder and Editor-in-Chief of Irish America *magazine.*

A Darker Shade of Green

Sometimes I wonder who I am. I'm Irish of course; my family's roots have been embedded in that soil for hundreds of years. But there's something else too.

I always felt a bit of an oddity growing up in rural Ireland. In my first Holy Communion photograph, I'm at least two feet taller than any of the other seven-year-olds, who stand around me like flower girls at a wedding. Recently I attended a Scandinavian function and I felt as if I'd found my people. Everyone looked like me — tall and fair-haired. People talk about the Celts but forget that we had several hundred years of Viking rule. And one of them must have been down our way.

My mother's side came over with Strongbow, the French-speaking Norman who landed in County Wexford in 1170 and ended up as King of Leinster, having married Aoife MacMurrough. This side of the family settled in Waterford and were inclined to join the British Army (my mother's early years were spent in India) and have pictures of Queen Victoria in their houses.

My father's family settled in Tipperary where I grew up, and was more inclined towards nationalism. (I was brought up on tales of the Black and Tans on the one hand and the sun never setting on the British Empire on the other.) Three "Wild Geese" Harty brothers fled to France and served in the Irish Brigade. A nephew of theirs, one Oliver Harty, organised the Brigade Etrangère that was part of the expedition that accompanied Wolfe Tone to stormy Bantry Bay. Later he would accompany Napoleon on his campaigns, and was created Baron de Pierrebourg of Alsace. I know all of this because the French side traced us back when I was a child, and we are still in touch. My paternal grandmother was Seymour. The name is English, as in Jane, Henry VIII's third wife. My Seymours were farmers who doled out the American corn to the needy during the Famine. We know this because of a Famine diary record that was handed down.

So who am I? We are part of all that we have met, as the poet said. I have a Roman nose, which makes me feel at home in Italy and Greece; white skin, which doesn't make me feel at home in either Italy or Greece or anywhere the sun shines. I'm taller than the average Irish woman and I have strange moments of complete inarticulateness when English seems like a foreign language; this I believe is due to a mix of ancestral genes and languages. But I'm Irish. It's in my soul.

My heart lights up when I see another Irish person. Like those two young construction workers I saw on my way to work today. I hate the Notre Dame Leprechaun, but I do believe in little people, and in the magic of the whitethorn tree. I love Irish music, and there are more Irish *seisiúns* in New York than anywhere else. When I hear an Irish fiddle I think of the miners and the railroad workers and the immigrant Irish who had little else but brought their music with them. When I hear an Irish fiddle I know I have a soul.

I believe I can tell an Irishman from the way he walks — the self-conscious gait, the way he holds his head. I believe I can tell an Irish American down to the generation. I learned that with Americans I have to communicate, and with Irish people so much is left unsaid. Or is said with a nod or a wink or an unspoken gesture. And there's a vulnerability there too, in the knowledge that another Irish person can read me — there is no hiding, they can see right through me. Like all people who have faced danger together, the Irish have a highly developed intuitive sense of each other.

Perhaps it's the fusion of blood of conqueror and conquered, of indigenous and colonist that we all are in Ireland — surely as mongrel a race as Americans — that makes me delight when I read about a Filipino-Irishman playing football for Dublin, and a Fijian playing hurling for Cork. Or meet with a Chinese-Irish family in Hawaii. Here in America, where I now live, the Irish have married into other ethnic groups more than any other race. I count among my friends Irish-Italians, Irish-Germans and Irish-Jewish. I hope for some dark-skinned, warm-blooded future partners for my red-haired, pale-skinned Californian nieces and nephews. We are far too white in my family to survive global warming.

And what of the Irish in America? Eugene O'Neill once remarked that "the thing the critics don't get about me is the fact that I'm Irish". O'Neill never made a visit to Ireland. Does that make him any less Irish? I don't think so.

Another famous writer, John Steinbeck, said, "I am half-Irish, the rest of my blood being watered down with German and Massachusetts English. But Irish blood doesn't water down very well; the strain must be very strong."

I know that's true. That despite everything we encounter, somewhere in the landscape of the heart those Irish genes refuse to lie quiet, but sing out no matter in what country, no matter with who they intermingle. Didn't we learn in school that "the Vikings became more Irish than the Irish themselves"?

My niece Caitlin, American by birth, with an English mother and an Irish father, loves Irish dance. I think of her with her red hair flying as she dances for my mother's 80th birthday, in San Francisco. Am I going to tell her that she's not Irish? Or my French cousins that they are not entitled to their Irish heritage?

What makes a person Irish, according to G.B. Shaw (who the *New York Times* insists on calling British), is a state of mind. Something to ponder as Ireland grapples with its first immigration "problem", and Lithuanians, Romanians, Bosnians, and refugees from Africa become the new Irish.

Tom Hayden

Tom Hayden is a long-time visitor to Ireland and a California State Senator. He is the author of Irish Hunger, *a collection on the Famine (1997), author of a law to include the Famine in the California school curriculum, and a frequent writer on equality issues comparing the civil rights movements in Northern Ireland and the US.*

When David Trimble said recently that Irish republicans need house-training, I heard my master's voice down through the ages, that of the Vikings, the British, and the WASPs, and knew why I am Irish.

Now and then someone has to shit on the master's rug.

They have tried to house-train us for thousands of years. And to a degree, they have succeeded. They have occupied our souls and minds, not simply our lands. We have tried to be good colonial subjects, even post-colonial subjects, learning their language, deifying their culture, denouncing our rebels. And we have trained ourselves to shit properly. We've made vaudeville paddies of ourselves, tried to become respectable, lace-curtain, corporate, won honours for everything from prize-fighting to literature, and even elected an American president. We've tried of wash off every trace of the bog, even from our memory. We've done our best to ethnically cleanse our race.

But it's not enough, and try as we might, it never will be. The Irish soul is not British, not WASP. Those people need dogs to train. We are not dogs, nor are we good at being masters.

Plenty of Irish, of course, would be embarrassed by this whole discussion. After all our sanitary progress in becoming white Anglos, they say, let's shut the closet door on the past, or excommunicate anyone who refuses to be house-trained. "The Filthy Irish Haven't Grasped the Hygiene Habit," screamed a headline in the *Irish Independent* this year, the author complaining that we "believe tidiness is not important" (27 February 2000).

Maureen Dowd of the *New York Times* excels at reinforcing our shame. For St Patrick's Day this year, she recounted how she "blushed in childish embarrassment" when her parents led Irish parades in her youth. Even today, "The mere tap-tap sound that signals the approach of *Riverdance*" fills Ms Dowd with "dread".

On the other side are sometimes found people of colour, applauded by self-hating Irish, who insist that we be classified with the master, that we are the Devil's kin, that we have chosen white skin privilege, and that the right to shit on the rug belongs only to descendants of Africa, Asia, Latin America and the American Indians. The Irish haven't really been treated like dogs, they say, only like pets.

These differences among the Irish demonstrate that the struggle for the conscience of our race continues from generation to generation.

The Irish are rightly touted as a grand success story, proof of the melting pot thesis, an example to new immigrants. But the continuing price of our material success is disregarded because it spoils the myth. For the past 150 years, we have experienced high rates of schizophrenia, depression, alcoholism and domestic violence. Irish immigrants in England today have the most serious rates of suicide and mental illness of any immigrants in Europe. Even the sanest among us have lost our bearings because our history has been forgotten or sanitised. Our major universities rarely tell our story, filing us instead under British or European civilisation.

The most extreme measure of running from our past can be counted by the thousands of Irish Americans who visit the old country without ever entering the North. It is not a fear of violence that keeps them out — New York is more violent — but a denial of our roots, and a preference for a more acceptable, if fanciful, identity.

We must re-inhabit our history. We are an old culture, ten times older than the United States. Our deepest identity is bound up with resistance to foreign domination. But we are more than warriors. Our forebears at Newgrange charted the universe through apertures that caught the rising sun on 21 December, the solstice. They were great scientists and dreamers long before they were yoked by colonialism to a shrunken concept of themselves. Our Celtic ancestor John Muir noted the conquest of our consciousness very well when he wrote that our God image "became very much like an English gentleman [who] believes in the literature and language of England, is a warm supporter of the English constitution and Sunday schools and missionary societies".

Why do I love being Irish? Because it makes me feel alive with all the possibilities and contradictions of the human condition. We are both tragic and triumphant. We have assimilated but not submitted. My hope is that we assimilate in a new direction. It is not being fully Irish to assimilate only into the "English-speaking world", as if that is where we belong. Because we have been colonial victims ourselves, we should identify with the non-English speaking world of indigenous cultures who live under oppression all to familiar to the Irish.

Our destiny is to be a global race, not a master race.

David Hewitt

David Hewitt, CBE, LLB, is an Evangelical Christian and Presbyterian Elder, a Senior Partner in a Belfast solicitors' practice, a member of the Parades Commission and a former Irish rugby international.

I was born on the Island of Ireland. I have lived there for 60 years. So I am Irish. I am not Scottish, Welsh or English. When the men of Munster met English opposition in rugby's European Cup Final, I had no divided loyalty. How disappointing that Northampton prevailed. Forty years ago, I proudly wore the green jersey at Lansdowne Road, Dublin. Under the tricolour and inspired as 50,000 sang "The Soldier's Song", we battled against the English. My Irish national pride was at stake. Yes I am Irish.

But not on paper. English, not Irish, is my language. My tax demands come from the British Exchequer. My passport allows me to "pass freely without let or hindrance in the name of her Britannic Majesty". Four years ago, Her said Majesty granted me "the dignity of an Ordinary Commander of the Civil Division of the Order of the British Empire" — so I am British, and Irish.

But I am only comfortably Irish when that Irishness is generous of heart. As when the disappointed Munster supporters applauded their Northampton victors. The friendships that grew out of encounters 40 years ago remain long after defeat and victory. Though Irish is not my language, a year of evening classes introduced me to its haunting sounds. I discovered a common identity with those who enjoy it as a first language. But when I hear it used provocatively by Republican politicians, I feel British again. I warm to those who invite me to share their Irish culture. I quickly cool when it is thrust in my face. My

Irish pride turns to shame when I see the depravity of twentieth century armed-force republicanism and tribunal-exposed corruption. The Celtic tiger could well demand a price too great, for "what shall it profit a man (or a nation) if he gains the whole world and loses his soul".

Even with Patrick, our patron saint, we have contradiction and confusion. He was a Brit born in the North of England in 389 AD. Held in high esteem by Catholic Nationalist Ireland, he is buried in a Protestant graveyard in Ulster. Perhaps it is no surprise that he is more celebrated at a distance where absence makes the heart grow fonder. New York and Boston are greener than Dublin. Deep feelings are aroused each 17 March between Catholic Nationalists and Protestant Unionists — was Patrick "one of us or one of them"? He was neither, and both. He came to Ireland at God's call to pagan druids, converting 120,000 of them to the way of Christ. Patrick, like his Master, saw national identity as of little importance. The Kingdom of God was what mattered, transcending petty loyalties and destroying the walls of partition they created. So it was that Europe was enlightened from this small island of saints and scholars. Today Europe and the world at large waits to see if we can struggle free from the burden of our history, and from the blasphemy that claims "God is on our side".

I want to be Irish, but would rather be British if to be Irish I have to be anti-British. More than either, I long for an Ireland at peace with itself when its people have rediscovered Patrick's God. His offer of peace beyond understanding is readily available to twenty-first century Irish men and women.

I am hopeful. Some of the perpetrators of yesterday's violence now give a positive political lead. The bankruptcy of the armed struggle has been accepted. The bitter pills of political inclusion, prisoner release and weapons decommissioning are at least being sucked, if not swallowed. Sworn enemies are discovering their shared humanity, previously hidden by distancing and demonising. The constitutional wheels in assembly, committee and councils are being oiled by occasional good humour from unexpected sources. Support for intransigent marchers and residents grows thin as TV cameras expose mean and sour attitudes, each side using "human rights" to wrong their neighbours.

The determined bridge-building of many people, the courage of victims and the professionalism of police and army have together kept us from the brink.

If trust takes root, everything is possible. Those who follow Patrick's Lord are free to take the risks and enjoy the blessings that peacemaking brings. For his Kingdom is not of this world, let alone this small island. Would He not delight in seeing green and orange accept each others' identity and enjoy each others' culture — Irelanders together? Yes, I am hopeful — even, at times, excited!

John Hume

John Hume MP MEP is the founding member and leader of the Social Democratic and Labour Party in Northern Ireland. He was joint winner, along with David Trimble, of the 1998 Nobel Prize for Peace.

Despite the fact that the world has become a smaller place, with the most far-reaching revolution in history — tremendous advances in technology, telecommunications and transport — a sense of the importance of our Irish identity has not been lost. Instead, it has been strengthened with positive developments in the peace process and a greater sense of national confidence in the global arena. Irish cultural, political and historical identity has evolved in tandem with the creation of this post-nationalist world where the European Union can be seen as one of the greatest examples in modern history of conflict resolution.

Our sense of community is of fundamental importance to our Irish identity. This is of particular relevance in a world where decentralisation and empowerment of those traditionally excluded from the structures of the nation state should be foremost on our list of priorities. My own Irishness is invariably linked to my identity as a Derry man. My pride in my country is fuelled by my love of my city, and its musical, cultural and historic traditions. The ideal behind the European Union is particularly important in the construction of a positive identity for our people. It envisages a union of peoples, of communities and of regions, and is not merely restricted to the day-to-day practicalities of modern political economies. For me, this ideal and respect of diversity is central to any positive sense of Irish identity.

Our Irishness is not confined to one piece of land. It is about our people, and we have traditionally been one of the biggest wandering peoples of the world. Because of our emigrants, the Irish Diaspora is one of the greatest in the world, represented in countries as diverse as Australia, Argentina and the USA. The first president of France was Irish and Irish roots have touched the political histories of many other countries such as Chile, the USA and Canada. The talent of Irish people has been used in promoting the cultural, social and economic development of many countries throughout the world, and is an important factor in our collective identity as an Irish people, transcending our political traditions. Recent murals in a loyalist area of Derry, Bond Street, replace the traditional paramilitary drawings with paintings of many men of Ulster roots who have been presidents of the USA, while the St Patrick's Day celebration is still celebrated by the Irish community worldwide.

The international Irish community has great potential for the development of modern Ireland and we should harness the massive strength of this Irish Diaspora for the benefit of Ireland as a whole. One way to do this would be for the Irish government to create a *Certificate of Irish Identity*, which could be applied for by people with Irish roots across the world. This would no doubt strengthen solidarity within the global Irish community and would promote more inward investment as well as the marketing of our products on a worldwide scale.

The talents and diversity of Irish people are our greatest strength. Our music and literary traditions are revered and respected across the world, encompassing the great yet diverse talents of literary figures such as James Joyce, Samuel Beckett, Seamus Heaney, Brian Friel and Roddy Doyle. In the world of music, U2 and The Corrs are heard alongside James Galway and Phil Coulter.

These are the sounds and talents of the Ireland that enters the new millennium, and in this new millennium we will continue to build a new Ireland based upon the strengths of our people, and upon agreement and respect for our diversity.

Fionnuala Hunt

*Fionnuala Hunt, violinist, is the Leader and Music Di-
rector of the Irish Chamber Orchestra. She has been
guest leader with the London Symphony Orchestra, the
Ulster Orchestra, the BBC Philharmonic Orchestra
amongst others, and is Honorary President of the Dublin
Youth Orchestra.*

Identity. For me it is all about identity. Growing up as I did in Northern Ireland, there was no room for vagueness about one's identity. It was black or
white (orange or green really!), this or that. There was no fudging or softening
of the hard edges of the pigeonhole into which people sought to place you.
Along with virtually everyone else, I conformed to this narrow and limiting
worldview and slotted meekly into my appointed pigeonhole: Catholic middle
class, not especially political, aware of but not overly disturbed by the divisions
in our society. As a consequence, I didn't establish an identity of my own but
all too readily assumed the one that was thrust upon me.

Like generations before me, I could easily have continued along this barren
path, but then fate intervened. Thanks to my burgeoning career as a violinist I
began to travel extensively, first to Vienna where I studied for eight years and
subsequently to many far-flung corners — Australia's Barossa Valley,
Jyväskylä in Finland, Wheeling in West Virginia . . .

The hectic travel schedule has continued unabated for 20 or more years
and while it undoubtedly has its downsides (a legion of delayed flights and a
mountain of lost luggage spring instantly to mind) it has also acted as a constant stimulus, urging me to re-examine my own sense of Irishness. Twenty
years ago, the world-view of Ireland was slavishly stereotypical, based either
on the belief that our island was permanently wracked by sectarian violence or

populated by a tribe of devil-may-care leprechauns. It was an image I constantly felt uncomfortable with yet, try as I might, I found I could do little to shake people's beliefs and help them to see a broader, more richly textured picture. It was the same with music — people either expected thumping rock and roll or, more likely, traditional jigs and reels. What was this classical violinist doing, coming from the land of the leprechaun?

I didn't fit their stereotype, they couldn't pigeonhole me and hey, I enjoyed the feeling! Slowly, over a period of years, my sense of Irishness filled out and developed. The narrow, straight-jacketing process of Northern Ireland receded into the past, to be replaced by a sense of identity that was rich, complex, comforting; but also at times confusing and contradictory, even to myself. I began to revel in the great diversity of things Irish, particularly in the cultural field, and found it much easier to proclaim myself to be Irish — and look the world in the eye as I did so.

Thankfully, that world is now prepared to throw away the tired picture-postcard image of our island, as well as its belief that Ireland is one of the world's most turbulent trouble spots. It is hard to pin down a time when this change began to occur but certainly the great hope engendered by the peace process allied to the current economic boom has helped to foster and stimulate the change. This has made things much easier for me. Ireland is now hot news and gone is the day when a revelation of my nationality was quaintly acknowledged. Now the response is more likely to be a plethora of well-informed, incisive questions about current developments in Ireland.

In a sense, my own career has benefited too. Recently I played in Washington DC along with the Irish Chamber Orchestra, premiering a piece written by Bill Whelan of *Riverdance* fame. Entitled *Inishlacken*, it featured myself as a classical violinist along with Zoë Conway as a traditional fiddle player, backed by the orchestra. For too long, classical violin and traditional fiddle players have regarded each other with something bordering on sniffy disdain. This piece demonstrated that the two styles could not only exist comfortably side by side but could also learn from each other in the process.

I would like to see this piece as a metaphor for the new Ireland that I hope will emerge as the coming century dawns. Not only should it be inclusive of all traditions, it can and should go further than that by promoting a new era of co-operation and development between them. I will continue to travel, though perhaps not at the hectic pace of heretofore, and I shall do so safe in the knowledge that my sense of Irishness is more secure than ever.

The great potential of our country is finally being realised. Truly we are taking our place amongst the nations of the world. It is an exciting time to be Irish and to feel part of the process. Personally, I feel that my long held, richly diverse concept of Irishness has at last been validated. Let there be no more stereotypes. Let the pigeonholes be banished forever!

Garry Hynes

Photo: Ivan Kymel

Garry Hynes is founder member and Artistic Director of the Druid Theatre Company and former Artistic Director of the Abbey. In 1997, she received a Tony Award for directing The Beauty Queen of Leenane, *the first woman to be so honoured.*

It is through the work of writers, poets and playwrights in particular that I've come to understand what it means to me to be Irish, and there are a couple of verses by one of the greatest of them, John Millington Synge, which always seems to me to catch the essence of that experience.

Prelude

> Still south I went and west and south again
> Through Wicklow from the morning till the night
> And far from cities and the sight of man
> Lived with the sunshine and the moon's delight
>
> I knew the stars the flowers and the birds
> The grey and wintry sides of many glens
> And did but half remember human words
> In converse with the mountains moors and fens

Jennifer Johnston

Jennifer Johnston was born in Dublin in 1930 and has lived in Derry since 1974. She has published 11 novels, some short stories and monologues.

I have to say that I don't reflect much any longer on my Irishness . . . or indeed on the subject of Irishness in general. There was a long draggy time in the 1970s and 1980s when we were all expected to examine our heads and our hearts and speak to the world about our "Irishness" . . . or lack of it as the case often was. At that time, we were persuaded that it was a useful thing to do. I'm not so sure about that. We bored the world and solved no problems.

"What does it mean to be Irish?" The question was thrown at you in England, France, Italy . . . of course also in America, but they don't count, as they think they know the answer and don't really care what you have to say on the subject. The same tired old answers were trotted out; Yeats was quoted, the dead heroes, Seamus Heaney, four beautiful green fields, also the fact that we were indubitably not English . . . .for God's sake, even the most loyal of Loyalists don't aspire to Englishness, just that amorphous notion of being and remaining "British" . . . one of the world's cop outs! The fact that so many people all seemed to be obsessed by this question of identity added an element of dementia to the problems we were already undergoing: how to cope with poverty, violence, corruption; how to present true democracy to an island with four and half million inhabitants, who had lived for so long colonised by their neighbour and by the Church . . . both tyrannical masters in their own different ways. It has been a lengthy and very painful process, not over yet by any means, but we seem to be moving along.

Neither the French nor the Italians spend their time asking each other what it means to be French or Italian; they don't need to, they know. We know too, in the same way that the French or the Italians do; each one of us has our own view, or vision, if you prefer, of what our nationality means to us. Maybe our view is not the same in every aspect as that of the person living in the next house, but we are learning to say "so what?"

I have never found another country in which I would rather live and die. I feel great pride when we do things right and a great anger when we get things horribly wrong. All my bondings (to use a loathsome contemporary expression) have happened in this country, with my family and their past, my city, and the whole landscape of the island, to the language we use and the way we have moulded it and made it different and vital, the stories we tell and the songs we sing and all the people with whom I have learned and worked and played. I feel comfortable here; the shoes of Irishness fit me well. What more can I say?

Photo: Sony Music

Brian Kennedy

Brian Kennedy is a singer from Belfast. As well as his solo work, he has collaborated with Van Morrison and Ronan Keating, amongst others. His latest album is Now That I Know What I Want.

You know, I would love to have a time machine and travel back to Ireland at the beginning of the last century. Apart from resisting the temptation to make a quick detour to Merrion Square to visit Mr Wilde, I would head north-east first to my hometown of Belfast. I'm sure it would be unrecognisable compared to now.

Historically, I would go so far as to say that the definition of "Irishness" has gone through some extraordinary interpretations, almost to the point of schizophrenia (murderers, saviours, geniuses, alcoholic virgin dunces). Also, what other land mass as tiny as ours has been so responsible for the breathtaking volume of creative expression in all its forms, which have gone on to be globally embraced, copied and celebrated almost to the point of obsession.

So just as the land and cityscape have been permanently sculpted by the weather of progress, then it is not unreasonable to suggest that the people have too, right?

Like so many of my ancestors, I left home for the bright lights of London at the first available opportunity when I was just 18 years old, because the message was loud and clear: *London = success* and *Ireland = failure*. I stayed for almost 14 years. Although initially I was cosseted to a degree (albeit in an overcrowded, starving squat) by an almost exclusive Irish circle of friends, it was really one of the first moments where I genuinely felt disconnected, simply because I was a foreigner, so I was forced to think about exactly where I was from, where I was going and indeed why I was different. It took a while before I finally ventured out of the safety net of "London Irishness", or more unkindly the "Plastic Paddies" or "Champagne Catholics" (if they had money). Irishness really had no positive currency beyond the building trade and I realised that my childhood experiences where for the most part the complete antithesis of everybody else's that I came in contact with.

I think that my initial personal experience of politically enforced negative identity coupled with religious fervour definitely contributed to the so-called uniqueness. When I was growing up on the Falls Road in Belfast, I was made violently aware that it was illegal to think of myself as anything other than a British subject. School favoured British history and Irish was taught like French, as a foreign language that almost everyone thought was a waste of time because it was dead. I took to it immediately, though, because our teacher Mr Austin was tough and brilliant and I loved the sound of the words. Although I was born in Northern Ireland, therefore eligible for an Irish or British passport, it never occurred to me for a second that I was anything other than Irish, mainly because of the political situation I found myself in and the seemingly unending punishment of that particular so-called crime.

As far as suffering goes, then you can rest assured that first prize always went to "Jesus on the cross" who died for all of our sins. The biggest sin of all, seemingly, being sexual desire. Again, this was something that was regarded as illegal, so it also had to be suppressed, silenced and kept under lock and key like some criminal disease. I'm really talking about what it is like to have to first explore your emotional vulnerability in the darkness of a confession box with someone in uniform not experienced enough to give advice to anyone, let alone a child, or indeed in the darkness of fear and misinformation at any age. How can anything be made clear in the dark? Isn't that meant to be the purpose of light? I think that whoever made up the rules for priests was just a bad speller. "Celibate" really should have been "Celebrate!"

I could go on all day about this subject but I want to talk specifically about the symptoms of this particular source because I think they are a huge part of this thing called Irishness. When anything is denied and suppressed, it just increases the appetite for it. We've been on an emotional diet for too long.

My friend, the Donegal poet Cathal O'Searcaigh, brought something interesting to my attention recently, which has to do with the power of language. In our mother tongue of Irish, if you say, for instance, you are hungry, then you say "*tá ocras orm*", which is directly translated as "hunger is upon me". So hunger is something that you feel as a separate thing like say, sadness, anger and so on. It's like these feelings that visit and leave you without warning. In English, however, because the sentence reads as "I'm hungry", then you actually become the very thing that you feel in the sense that you take it over completely. Hunger is no longer "upon" you like an item of clothing that can be removed; you have actually become hunger itself, as a declaration.

I'm reminded of a scene near the end of Monty Pythons' *The Life of Brian*, where an officer is looking for Brian because he has been pardoned at the last minute. As soon as the rest of the crucified prisoners find out, they all pretend to be him one by one, and it has this sort of domino effect whereupon this very English man calls out "No, I'm Brian . . . and so's my wife".

As far my memory serves me, the word "Irish" was always wrapped up in thick layers of negative definitions, one of the favourites being "stupidity". If we focus on the sound of the word "Ir-ish" it sounds like we are something not quite complete, like describing someone as Small-ish or Tall-ish. Again, I am reminded of child-ish (there it is again) school days when the person that suffered the most abuse was the one that exhibited some kind of difference to what was considered normal, and therefore was immediately a threat.

Given that, historically, our Irish language was forced into the hills of minority, it is interesting then that the most celebrated writers in the English language are people like our own Oscar, Yeats, James Joyce, Samuel Beckett, Sean O'Casey, Seamus Heaney, Brendan Behan, Maeve Binchy, Patrick Kavanagh, Brian Friel, Sebastian Barry, Patrick McCabe, Colm Toibin, Joe O'Connor and so on and so forth, and that is just the tip of the iceberg in terms of the global written word.

Irishness, thankfully, no longer means having to be only one thing. For me, music replaced guilt as the petrol in the engine of change. Given that it is the language of emotion universally, songs are a safe place to visit how you really feel, regardless of the intensity. In trying to explain being Irish, I would say it's like taking a picture of the word "sadness" and then taking another picture of the word "joy". When the film comes back from the chemist, it's been double-exposed and the two words have become superimposed like some strange hybrid.

Like a lot of cultures that have a history of profound loss as a result of war or famine or both, there is an underlying melancholia that seems to exist in the very blood, like some kind of ancient algae that the water depends upon for clarity, almost like a gene. Someone told me they could hear it in my voice, especially when I sang an old Irish song. I suppose it's possible given that songs and poetry were really the only safe way to record history because for the longest time it was too dangerous to write anything down. It's interesting too how sometimes the most difficult words are easier to sing than to say.

On a reluctant final note (otherwise we will be here all day!) I think it's important to mention the phenomenon called *Riverdance*. In one three-and-a-half-minute segment as part of something that is as equally cool and naff as the Eurovision song contest, Bill Whelan, Moya Doherty, John McColgan, Jean Butler and Michael Flatley made Irish dancing truly sexy around the whole world.

Now that's what I call Irishness!

Dennis Kennedy

Dennis Kennedy lectures at the Institute of European Studies at Queen's University in Belfast and is President of the Irish Association for Cultural, Economic and Social Relations. He was formerly Deputy Editor at The Irish Times *and from 1985–91 was Head of the European Commission office in Northern Ireland.*

The only unique thing about the Irish, perhaps, is their utter conviction that there is something unique about being Irish.

This sense of a totally distinct identity may be common to many peoples, but in the case of the Irish, the fervour with which it is embraced is in stark contrast to its shaky foundations.

Conor Cruise O'Brien once defined Irishness as "not primarily a question of birth, blood or language, but the condition of being involved in the Irish situation and usually of being mauled by it". He was examining the writers selected by Donagh MacDonagh and Lennox Robinson for inclusion in the 1959 Oxford Book of Irish Verse and was finding their geographical basis for Irishness very unsatisfactory.

Forty years on from that review, the Belfast Agreement reverted to geography, decreeing that it was "the birthright" of all the people of Ireland, including Northern Ireland, to be Irish. But this definition was not just geographical; it was a voluntary sort of Irishness, for in the Agreement the Irish Government formally acknowledges that the entire Northern population is Irish only if it so desires, and conversely is not Irish if it so desires.

The revised Irish Constitution, altered after the Belfast Agreement, now reflects this optional dimension to being Irish. In its original form, the Constitution clearly linked the "Irish nation" to the "national territory" of Ireland, which was defined as the whole island. Now Article 2 speaks grandly of the birthright of every person born in the island to be part of the Irish nation, a right, incidentally, extended to anyone else entitled by law to be a citizen. As that includes any Arab sheikh or Mongolian magnate prepared to invest £1 million in Ireland, Irishness is both made a much vaguer concept and left clinging to the geographical island as its only touchstone.

This fixation with the island is understandable. As an island it is, after all, distinct, unique, unlike the people who live in it, who speak English, belong to a universal religion, spring from a mixed ancestry and over the years have displayed both a zeal and an ability to leave the island and settle down elsewhere. Even while on the island, they have had great difficulty agreeing on a definition of Irishness, disputes leading both to split hairs and split heads.

The follies and frustrations of geographical nationalism were graphically portrayed in Flann O'Brien's *The Poor Mouth*. The hero, Bonaparte O'Coonassa, is pursued across the Paradise of Ireland by an evil-smelling great hairy quadruped that threatens to devour him. When asked to put down on paper the shape and appearance of this savage thing, O'Coonassa draws an outline which, the author notes, bore a close resemblance to "the pleasant little land which is our own".

For most of the past 30 years, the inhabitants of part of the island have been pursued by the same evil-smelling monster, this time armed not just with fangs, but with armalites and semtex. Its baleful influence is still around, and both permeates the Belfast Agreement and threatens to destroy it.

Political nationalism is the enemy of proper enjoyment of the real sense of Irishness that can exist for those "involved in the Irish situation", which, the politicians now confirm, means little more than living on the island. Living on a reasonably small island means we share its geography and its geology, its history and its various traditions. We can delight in and feel special affinity with the artistic and literary works of others who have also lived here. We can cheer our heads off when Ireland win at Lansdowne Road, and roar home any horse born, bred or trained in Ireland. And when both the rugby team and the horse let us down, we can say too bad and forget about it. For, in truth, it is not that important.

For the tourist, we can invent an Irishness that is a byword for hospitality, conviviality, and conversation, practised by a non-materialistic people given to porter and poetry, who, at the same time, have somehow managed to become the smartest entrepreneurs of Europe. There is no harm in that, provided we don't go taking it seriously and believing it ourselves. Much the same could be said of any concept of Irishness.

Sr Stanislaus Kennedy

Photo: Derek Speirs/Report

Sister Stanislaus Kennedy is the Founder and President of Focus Ireland. A native of Lispole, County Kerry, she joined the Sisters of Charity in 1958, and has been instrumental in developing and implementing social service programmes that have benefited thousands of needy people.

Growing up on the Dingle Peninsula during and after the Second World War, I had the archetypal traditional Irish rural childhood. I lived my childhood years among fishermen and farmers, the caretakers of a peasant Irish tradition. There was story-telling and card-playing, music, dance and drama, in the place of radio, cinema, television and personal computers. It was a life of great simplicity and spirituality. The institutional church was very important but the spirituality of the people went deeper than any church or institution. The pattern of day and night, the coming and going of the seasons of the year and the rhythm of life itself were lived unselfconsciously in the presence of God, as the people saved the hay, fished for trout and salmon, went to stations, wakes, funerals, weddings, cut and footed the turf or brought tea to the fields or the bog. Being Irish means to me being at home with that traditional culture and way of life and continuing to cherish it.

But it was a hard life too, there on the Dingle Peninsula in the 1940s and 1950s. The people had lived through the Depression, two world wars and the terrible strife of civil war. History was but a generation away. The older people had known people who had been forbidden to speak their native tongue, who knew what it was like to lose parents, family and friends to the Famine. They all knew the hard times that drove their neighbours from the land.

Being Irish means to me the experience of having lived close to poverty and oppression and how that experience can open us up to a new understanding and a new compassion. Hardness of heart cannot be maintained for long in the face of human suffering. I saw the courage and faith of people who had little, for whom everything was a challenge, and they taught me how to let go of conventional values and follow my heart, setting myself apart from the support of a society with its promises and illusions and embarking on a journey that does not give immediate certainties or immediate rewards.

The life I live in the Ireland of today is almost the polar opposite of the life I lived as a child. It is urban, hectic, clock-bound, rather than rural, peaceful and seasonal. And yet, in the midst of the frantic days that make up my life today, it is to that childhood world that I look for my sense of who I am as a person, as a spiritual being and as an Irishwoman. Being Irish means to me having a creation-centred sense of spirituality, rooted in silence and solitude, centred on God but not separate from the world.

The people I grew up among had a strong sense of themselves and of community. Being Irish means to me valuing the sense of community and working towards creating a more inclusive society, where the gifts of everyone are realised.

Being Irish to me is being part of the first generation of our family to go to university. It is also seeing the next generation flooding into the schools, colleges, institutes and universities, expanding their knowledge and the national knowledge and being glad of it. Sometimes being Irish is to be smug about our own achievements, but we have not achieved what we have achieved on our own. For every one of us who has created a place for ourselves in society, there has been at least one and usually several people who have helped us to find that place, who have encouraged us, recognised our abilities and helped us through the system. I have known so many people whose lives would have been enriched and expanded beyond recognition if they had had the opportunity for education that others of us have had, and being Irish to me means working to make education available to people who have missed out on that chance because of the circumstances of their lives. I am thinking particularly of young people who leave primary and secondary school each year without being able to read or write, and whose frustrated, destroyed potential leads to lives lived at the margins.

Being Irish in this flourishing, confident, successful, educated little country today is to be challenged as our people have never before been challenged. The challenge to us now, in this sophisticated, high-tech, high-achieving economy, is to decide that we will not be satisfied until the potential of every single Irish person is realised and their energy released. The challenge is to be determined not to be satisfied with a country where there are large numbers of people still living on the margins, but to create a society where there are no them and theirs, where all is one. Our challenge as Irish people is to create a country that welcomes the strangers who seek refuge here, that respects their culture and enables them to make a new life for themselves here as other countries did for our people in previous generations. This ethos of welcome and community is the ethos on which our state was founded, and being Irish today is to hold the responsibility of those values. It is up to us to ensure that these values survive the changes that are occurring in our country and are passed on to the next generation. It all depends on us.

Tony Kennedy

Tony Kennedy has been Chief Executive of Co-operation Ireland since 1992 and is also involved in a number of community initiatives. He was active in the non-violent civil rights movement before working in the Northern Ireland Housing Executive and as Chief Housing Officer in Wakefield MDC.

My mother was born a Protestant in Dublin and moved to Belfast in 1947. She was never in any doubt that she was Irish, though she spoke of celebrating the end of the Second World War in Trinity College Dublin waving the Union Flag. My son was born in West Yorkshire to parents from Larne and Belfast and was sure when he came to Belfast at the age of eight that he was English. Now at age 15 he says he is Northern Irish. My daughter born in Londonderry (or Derry) living in England from age one to age eleven recently defined herself as "not English" in a discussion with a friend. When asked what she was, she said "mixed up, like everyone else here". Their stepmother, born in London to a father from Mayo and a north of England second-generation Irish mother is sure she is Irish. The amendment to Article 2 of the Constitution of Ireland stating that "the Irish nation cherishes its special affinity with people of Irish ancestry living abroad" brought tears to her eyes.

This long introduction is by way of illustrating the complicated issues that are generated within one family by the simple request to consider what being Irish means. For myself, at one level I am sure that I am Irish — I love the countryside and the character of (most of) the people, North and South, I cheer for the national teams in rugby and soccer (both of them) and rejoice when England are defeated — thus satisfying Enoch Powell's citizenship test, though not in the way he intended. But it is more complicated than that.

Irishness is a part of me, but it is mixed with other elements. I identify strongly with the views of John Hewitt who stated that he was an Ulsterman, Irish, British and European and that to remove any of these elements was to remove an essential part of his identity. In fact, I remember the relief I felt reading this in my late teens and receiving an endorsement of the feeling that I could be Irish (or anything else) without being required to be exclusively Irish.

The creation of an exclusive national identity creates pressure to opt out rather than opt in. If being Irish involves accepting the full cultural and political package of a Gaelic Nationalist Ireland and a rejection of any form of Britishness, I along with many, if not most, non-Catholics will reject it. This is particularly the case if the national identity is reinforced by violence. If I see a murder being committed in the name of Ireland, my feeling of Irishness is reduced, just as if I see a murder being committed in the name of Ulster, or Britain, I lose some of the feeling of identity with those groupings.

This change in the strength of my feeling for a particular identity over time, or in response to events, is an experience shared by many. Perhaps the starkest example is the reduction of Northern Ireland Protestants describing their national identity as Irish from 20 per cent in 1968 to 3 per cent in 1986. It may also be due in part to the fact that, like many people, it is frequently easier for me to describe national identity, as my daughter does, by what I am not, rather than what I am. In a similar way, the Irish, Scots and Welsh for years defined themselves as not English, while the English nowadays tend to define themselves as not European.

However, one of the advantages of membership of the European Union observable in the Republic of Ireland is the development of a more positive Irish identity. This involves rejecting the old insular attitude of the absolutism of Irishness in favour of a more relaxed outgoing feeling of nationality. This can be hurtful to those who feel their Irishness under threat, as many Northern nationalists still do, but paradoxically it increases a sense of identification of Irish with those who, like me, feel a mixed allegiance.

When I choose to identify myself as Irish, I can now do so in the comfort of feeling that my other identities are secure and respected; that I can enjoy recitations and dislike traditional music; that I need not feel guilty about being unable to speak the language. I can identify with an outward-looking nation that is confident in its external relationships to play its full part in a modern Europe and confident enough in itself to start respecting internal diversity. I can feel that I can contribute to the continuing development of Irishness to encompass black Irish or Irish of eastern European origin in years to come. I can recognise the flaws in Irish society without feeling that I should somehow overlook them, or that they should lead me to reject that part of me which is Irish. And most of all, that I can be British, European and an Ulsterman at the same time.

Lainey Keogh

Lainey Keogh is a fashion designer based in Dublin.

Being Irish . . .

. . . is born free . . . open . . . trusting . . . true . . . in heart . . . healing . . .
green . . . spontaneous . . . storytellers . . . mesmerising . . . revellers . . .
irreverent . . . poetic . . . playful . . . generous . . . funny . . . dreamy . . .
friendly . . . fluid . . . sensual . . . initiators . . . responsible . . .
intuitive . . . naïve . . . respectful . . . wild . . . childlike . . .
child-friendly . . . unpunctual . . . nature babies . . .
protective . . . caring . . . conscious . . .
aware . . . wise . . .
old druids

Virginia Kerr

Photo: Keith Saunders

Virginia Kerr is one of the most distinguished Irish so-pranos of her generation. She has sung with many of the world's leading orchestras and is a frequent performer on radio and television, both at home and abroad.

"We are the dream makers
And we are the dreamers of dreams.
Wandering by lone sea-breakers,
And sitting by desolate streams:
World-losers and world forsakers,
On whom the pale moon gleams:
Yet we are the movers and shakers
*of the world forever, it seems."**

The question of "being Irish" is something to which I have never given much thought — I have just taken it for granted. Writing this essay has made me sit down and think deeply, not only about the changing face of my country but also about the changes in myself. Perhaps I have the best of both worlds: my base is here in Ireland but I spend most of my time abroad so I am able to observe this rapidly changing country from both a national and international viewpoint.

While studying at music college in London, back in the late 1970s, I remember reading an interview with a well-known Irish singer who had made her life outside Ireland. One remark she made stayed with me for a long time. She said "The Irish apologise for living." I remembered that phrase many times during my student years and later. Sometimes whilst sitting with friends

---

* Quotations at beginning and end are from "Ode" by Arthur O'Shaughnessy (1844–1881).

and hearing of a bomb going off somewhere in London, I would feel a terrible sense of shame that such atrocities were being carried out in the name of my country. It was a strange time to be living in England then and I often felt a need to defend Ireland and to point out all the wonderful things about the country that were being overshadowed by these terrible events. Our history of being the underdog for such a long time caused us to have a kind of collective low self-esteem, but in another way it was a forcing ground for our language and folk tradition.

Visiting other countries during those years seemed to be easier — they appeared to focus on our good qualities and were always eager to learn more about the wonderful countryside and friendly people. America, of course, was the easiest place of all but I often got a sense that the Ireland they knew about or wanted to learn about was more likely to have come from the world of stage and screen.

As a young musician starting a career, opportunities were scarce at home and one inevitably had to go abroad. Unfortunately the same thing happens today but because we are no longer isolated the transition seems much easier. In the early 1980s young singers had little or no chance to work with professional orchestras or with professional conductors and directors, so much so that we had to take matters into our own hands and start a company ourselves, which we did, and the Young Irish Artists was formed in 1981. We operated for four years and by then things had started to happen musically throughout the country and we went our separate ways to further our solo careers. Though I think it's a very sad state of affairs that we still have no opera house in Ireland, wonderful work is now being done countrywide in the classical music field and there are opportunities available to Irish musicians that one could only have dreamt of in the past. Today we have singers, pianists and instrumentalists across the globe in all the art forms from pop to traditional, classical to folk — all living happily with their international counterparts, both drawing from and enriching them with an eagerness never before experienced.

I recently visited County Kerry and attended performances at the Fleadh Chiarraí and also Siamsa Tíre. It was such a joy to see our traditional dancing and singing being performed with such enthusiasm by even the youngest children as they displayed their talents. For many years it was left to the emigrants to nurture and treasure this wonderful cultural heritage but thankfully now in every school in Ireland, children are being encouraged to learn a whole variety of instruments and traditional musicians are passing on their precious skills.

Performing in different parts of the world has given me the opportunity to compare and contrast different ways of life and I have observed Irish society emerging with a self confidence and pride that was alien in former times. Our new found success, wealth and place in the world have attracted attention everywhere. People want to share in the new improved Ireland. It is true that some outsiders view our country as a dreamlike place of misty hills and valleys with everyone having a ball all day every day. The reality is a little different but at the same time whenever I think of home I think of a rural, friendly warmth and welcome that I hope we can retain side by side with the five star lifestyle now available to so many (but sadly not to all) We now have knowledge and choices and must take care not to find ourselves, in years to come, lamenting the loss of the very things that make us so special. Being known as Ireland of the Welcomes may be put to the test in ways that cause us to look inwards at what exactly Irish values encompass.

"For each age is a dream that is dying
Or one that is coming to birth."

Avila Kilmurray

Avila Kilmurray is Director of the Northern Ireland Voluntary Trust. She helped to conceive and establish the Northern Ireland Women's Coalition and represented the Coalition in the talks that resulted in the Good Friday Peace Agreement.

Being Irish may be too comfortable, may even invite complacency, given the chic national status that all things Irish have achieved since *Riverdance*. What my grandmother banned from her matriarchal home as "peasant" is now cultural *haute couture*. Roots, albeit with a modernist gloss, are definitely in, rather than being discreetly hidden as was the fashion in the 1960s and 1970s.

Born and reared in Dublin in a family that never indulged in foreign holidays, being Irish was taken for granted. The only clear consciousness of that status came from a study of school-taught Irish history where Irishness was a concept that emerged in opposition to Britishness, and where the term "West Brit" was seen as a deliberate insult. The "Wrap the Green Flag Round Me" commemoration of the fiftieth anniversary of the 1916 Rising was the ultimate exercise in the creation of a hegemonic nationalist political culture; what was lost in the process was any sense of complexity. Ó Riada's stirring "Mise Eire" spoke to the soul rather than to the intellect. The spare, ageing figure of De Valera presided raven-like over the transformation of the 26-county Republic into the national state.

However, as with many others, it was only in leaving Ireland that a clearer personal perspective of Irishness was discovered. First of all there was the gleeful realisation that the presentation of an Irish passport generally elicited a warm response in foreign parts. The Irish were not seen as colonisers, or a feared superpower, or even as having specific objectionable national characteristics. That many Irish people actively engaged in the British colonial enterprise seemed to go unnoticed; and the only complaints appeared to be related to the perceived national pastime of drinking. If anything, there was the cuddly feeling that the Irish were the talented, good-humoured, if somewhat obstreperous youngsters of Western Europe. Playing along with this rather patronising stereotype won many a student job and expanded social circles.

If absence is said to make the heart grow fonder, what came as a complete shock was the longing for the physical landscape of the island. Sequestered in the landlocked Australian capital, Canberra, the most acute absence for me was the roar and crash of the sea. Faced with the immensity of a country-continent, thoughts of the sheer diversity of the home scenery inspired a sense of loss. The vividness of the colours of bog and coast, together with the ever shifting light patterns in the western skies, came to characterise Ireland in the mind's eye. Clearly there was greater scenic drama in other countries of the world, and more striking terrain, but the physical compactness of the island emphasised its kaleidoscope of colour and texture.

Divided Irishness

By the mid-1970s Cathleen Ni Houlihan was more likely to be found on the plane to Brussels rather than dancing at the village crossroads. Northern Ireland was in flames and the Republic was embarrassed by the sight. Working regularly between war-torn Derry and complacent Dublin was not good for one's mental stability. Crossing the border was not just a physical reality and a security ordeal, but required a psychological shift in gear. If people in Dublin asked, "How are things in the North?", any answer that lasted longer than two minutes in length was likely to elicit a glazed expression and a polite, apologetic comment as the enquirer moved away. People really did not want to know, or else felt that they had the measure of the situation and did not welcome any complicating explanations. Unspoken was the underlying question — Why can't they be more like us here in the Republic?" The non-Catholic, minority communities in the Republic stayed quiet.

My sense of Irishness became confused and confusing. The experience of being a southerner living in the North highlighted the identity issue. For the first time in my life, my identity was directly challenged by Unionists, who saw themselves as British, and any immigrant from the south as an interloper. As a community worker in loyalist communities there was the realisation — somewhat surprising to a southerner — that one could not simply dismiss or explain away the local sense of British identity as "false consciousness". That British identity might well be uncertain and defensive in nature (which often took the form of deriding aspects of Irishness), but it was no less genuine and deeply held for all that. Equally, the Irish identity of nationalist communities in Northern Ireland was fashioned by their experience of being a distrusted minority within a contested state. The "double minority" thesis was at work — nationalists within Northern Ireland and unionists within the island of Ireland. On a personal level the conundrum highlighted the complexity of Irishness. On a political level, it encouraged a devil's advocate stance — arguing the northern republican position in the face of deliberate southern incomprehension, and being conscious of unionist fears in the face of an increasingly narrow Gaelic, Catholic nationalism in the North.

One of the saddest developments of the 1980s was the strategy that sought to translate the political message of "ourselves alone" into a cultural and social hegemony within nationalist communities. Clearly this was a tactic that drew on the historic example of the Gaelic League which provided a nascent political culture for re-emerging Irish republicanism at the turn of the 1900s. In Northern Ireland, the tactic was equally politically effective, although the results of the strategy were rather less inclusive in nature than they had been almost a century earlier. The Gaelic new wave was fashioned after the pattern of the Patrick Pearse philosophy rather than that advocated by Gaelic League founder, Douglas Hyde. An immediate consequence in the north was the sharp political edge provided to the responsive assertion of an Ulster-Scots language and culture; again, tending to emphasise difference rather than diversity. In the longer term, an optimist might argue that the thesis of a burgeoning northern Gaelic identity, and the antithesis of Ulster-Scots, could yet have the potential to evolve into the synthesis of a broader, more inclusive definition of

Irishness. In the interim, however, the prospect of co-existence as a *modus vivendi* in place of any recognition of mutual interdependence becomes more marked; with the boundaries of that co-existence being jealously policed by the political guardians of "parity of esteem".

In the Republic, historical and attitudinal revisionism were a poor substitute for critical analysis. By the 1990s degrees of complexity began to emerge in consideration of Irishness. Thought in the Republic seemed to be moving from uncritical southern nationalism, to rejectionist revisionism, to an optimistic "All's well that ends well" sigh of relief after the Good Friday Agreement. The consensus is that its time to relegate the past to history and get on with things. Perhaps this is an explanation as to why there is still a resistance to the idea that peace building and reconciliation, which are so glibly spoken of as being essential within Northern Ireland, might have any relevance to people within the Republic itself; and if so what such relevance might be.

Coming to Terms with Irishness

The combination of the hesitantly successful peace process, the emergence of a strong economy in the Republic, and the recent cultural renaissance has resulted in a new self-confidence in being Irish. The "broth of a boy" image of a Behan has been replaced by the considerably more stylish presentation of a Heaney or the sharp intellect of Mary Robinson. Three decades have moved the Irish from being patronised to being acceptable and accomplished patrons in many spheres of activity.

What the new sense of national self-confidence does is to offer us the potential to recognise the essential diversity that lies at the core of Irishness. Even a superficial examination of any family history provides evidence of this. My personal family litany reflects the waves of influence across the centuries. A clear Anglo-Norman inheritance from my mother's side was complicated by the economic disinheritance of a great-grandfather who had the temerity to marry a Catholic in the mid-nineteenth century. This left a grandfather with a palpable land hunger and a drive to restore the family fortunes. On the paternal side, there were influences drawn from the Murphys of Wexford as well as the long-settled descendants of fourteenth-century gallowglasses from Scotland. This pot pourri of Irishness was given additional piquancy by parental family connections through marriage that included a colonial High Court Justice in Africa and his brother, a priest in North Belfast's Ardoyne, with decided republican sympathies. In short, nothing that was particularly out of place in an Irish family and that had all the makings of a gregarious, and at times garrulous, family Christmas.

Nevertheless, continuing political divisions within the island have raised queries over the genuine diversity of the concept of Irishness. By definition, those that advocated the British identity excluded themselves, and were eventually excluded, from any sense of Irishness. Adherence to a sense of Britishness remains strong, and has in all probability been strengthened by the past 30 years of the Troubles. Unionist Ulster is no less thran than its nationalist neighbours. If anything, its dogged determination not to be Irish is an indication of a negative sense of identity, rather than any sense of coherence between a British identity held in Cullybackey and that held in Birmingham. However, political hurts and uncertainties are still too raw to allow any creative examination of the implications of a multinational sense of Britishness, let alone of Irishness.

The careful crafting of the Good Friday Agreement has finally set out an alternative conceptual agenda. For the first time, there has been an attempt made to untangle the concepts of identity, allegiance and citizenship. A possible *à la carte* approach is on offer if there is sufficient imaginative political leadership and community confidence within Northern Ireland to allow a creative examination of the options. While copper-fastening the right, as expressed by the majority of the electorate of Northern Ireland, to decide the constitutional status of the region (i.e. the exercise of sovereignty), the Agreement reaffirms the right of the people of Northern Ireland to hold diverse identities, traditions and aspirations; and to identify themselves and to be accepted as Irish or British or both. Furthermore, the right to hold both British and Irish citizenship is accepted by both governments. In other words, it is now possible for political unionists to be able to participate in the concept of Irishness without jeopardising their preferred constitutional position. What is now required is the context which will make it reasonable and attractive for them to do so. This presents a challenge to those that seek to advocate a genuinely inclusive sense of Irishness.

Negotiating Irishness

If the flaring skirts and the high-kicking reels of *Riverdance* questioned the accepted perceptions of traditional Irish dancing, then the changing image of Irishness must also be recognised. Escape from the squinting windows of petty localism and rural Catholicism that stunted potential in the 1950s and 1960s has allowed individual initiative to flourish. What is less certain is the sense of collective identity. The replacement of the local gossip by the gossip column does little to guarantee a more acceptable, accepting, view of ourselves. It is this collective self-perception that still has to be negotiated. As President, Mary Robinson may well have encouraged us to commence the process of reflecting on the social, economic and cultural diversity that is Ireland; however, reflection needs to be followed by analysis and conclusions.

There is still the common factor of a small, shared island on the western fringes of Europe. There is still a sense of pride in the creativity and occasional eccentricity that Irishness can sometimes denote. There is the awareness that the Irishness of the native islanders is supplemented by the diverse Irishness of a wide Diaspora across the globe. There is now the opportunity that, when we consider Louis McNeice's insight that:

> *Pride in your history is pride*
> *In living what your fathers died,*
> *Is pride in taking your own pulse*
> *And counting in you someone else,*

the "someone else" will take account of the wide diversity of what has comprised our Irishness over the generations. Negotiating an inclusive sense of Irishness with ourselves may yet create the context within which the currently mutually divisive community identities in the north of the island may find a place, not by forgetting history but through reconciling it.

Maeve Kyle

Maeve Kyle represented Ireland at hockey (1948–1968) and athletics in the Olympics, 1956, 1960 and 1964. She continues to coach athletics.

I am Irish — and very proud of it! Being born and bred on the island of Ireland, what else could I be? This is neither an ethnic nor a political statement, merely an acceptance that I have a recognisable identity — I belong to the Island of Ireland, and the island belongs to me.

I grew up in Kilkenny, in a strongly Protestant family — a good marriage of Anglo-Irish and Irish stock, but was blessed to be in an environment where people were valued for themselves and not for their accident of birth into any particular religious or political strand. With both parents highly qualified scientists, we were taught to question and to enquire before we made any decision on the actions or values of others. As small children we were entrusted to those who cared for us, be it the gardener to take us to the hurling match or the nursemaid to take us to see the various cribs at Christmas. These activities were considered at least as valuable to our development as the more expected activities of a rural Protestant family. We learnt to love and to treasure the countryside and seaside of our beautiful island — long before we reached the questioning teenage years!

My full Irish identity came to fruition when I was selected at 20 to represent Ireland in Field Hockey in 1948 — an ambition since childhood, nurtured by parents and teachers. My first appearance in the green of Ireland was in Belfast. The reception and support for the whole team was immense, and we were a glorious mixture of every tradition in Ireland — North and South, Protestant and Catholic! These team-mates became my friends and confidants and helped me to appreciate the many strands of Irishness on this island, and through these friends, some five years later, I met and married my beloved Sean, son of strong Ulster Presbyterian stock who happened to be a sports fanatic. Sean added another strand to my sporting portfolio — track and field athletics. Once again I was selected to represent Ireland — this time as a sprinter in Melbourne at the 1956 Olympic Games. My joy and pride knew no bounds when I walked into that huge stadium representing my native island — with my team-mates from Belfast, Dublin, Donegal, Cork et al. We were there for one purpose: to represent the best of Irish sporting youth in our chosen sports in the greatest sporting festival that there is.

This expression of who I am is not readily understood; because I represented "Ireland" in sport, in the eyes of some I must have at least Nationalist/Republican sympathies. The fact that I was never eligible to represent any other country under the existing rules has escaped notice! Being raised in a strong church-going, Church of Ireland, Christian family leads many to put me in the "support British" box, especially as my Yorkshire grandfather was a prominent member of the Church of Ireland. He was also a member of the first Dáil, holding a University seat. Neither his birthplace nor his religion prevented him from serving his adopted country to the best of his considerable ability.

I have been very fortunate to have experienced family life, education, sport and work in both North and South and have been happy to contribute wherever I can to whichever society I live in. I have many friends in every tradition and though we do not always see eye to eye, our friendship and tolerance for our different views is never in jeopardy. Rather our differences are as important as our similarities and certainly more exciting!

Being Irish is for me not an expression of my political identity. It is far more important than that; it is an essential part of my psyche and my emotional security. Like the vast majority of all the people of this island, no matter where I am in the world, I am proud to declare my "'Irishness" and will gravitate towards those of like mind and outlook.

Southern Maeve married to a Northern Sean — difficult to put us in the politically or religiously "correct" box! And does it matter? History is only our interpretation of what happened yesterday — or what we like to believe happened. We do not know the human background of the small individuals like myself, who are but single threads in the complex and colourful tapestry of this lovely island of Ireland.

Louis le Brocquy

Louis le Brocquy is Ireland's most distinguished living painter, arguably best known for his long series of head images of subjects including Yeats, Beckett and Joyce. He has received many awards and honours, nationally and internationally, and was elected Saoi in 1994. He has lived in France for many years, but has recently returned to Ireland.

A Painter's Notes on his Irishness[*]

Although I was born in Dublin in the year of the Rebellion and brought up entirely in Ireland, I do not remember feeling particularly Irish. I remember being *human*, for as a child it seemed to me that I might just as well have been born a goat or a hedgehog — an animal for which I had an early sympathy.

Besides, my immediate paternal forebears were of Belgian stock. My great-grandfather was supposed to have been involved as a boy in the Belgian war of independence of 1830, capturing riderless Dutch horses for the rebels. Afterwards, on manoeuvres with a battery of field artillery, he was thrown from his horse under a gun-carriage, injuring his leg. Unable to ride thereafter, he maintained his love and extraordinary judgement of that animal, which eventually led him via Chelsea, London, to his last home at Newgrove, Raheny, Dublin, where he married a Kilkenny girl named Anne Walsh and passed a good-humoured and expansive life buying strings of Irish horses for the Belgian remount.

---

[*] Original version appeared in *The Recorder*, Volume 42, The American Irish Historical Society, 1981.

My mother's people included earlier foreigners — Normans, Cromwellians — who somehow managed to remain Catholic along with the yet earlier Celto-Iberian stocks with which they intermarried.

When I was a young man (with the derisory term *West-British* in mind) I occasionally referred to myself ironically as "a West-Belgian". No one seemed to me less manifestly Irish than that small family whose name I bore. Then, one day in my twenty-second year, I precipitously sailed from Dublin into a new life as a painter studying in the museums of London, Paris, Venice and Geneva (temporarily the home of the Prado collection). Alone among the great artists of the past, in these strange related cities I became vividly aware for the first time of my Irish identity, to which I have remained attached all my life.

Yet within this vital inner discovery lay the peril of insularity. Art begets art, however, and my imagination was full of the paintings of Rembrandt, of Manet, of the great Spaniards — each simultaneously himself, his race and *universal*. From the very beginning, their transcendent universality helped to protect this incipient painter from self-conscious nationalism, inducing picturesque images, perhaps, of Irish country folk dressed in the clothes of a preceding generation, or of thatched cottages arranged like dominoes under convenient hills; images no more respectable in themselves than the sterile Nazi *Kultur*, or the ordained Stalinist aesthetic of "social reality" with its invariably happy peasants.

Country people by all means, but those humbly and critically approached or obliquely overheard by a John Millington Synge, or by a Federico Garcia Lorca, whose whole being gave form and utterance to their stifled cry. For art is neither an instrument nor a convenience, but a secret logic of the imagination. It is another way of seeing, the whole sense and value of which lies in its autonomy, its distance from actuality, its *otherness*.

I believe that true art is a form of intelligence nine tenths of which, like the iceberg, lie below the surface. It is as artificial and as natural as riding a bicycle. You may say that sham art is quite simply self-conscious art and, since we are all more or less self-conscious, every artist is in some danger of manipulating his art. Art does not survive being used or manipulated. Essentially autonomous, it is the leafing, the flowering of our imagination nourished by roots hidden in our native soil. Every artist faces that self-conscious danger, I think, and the recurrent fear of it throughout his life. As a child my favourite nursery rhyme was not strictly a nursery rhyme at all, as I remember it:

> *The Centipede was happy quite*
> *until the Toad in fun*
> *asked him which leg came after which.*
> *This set his mind to such a pitch*
> *that he lay distracted in a ditch*
> *considering how to run.*

I think all art is essentially as unconscious, as complex, as simple and as mysterious as the Centipede of my childhood. I have done my best to steer clear of the Toad.

Joe Lee

Photo: John Sheehan

Joe Lee is Professor of Irish History at University College Cork. He is the author of Ireland: 1912–1985, Politics and Society.

Being Irish today is, for a historian intrigued by issues of identity, like living in a participatory laboratory. The Irish are at one of the periodic hinge moments in their history when they are reinventing themselves. Remaking always involves a degree of refaking, which requires in turn a capacity for both unctuous self-righteousness and massive self-deception, both in ample supply.

The significance of this remaking extends far beyond the experience of the five or more million people on the island. At one level, one might ask, what does Ireland matter anyway, for that five million is a drop in the global ocean of six billion. But Ireland has often punched above its weight in world history. Four features which seem to me to mark out the Irish experience today as worthy of wider notice are the peace process, the changing sense of British identity, the Celtic Tiger and globalisation.

The peace process deals directly with only a tiny area. But if the scale is local, the issues of principle are universal. The history of the area that became Northern Ireland under the Government of Ireland Act in 1920 has taken many a twist and turn over the centuries. Who knows what further twists may be in store? History did not end with the Good Friday Agreement.

To get agreement at all required one of the great works of necessary creative fiction of modern diplomacy. As the Agreement is based on fundamentally incompatible assumptions among the various participants, some must be disappointed with its fruits in due course, unless the process itself changes their sense of self. How it works out will be partly influenced by the fact that the sense of British identity is changing more rapidly in Britain itself than for several centuries. It would be ironic if the last bastion of British identity in the "British" Isles were to be the unionist parts of Northern Ireland!

Further south, the Celtic Tiger is a truly striking phenomenon, as much for its psychological as for its economic consequences. It makes unionists work even harder at sustaining the image of axiomatic Catholic inferiority — and it is no consolation to that mindset that the Catholicism is itself changing rapidly, indeed in some respects declining.

The generation of the 1990s is the first to have been reared on expectations of constant success. But can they cope with success? The Celtic Tiger is nothing if not eager to be global. It is not that Ireland is new to globalisation. It underwent one of the earliest versions of it. It was then called anglicisation. It was resisted politically and, partly, culturally, because it came in the gun carriage of the conqueror. Globalisation, now meaning cultural conquest by the strongest media power, infiltrating with no such obvious political baggage, rouses little resistance.

The perception of Ireland as Little America — or at least of Dublin as Little New York — is already familiar. "If you take a stroll down Grafton Street," Niall O'Dowd observes from New York, "it is like any American shopping mall nowadays. In the rush to conform to the latest fashions, Irish kids are indistinguishable from an American high school class. None of the traditional individualism of the Irish is immediately apparent . . ." The sceptic might wonder if the only real question is whether it is London or New York that is the cultural capital of Ireland, through its proxy, Dublin? Patrick West makes his pitch for London in the *Sunday Independent*, on the grounds that "We are all tea-drinking, pub-going, Anglo, Manchester-United supporting, *EastEnders*-watching peoples together." Can we preserve a little Anglo-Hibernian time warp? So much for Romantic Ireland — or even Romantic England! Was Yeats right after all — just a bit previous?

A pluralist Ireland can enrich Irish culture. But where pluralism is really a fraudulent ploy for the destruction of everything distinctively Irish, then it becomes simply an agent for global homogeneity, contributing more to conformity than to diversity. That is why so much of what passes as cosmopolitanism in Ireland is so redolent of provincialism, with globalisation in place accompanied by provincialism in time, fostering an obsession to rubbish the dead in order to enhance the self-importance of the living. So tiny a country must always be a taker to a great extent. But what it takes, and how it takes, determines largely who it is, and what it can give back. And if it cannot make those choices on the basis of something distinctive to itself, then there is no particular reason for it to exist at all. Being Irish becomes simply a convenience networking for careerists rather than a commitment of conviction.

It is an exciting time to be Irish. The opportunities opened up by the peace process and by the Celtic Tiger are immense. There is still a marvellous vivacity about many young people, whatever the pressure to conformity. If identity increasingly depends on imagination rather than inheritance, how the inheritance is used is crucial to the nature of the creativity. A new Irish identity is still all to play for.

Photo: Derek Speirs

Ronit Lentin[*]

Ronit Lentin is Director of the MPhil in Ethnic and Racial Studies, Department of Sociology, Trinity College Dublin and an antiracism activist. She has published extensively on racism and ethnicity in Ireland. Her latest book is Israel and the Daughters of the Shoah.

The New Bloomusalem: Being Jewish in Contemporary Ireland

What does it feel like to be a Jew in today's Ireland? My attempt to narrate the peculiarities of being a Jewish-Israeli woman in the Ireland of the twenty-first century, as the country is grappling with the dark shadows of racism, must begin with an amazing account of racialisation: the encounter between Joe Cohen, expatriate Jewish Corkman, "new boy in accounts", and the black porter Gary, in the London firm of Levin Brothers in David Marcus's poignant story "Who Ever Heard of an Irish Jew?". It takes the ethnically conscious Gary to racialise Joe, whose father moved from one ghetto in Russia to another in Cork. It is Gary who makes Joe understand that those who suffer racial discrimination should stand up for themselves and stick together. In today's ethnic relations parlance, it would be called antiracist coalitions.

I have often wondered why the tiny Irish Jewish community, in the face of historical adversity and of decreasing numbers, has attracted such disproportionate attention from writers, historians, media producers and students. Is it because literature's archetypal Jew, Leopold Bloom, was created by Ireland's own prodigal exiled son? Or rather because of what Edward Lispet, Dublin Jew

---

[*] A version of this article appeared in *The Irish Times* on Bloomsday (16 June) 1998.

turned convert, journalist, novelist and contemporary of Joyce, called the "peculiarly peculiar" position of Jews in Ireland?

In today's Ireland, as the moral panic created by the trickle of asylum-seekers manifests in increasing government and media racist discourses as well as overt racist violence against people whose skin colour does not fit, people tend to forget Ireland's home-grown "old" ethnicities — Travellers, Jewish people and black-Irish people. Racism, as well as restrictive immigration policies, are nothing new.

In Irish-Jewish history there was the 1904–6 Limerick "pogrom" which, although no one was killed, as Jews had been in the Russian and Polish turn-of-the-century pogroms, raised the fear of the newly arrived small group of Lithuanian Jews and resulted in the near decimation of the Limerick Jewish community. There was also the shameful history of the closing of doors to Jewish refugees fleeing Nazi-controlled Europe: between 1933 and 1946, only 60 Jewish refugees were given asylum in this country. No one knows what happened to those who were refused, just as no one bothers to track asylum-seekers who are destined for deportation from contemporary Ireland.

So what does it feel like to be a Jew in today's Ireland? With daily attacks on asylum-seekers on the one hand, and with the continuing racialisation of Travellers, is it fair to speak of anti-Semitism?

Is it fair, considering the fact that in recent years there have been very few manifestations of overt anti-Semitism (such as daubings, grave desecration, physical violence and verbal abuse)? One of the commonest manifestations of anti-Semitism Irish Jews encounter are jokes, which, Freud reminds us, make it possible for us to hear the unconscious speak in the psychopathology of everyday life. And, of course, inappropriate comments, such as the comment on a television programme, by the late writer Francis Stuart, that "the Jew is the worm that got into the rose and sickened it", comments which hurt, particularly considering Stuart's history of broadcasting from Nazi Germany during World War II.

In today's Ireland, we should perhaps be speaking about what sociologist Zygmunt Bauman calls "allosemitism" — the practice of setting Jews apart as people radically different from all others, needing separate concepts to describe and understand them.

It is perhaps understandable why the Irish-Jewish community has not joined the anti-racism struggle, which I, as an individual Jew, am committed to: best let sleeping demons rest. Ireland's Jews have been successful in business, politics, the professions and the arts, although we are far from "wielding power' and control in money matters far out of proportion to our numbers" as 33 per cent of the respondents to Father Micheál MacGréil's 1996 attitudes to prejudice survey believed.

Jews, I would argue, are the archetypal "others" of Ireland's national Catholicism, seen variably as displaying dual loyalty (to Ireland and Israel), or simply as "not really Irish". In private conversations, some of us admit to feeling the "odd man out". And, if we choose to operate as publicly Jewish, we must face the consequences. These can be "only" jokes, or anonymous phone calls and letters — last St Valentine's Day brought me a postcard warning me, in German, that "our day will come". I was seriously disturbed at the thought that a neo-Nazi group, using Republican slogans, may be watching me, noticing, for instance, the article I had written about the Holocaust-denying historian David Irving.

However, the main price we pay is the continuing emigration of young Irish Jews, even in these times of economic boom, many of them to communities where they can lead a Jewish life.

If Jews are indeed "peculiarly peculiar" in relation to Ireland's self-perceived ethnic and religious homogeneity, I, for one, welcome the shifting of that homogeneity towards a genuine multi-ethnicity. The new Bloomusalem, as envisaged by Joyce for Leopold Bloom, could still be my, our, new Ireland.

Fee Ching Leong

Fee Ching Leong was born in West Malaysia and has lived in Northern Ireland for twenty-five years, where she has two daughters. She has edited and written six books on racial equality and anti-racism training. She enjoys drumming and dancing.

If you were to enter the living room in the home of my childhood days, you would have been confronted by an elaborately carved table displaying statues of Buddha, "Goon Yum" (the Goddess of Fertility), the Earth God and the Monkey God. There was also a specific tabernacle with fresh fruits being constantly offered to my ancestors and their blessings would have channelled into us via the fruits as we consumed them. Joss sticks were lit morning and evening — these were stuck into porcelain pots two-thirds filled with light brown ashes.

On the first and fifteenth day of every Chinese lunar month, I would have been obliged to participate in praying to the Gods and to my ancestors. Clasping smoking joss-sticks in my hands, I would have waved them gently up and down before I stuck them, three at a time, into the ash-filled containers. I was instructed by my parents and elders to ask for good health and the ability to perform well in my school examinations. I would also have engaged in going on my knees and kow-towing — with hands sprawled in front of me, I brought my head to meet the ground three times.

I was brought up in a Buddhist-cum-Taoist home environment in a town called Ipoh in West Malaysia. The Irish influence on my life began at the very beginning of my school days and has lasted right through to this day. The principal of the convent school I attended was an Irishwoman; Sister Fidelma was strict but other Irish nuns were less so. They had different roles in the school. A few were teaching staff whilst others cared for the children living in an orphanage attached to the school. There were French nuns too and together with their Irish compatriots, they helped to instil within me a deep sense of compassion and an aspiration to real humility — qualities which were more artificially expressed by those who constituted my more worldly upper-middle-class upbringing.

And yet, my ending up living in Northern Ireland for the last 25 years was not exactly what I would have desired two and a half decades ago. The lights of London and other cities in England were more appealing to the younger me, but my parents chose Belfast for me because I already had cousins studying there at the time — also, what would Belfast have to offer socially to a teenager? Whilst the bombs presented a life threat, my parents were more concerned that I had as little opportunity as possible to avail of what they consider unnecessarily distracting social activities.

Armed with instructions to achieve academically and a threat of being disowned if I married anyone outside of the Chinese "race", I promised myself to excel in my studies but within a month of arrival on the island, I knew the charms of Irish men would be difficult to resist and it would be in my destiny to rebel. I was swamped with dates and was courted with fervour. My weakness for tall men greatly influenced the choice of my first husband. He was a working class Protestant and an only son, which, in Northern Ireland, is a combination that typically still spells an interdependence that paralyses the offspring's ability to plan and act accordingly. I became a wife who replaced the mother to whom he then promptly returned when we separated.

For ten years, I listened to but was not persuaded by the unionist viewpoint, wondered about the negative stereotypes of Catholic people and strived to feel fulfilled as the wife of a white man. I became, as a Chinese friend confided one day, "a white woman in a yellow skin". Whilst my first rebellion had been about following my heart, my second rebellion, a decade later, resulted from allowing the real me to emerge.

As I subsequently engaged in working with community groups and representations from a range of organisations to challenge their own assumptions and prejudices, I found that attitudes were only slowly moving from the perceptions of other "races" as "foreigners" who should "return to where they have come from", despite the fact that there are many in Ireland today who, like my daughters, are born in the country and hold Irish and/or British citizenships.

We have, however, not allowed snide remarks — made in ignorance or otherwise — to dissuade us from wanting to belong, to be Irish. We try to understand the confusion that is in many a person's mind that Ireland is and, perhaps, should remain white, its culture has remained static, and inclusivity refers to simply enabling better relations between the two predominant religio-political communities. The diversities of backgrounds must surely lend a richness to an island too long divided by suspicion, conflict and violence. The Paddy jokes should no longer apply, not only because they reinforce the stereotypes of Irish people, but also because they lead to the continuing denial of Ireland as a multidimensional and multiethnic society.

In the meantime, I shall continue to dream, to dream of the day when I can be, first of all, an individual, rather than a second or third class citizen of Ireland.

Gretta Logue

Gretta Logue was born in London and reared in Derry. An archaeology graduate of Queen's University, Belfast, she is completing her Masters in forensic archaeology in Bradford University. She is 21 and is having a year out backpacking in Australia.

Backpacking for a year in Australia with other young people from all over the world is making me think for the first time about what being Irish means to me.

When you meet someone from back home, it's straight down to Irish nosey business. Skipping the polite stages of normal conversation, you proceed directly to the quick-fire-interrogation of "who are you?", "where are you from?" and "who do you know?". James O'Donnell? No. Robert Johnston? Yes. Susan Devine? No. Sinead Gallagher? I think so. Hanna Mullan? Yes. Aine Mullan? Yes. No extra points scored for knowing entire families.

The "Yanks" and the "Pommies" don't seem to be too popular here. But it's great being Irish. When I arrived in Sydney for a one-year working holiday visit I had white skin, impractical clothes and a Northern Irish accent. The people here love the way I talk and always have time to find out where I'm from. Serving behind the bar in an Irish pub in Brisbane, one customer asked, "Is it part of your training to have that accent?" Hey, man, I'm the real thing.

I got a job as a dishwasher in an Italian restaurant. The Italians (known for hiring only their own) hired me, "a wee Irish girl", someone they knew would work as hard as themselves. On my first night I was putting away an instrument which crushed potatoes. It was about a foot long and I asked the chef: "Where does the garlic crusher go?" I just assumed that because they were

Italian they needed a lot of garlic! I laughed with them, even though they thought it was a typical "Irish" thing to say. I thought it was a typical Gretta thing to say, but hey, we all got on well and I fitted in.

There are other communities out here like the Italians, the Chinese, the Greeks, all communities that migrated, set up home in Australia, started businesses and worked hard. They all seem to relate to the Irish, struggling like themselves to start off a new life away from home. I made good friends in Sydney.

In all the countries I stopped in on my way out here I met Irish people. We must be everywhere. We are known as fighters. Ned Kelly was Irish and is renowned for his last stand against the law at Glen Rowan, Australia. According to the legend, he was a vigilante-type supporting the underdog in society. Sovereign Hill, a goldmining town a few hundred kilometres from Ned Kelly land, had a large Irish community. The Irish fought against terrible working conditions and formed unions in the 1800s. We have built the foundations of cities and the economies of some of the greatest nations in the new world. Yet we are known as self-destructive, crazed lunatics fighting over a piece of land in Northern Ireland the size of an Australian farm.

We cover the globe. Our hearts are huge, yet our home is small.

There is one downside to being Irish overseas. You can never escape the strong connection with Ireland. To flee completely and be totally independent is hard. Everywhere you go, everything you see, everything you do is being relayed back home. I find it impossible to have an adventure that nobody knows about. Somebody has phoned somebody in Ireland and soon everybody knows. The stories and anecdotes you wanted to keep until your return have lost their sparkle simply because of one phone call. This annoys me, but in the back of my mind it's a great security blanket.

Between ourselves, I am a bit scared of the older generation in Northern Ireland. They have been through the Troubles and know a lot about who died when and in which bomb. To me, all the bombs have melted into one, and the names of the dead? Well I'm just lucky not to recognise any.

I feel that my knowledge of the Troubles is inadequate and that my education about Ireland and Irish history is deficient. On the other hand I could tell you the contributing factors to the demise of Napoleon and the causes of the First World War. I can't speak Irish and barely know the geography of my country. Yet I have completed my degree in Archaeology at Queen's University, Belfast, and will shortly begin a research masters at Bradford University. Is my ignorance of Ireland my fault? Maybe my generation's limited education was part of a BIG PLAN to avoid educated anger, but ignorance about your own country isn't bliss. The children in school in the future should have a more in-formed and balanced curriculum with the Good Friday Agreement's new Executive in place.

It'll be alright. I have hope for Ireland and the Irish, because I have hope for myself. I love being Irish.

So who are we anyway? We're great craic, we're stupid, we're intellectual, we're lucky, we're thran, we work hard, we're caring, we fight, we're drunks, we love sport, we're charming, we love dancing and singing . . . we're simply us. Being Irish is being part of a worldwide clan which knows roughly where it's come from and knows exactly where it's going. Straight to the South Pole's newly opened Dirty Nelly's Irish Pub. See you there!

Nell McCafferty

Photo: Sunday Tribune

Nell McCafferty was born in the Bogside in 1944. She got her first job in Dublin in 1970. She moves regularly between North and South. She writes for The Sunday Tribune *and* Hot Press *magazine.*

I was told once that Karl Marx said people have to go through nationalism before they can espouse an independent complete identity. This came as a great relief, since every attempt I'd made at freedom came up against the rock of being Irish — whatever that meant. We tried for socialism in the place of my birth — Northern Ireland — and failed miserably to unite the working class because those of Protestant/unionist background suspected that we wanted to abolish British royalty (which we did, but not because of Irish national allegiance). We struggled for feminism in the Republic of Ireland, which meant abandoning the Northern sisterhood because the Northern question would split the Southern sisterhood. We tried to achieve a secular state, North and South, alienating most people, who did not wish to abandon the saints and scholars heritage of Christian Ireland.

My own ideological head was done in by Bloody Sunday, 1972, when the British army shot 13 people dead in Derry. They, like me, had been marching for civil rights. That is to say, parity of esteem — allegiance to any flag, union jack or tricolour, was anathema to us, we assured each other. There had been no question that day of using civil rights as a Trojan horse through which to advance the march of Catholics into a United Ireland. By late evening, as the death toll came rolling in, being Irish seemed a very good idea to me. Only an idiot, after that massacre, would accept British rule. The British government had ordered that its own citizens be shot. I was shocked. It was, and is, the most profound event in my life but — what did it mean to be Irish and how did one become an Irish citizen?

There was no use in the Dublin government giving us all passports, which were handed out like confetti. Tax was still paid to Britain, the British ran the education and health and welfare and legal system, and if we wanted any material or political change in our lives, it was to the London government that we pitched our demands. Dublin was a stranger, and a powerless one at that, if you lived in the North.

Still, under Dublin rule, you wouldn't be shot dead. The facts of history tell otherwise of course — groups and individuals had been put to death under Irish governments — but only if they reared up in arms against the state. You wouldn't be killed for seeking civil rights.

It was not a great reason for commending Irish citizenship and I did not argue it wholeheartedly. Apart from dying a natural death, there was not, on the face of it, any great advantage to being Irish, and there were loads of advantages to being even nominally British — a better education and health system, for instance.

Except that it was all but impossible to influence the British government. London lay across the sea, there were more than 600 MPs over there, we had less than a dozen representatives and the population of England, Scotland and Wales was 55 million versus our measly one and a half million Northerners.

As it happened, I got a job in the South and made do with my lot, which was to be a silent (and silenced) social, political and cultural orphan — whatever I did, it was better not to mention the war (in the North). Then one day, in a Dublin hotel, I ran into the Dublin Minister for Foreign Affairs, Paddy Hillery. There was something I wished to say to him about contraception, then illegal in the South. My argument was robust, he wished to move away, and I took him by the necktie and forced him to listen. It was a moment of epiphany. So this was what it meant to be Irish — you could take government by the scruff of the neck and not be shot for it. I was filled with a sense of power and well-being. It took another two decades to legalise contraception, but at least we were in there with a chance — reason pitted against reason, the most persuasive person to win the day.

I never looked back. Being Irish was just great. It meant taking and having control over one's own destiny. Being in there with a chance, not just on the island of Ireland, but on the European stage where the Irish voice had parity of esteem and on the world stage where the Irish voice could be distinguished from the British voice that had so long spoken on behalf of the silenced people of Northern Ireland. It feels first class to be Irish. To be a first class citizen of the world. There are other attractions to being Irish, but if I had been born in any other country I am sure I would feel just as much love for it. All I want is to use my own voice.

Sean McCague

Sean McCague is President of the Gaelic Athletic Association.

This is the world of e-commerce and the Web, where boundaries have disappeared and borders have opened. Freedom of movement and access to places that were once inaccessible have made this world a smaller place. And yet there is still something tangible about "being Irish".

Maybe it is because we are an island and even more because we have been a divided island, that a sense of national identity has remained so strong amongst a population entering the twenty-first century. The Irish still travel the world and fully participate in the Internet revolution. All the time, though, the lure of the homeland remains the strongest influence.

The modern signature of the identity is the global awareness of all things Irish. Rather than being swamped by the international explosion of the last few years, the Irish people and our culture have gained in stature and recognition in a way that has never been achieved before. There is a knowledge of Irish music, dance, business and sport in all corners of the world that could not have been imagined in the past.

Just as important is the awareness at home. Our national games have faced the challenge presented by world sports beamed into our homes by satellite television and have thrived. More people are playing the games and many more people are actively participating as supporters.

As Irish people have become part of the global community, so their sense of being Irish and pride in things Irish has become even stronger. The younger generations now participate fully in the global market, adapt to the needs of the international community and prosper. They are the leaders, innovators, builders and dreamers in the new world and all the time they carefully manage to protect their national identity. Because we so clearly look outward today there is no longer a fear of looking inward. We can examine where we have come from, where we are and where we are going and be confident we will be pleased with what we find.

The Irish were once described as great builders of the world who failed to be constructive at home. That has changed utterly. The modern Ireland is a bustling land, a thriving economic entity that has still managed to treasure most of its traditions. Our rich cultural heritage has been protected while at the same time we welcome the world onto our shores.

Of course, we have our failures. The failure to reconcile the differences between the communities north and south is still a cross we all must carry. What has changed is that there is a palpable desire now for reconciliation, where once there was despair and hopelessness.

There is a unity of mind in being Irish. Our games, our heritage, our music, dance and our built and green heritage are all part of what we are. There is a bond that means we care. In crisis, we come together like no other nation. Our generosity to others is world-renowned; our generosity to each other is often hidden but no less significant.

Colum McCann[*]

Colum McCann's novel This Side of Brightness *was shortlisted for the International IMPAC Dublin Literary Award. His newest book, a novella and stories, is entitled* Everything in This Country Must. *He was born in Dublin and currently lives in New York City.*

"I have lived so long abroad and in so many countries that I can feel at once the voice of Ireland in anything." — James Joyce, in a letter to Frank Bludgeon.

A Man of Two Countries

A story: In the early 1940s, a young and popular nun from Louisburgh in Mayo — under the dark shadow of Croagh Patrick — was asked to leave her native land to help a struggling church in the Bronx. Reluctantly, she agreed to the move.

When she got to the north Bronx, she found herself peculiarly ineffective. Her spirit seemed drained. Within the community she felt as if she wandered ghostlike. Nothing she could say or do brought peace to what she saw around her. These were hard streets. There wasn't much sky above them. Things went from bad to worse and one morning, in a small convenience store where the young nun went to buy cigarettes, she entered to find the owner slumped across the front counter with a gunshot wound to his head.

---

[*] This essay originally appeared in the October/November 2000 (15th Anniversary) issue of *Irish America* magazine. Reprinted with permission.

The shock of it caused a strange neurological reaction which baffled doctors — the nun went blind.

She walked the local streets wearing dark glasses, her eyes closed tight, tapping a white cane on the ground; being so visible, she soon became well known amongst the locals. They began to hail her on the streets. After a while, she began to work more closely with them. As the years went on, she became one of the most effective agents of change in the poor Bronx neighbourhood. She developed a gift of humour and wisdom and there were times when even some of the street kids listened to her. The murder rate within a twelve-block radius decreased dramatically and the attendance at church rose slightly. She lived 45 years in the Bronx, never once returning home, until — at the age of 74 — she was given a ticket to Ireland by members of the diocese. She returned to Louisburgh and together with three other nuns she made a pilgrimage, blind, up the holy mountain which had shadowed her youth.

At the top of the mountain, she said to her companions: "How lovely this looks." They turned to her, startled. She had taken off her glasses and she was squinting her eyes against the sunlight.

The women thought they were witnessing a miracle, but the nun just turned to them and said: "I've never been blind. I simply just closed my eyes a long time ago in order to remember all that loveliness I had once known."

She had, in effect, brought herself back to Ireland by becoming blind.

The story doesn't end there, of course. In fact, stories should never really end at all. But the Irish nun, at this point, raises a peculiar question. Are we formed by our early weathers? Does the geography of our childhood affect the intricacies of the human heart? Do the peculiar vagaries of our country — our nationhood, if you will – lend a consequence to every single moment of the rest of our lives? Can we shed a country and can we adopt another? Do we operate with a certain blindness when we leave?

It is true that whoever we once *were* is whoever we now *are*. We are built up out of our past. The only way we can essentially change our past is by telling stories (or lies) about it.

I have been in the United States on and off now for the best part of a decade. For the first couple of years I took a bicycle around, vagabonding. Then I

worked as an *educateur* in a programme for juvenile delinquents. For the last
five years I have lived in New York. For most of that time I have consciously
denied any inherent link with being "American", as if I am just on an extended
visit, a blow-in, a curious happening. But the truth is, I married an American. I
then had an American daughter. Followed by an American son. In an American city. Working on a novel that centred around American questions of race
and identity.

All this "American-ness" was suddenly a scaffold to my heart. But what also
held me together throughout all of this was the notion that I never wanted to
lose my "Irishness". I have tried to fiercely protect that corner of myself that
was my early weather.

Yet recently I have grown accustomed to the notion that I am, in many
ways, a man of two countries. I have a foot planted in the dark corners of each.
Every year, I try to spend long enough in Ireland in order to rediscover why I
left it. I also spend long enough in the States in order to question why I would
want to live here. (Overheard recently in a bar. "If you could live in New York
you can live anywhere." "Yeah, but why live in New York if you can live anywhere?!")

Possibly the most enduring question for any of us is: Who are we? To be
Irish in America is vastly different to being American in Ireland. To be Irish in
Ireland is different again. And yet I would argue that the two worlds — American and Irish — are beginning to converge in significant ways. The world is
shrinking so dramatically that the notion of "country" or even a "national consciousness" might soon be brought into question. With the Internet; with emigration no longer an issue (most people don't emigrate any more, they
commute); with global media; with our lives becoming jumbles of co-
ordinates, it is possible that we can belong to no country whatsoever. It is also
possible that we can belong to more than one country.

Which begs the question: How do we define ourselves?

Perhaps through stories.

And the story, as I said, is not quite finished . . . if it was ever begun in the
first place.

The nun — after two weeks in her hometown of Louisburgh — returned to the Bronx in order to work with the people she had grown to love. But she realised that her self-enforced blindness had been a currency of sorts, that it had been a sort of spiritual passport into people's lives. She worried about revealing the truth to the people in her area, perhaps losing their support, maybe even damaging their faith.

In the end, she hit on quite a simple solution — she continued to wear her dark glasses everywhere she went, even indoors, but behind the glasses she now kept her eyes open. She began to see the world around her: the doorways, the tenements, the churches, even the grocery store where she had once found the murdered shopkeeper. Her spiritual mission in the Bronx was stronger and more successful than ever.

Upon retiring, the elderly nun was given the choice of living anywhere she wanted. Instead of either the Bronx or Louisburgh the nun decided that she would make another trip, this time to Guatemala, where, before she died, she was often seen wandering narrow streets, being guided along by a number of children, all of whom wanted to hold her elbow in order to show her the way. She was famous locally as the holy woman with dark glasses who walked around with the constant suggestion of a smile on her face. And she was often heard to say that she had been so long in different places that she could hear the voice of everywhere in just about anything.

Felicity McCartney

Felicity McCartney was born and brought up in Lurgan, County Armagh. She joined the staff of Northern Ireland Voluntary Trust in 1992.

I am Irish. Even though I am not a Catholic, cannot speak the Irish language, don't drink whisky and would not fight for Ireland or for anybody else, still I am Irish. So how do I know I am Irish? The first thing is that I feel Irish and I enjoy being Irish. Ireland is an island and I was born and grew up in County Armagh and that is where I am "from" regardless of political boundaries. Being from somewhere is an important concept to Irish people. How many times is an Irish person asked the question "where are you from?"

The second way know I am Irish is that it is confirmed every time I leave the island. At one time, people in Britain and beyond did not recognise an Ulster accent. When James Ellis first appeared in *Z Cars* on television, the BBC got letters saying "at least give him an authentic accent". But due to "the Troubles" we have had a lot more coverage internationally and an Ulster accent is now recognisable across the English-speaking world. I say "Ulster" in the widest sense because a Donegal or Cavan accent is indistinguishable from one on the other side of the border. Accents, like flowing water and wildlife, don't suddenly change at a political frontier.

As a Scot might say she was Scottish, so I would describe myself as Irish and not normally as British, though I sometimes travel on a British passport. People abroad are now aware that there are those in the northern part of Ireland who call themselves British. I have found as I travel round the world, people may probe a bit more into the details of "what kind of Irish?" While living abroad, I once had the experience of an English friend carefully not inviting me round at the same time as someone from County Cavan, whom she knew to be a Catholic, in case she caused embarrassment! Later when we did meet there was great amusement and explanation that most of us enjoy meeting anybody from Ireland, north or south. That was in the South Pacific where I became the number one fan of the "Mfutu Street Ceili Band" an outfit which consisted mainly of Australian and English musicians and only one Irishman but which popularised Irish music before it became the cult it now is throughout the world. St Patrick's Day there was a big event and I often reflected that I celebrated more when I was outside Ireland than I did at home.

Living in other countries, I have always found Irish people keen to meet one another, even if they are not going to be bosom pals. There is a ritual of establishing where the person is from and whether you know any people or places in common. Then the conversation usually moves on. This is in complete contrast to some other nations. For example, a German friend living in Ireland thinks it is a strange idea to want to introduce her to other Germans. "Why should we have anything in common just because we are both German?" she asks.

Nationality and cultural grouping are not always the same. In America and other multicultural nations, new nations were created out of a mix of cultural groups. It isn't always easy, but it is a matter of survival. On an American bus, I was asked "Where are you from?" When I said "I am Irish", the reply was "I don't mean that; I mean where are you from?" This traveller was under the impression that Irish people came from Boston or Philadelphia; it wasn't part of his understanding that being "Irish" meant being from Ireland. Creating an American nation with "one flag" and a constitution embodying equality works to some extent. Civil rights still had to be won, but there was a foundation laid down to respect everybody. The Ulster Scots contributed to the building of the United States as well as the Catholic Irish, but they didn't tend to stay together, so they are not now such a cultural force as the group known as the Irish Americans. In fact, the idea that a typical Irish person is an oppressed Catholic fighting against Britain for a Gaelic Ireland is still popular in parts of the USA. Similarly, Protestants are identified in many an American mind as the landed gentry owning the wealth and probably mistreating their tenants. The present day news coverage creates another variation. But these stereotypes are not the full story. The only way to show that is to be there and demonstrate that there are other ways of being Irish and of belonging to Ulster.

How do I feel about Britain, the neighbouring island? More of my TV programmes come from London than from Dublin or Belfast. The communication age means that there is altogether more choice of information and entertainment. Culturally I am Irish; nationality-wise, it would suit me fairly well to have dual nationality, British and Irish. It reflects how I feel. But it isn't a big issue for me. It doesn't matter so much which country I am part of but what is very important is that my right to be what I am is recognised. If that were to be in a federal Europe, an alliance between Britain and Ireland or a provincial set-up within an all-Ireland, it could satisfy that aspiration. I would be happy to belong to an Ireland which wanted me as a member — that is, an Ireland which respected all traditions and backgrounds and where the Catholic church was not a dominant political force, where the right of conscientious objection to military service was recognised and where the foundation of the state was equality for all, including the many racial groups arriving on its shores. I would not like an Ireland of the Celtic twilight, monolithic religious institutions and conservative social attitudes. But I have a feeling that older Ireland is going anyway, at least in urban areas. One thing is certain: it would be an Ireland where Ulster people would play an important part because we have something to offer and it's about time we worked out what our positive contribution here at home is going to be. Not guns and bowler hats, but hospitality and industry and organising skills and a sense of belonging to a place with a history.

Muiris Mac Conghail

Muiris Mac Conghail is a writer, broadcaster, film-maker and university teacher. He was formerly a public servant, Controller of Programmes at RTÉ, Chairman of Bord Scannán na hÉireann (Irish Film Board), member of the Abbey Theatre board, Trustee of the RHA Gallery, Assistant Secretary at the Department of An Taoiseach. He is the author of The Blaskets: A Kerry Island Library.

I am Irish because, in the lines of the old refrain, "my mother and father were Irish" too. Not quite though; my mother was of Jewish descent on her mother's side and some of her relatives were murdered at the hands of the Nazis during the Second World War. My father was a landscape painter who worked in the west of Ireland, mostly in Irish-speaking areas, fought as a young man in the War of Independence and spent some time as a prisoner of war in County Down. He refused to fight in the Civil War. My mother's people were socialists and trades union activists. Her father and mother ran a newspaper shop in Amiens Street where Seán O'Casey bought his newspapers and it was they who brought O'Casey to the Abbey Theatre for the first time. Many of my mother's relatives fought in the First World War. My mother, who had been a student of my father's at the Metropolitan School of Art, was a writer and critic completely resistant to violence in pursuit of political objectives and sneered, as only she could, at misty Cathleen Ní Houlicism or bedraggled spectres of history. She spent a lot of time researching the network of spies and informers who, she believed, brought about the collapse of the 1798 Rebellion in Dublin. Pearse she thought of as a squinty-eyed useless romantic figure and headed me off from St Enda's and all of that. My father never spoke of the War of Independence nor of his part in it, although he was quite proud to have the military decoration and the certificate of his membership of Fianna Éireann. When my father died, he was buried with full military honours at Goirtín graveyard in Roundstone below Iorras Beag in Conamara, right beside his friend Bulmer Hobson, a founder member of the Irish Volunteers. My mother followed my father west shortly after his death and her coffin was enshrouded with the starry plough.

I am Irish also because my first language since the age of 18 is the Irish language. Neither of my parents spoke Irish with any great facility but sometime during my preparatory school days they took the decision to send both my brother Ciarán and me to school for two years to Scoil na Leanbh in the Ring Gaeltacht of County Waterford. This was a seminal moment in my life and there it was I learnt to speak Irish. At some time when I was an undergraduate at University College, Dublin, I took the decision that Irish would be my first language and perhaps my secret and private language. Well, in a state committed to the revival if not the restoration of the Irish language, this turned out to be a difficult choice for a first language; for all that I have seen since, my impression is that collectively the Irish people and their state had no intention of doing anything about the language. One of the first things I observed about the Irish language was that the party supposedly most committed to its restoration was truly ambiguous about it. My professor of Irish at UCD in the first year was Michael Hayes, who had served as Ceann Comhairle of Dáil Éireann for the first ten years of the State. A Dublin man, his command of Decies Irish was truly remarkable. One evening at the Damer Hall in St Stephen's Green I attended a drama production mounted by Gael Linn and amongst the audience and together were Michael Hayes, Richard Mulcahy and Ernest Blythe. These gentlemen were, in the parlance of the time, "blueshirts", which roughly speaking meant anti-national. They spoke to each other and to anyone else who might speak to them in Irish and very fluently. During my childhood and early adult life, I had occasion to meet socially with senior Fianna Fáil ministers, none of whom could string a sentence of Irish together.

I am Irish because I know that we Irish don't quite mean what we say or we say things which we don't quite mean. I find solace in the writings of John B. Keane when confronted with the problem — he knows we know he knows; and that is why the academic and literary establishment try to down-grade him. We use symbols within a grammar of usage which is unclear to the outsider and indeed to those outside the inside. We often transmit important messages in a sort of heliograph technology which is often misunderstood by those who are not familiar with the use of mirrors. There is, at times, an urgency in the message and it can be sent directly and promptly without any ambiguity. One of the most significant moments in my life was to attend as a civil servant to the government delegation lead by Liam Cosgrave as Taoiseach at the Sunningdale Conference in December 1973 where, for the first time, the twin aspirations of the people of Northern Ireland were inscribed in parallel texts — no winners, no losers. On the first morning when I went to work at the Department of the Taoiseach following on the General Election of 1973, there was a brown paper parcel awaiting me on my desk. It was full of vomit.

I am Irish because when I get away from the island, I love her most of all. I can put it all together again for me and forget the ferocious meanness of an island people. I understand well how the seventeenth-century priest poet Pádraigín Haicéad felt when he wrote while working as a Dominican in France. The Michael Hartnett translation gives full flavour to the original.

Isan bhFrainc im dhúscadh dhamh	*When I'm awake I am in France;*
In Éirinn Chuinn im chodladh;	*Asleep, I'm in my native land,*
Beag ar ngrádh uaidh don fhaire —	*I love my vigils less and less —*
Do thál suain ar síorfhaire.	*Yet sleep feeds my wakefulness.*

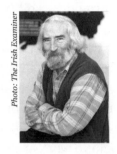

Photo: The Irish Examiner

*Cormac MacConnell**

Cormac MacConnell is a columnist with national and international newspapers and news editor with Clare FM radio. Originally from Fermanagh, Cormac now lives in Clare.

Being Irish?

Is being a clannish islander with all the good and all the bad that comes of that. Is being pagan and spiritual at the same time, in the same bone marrow, with all the good and all the bad that comes of that. Is not knowing how different you are until you meet the other islanders of all the world. Sad and happy in the one minute, changeable as the weather; sober when drunk, drunk when sober, fiery when gentle, gentle when fiery, flawed, zany, crazy, unpredictable, predictable as Hell. With all the good and all the bad that comes of that.

Being Irish?

Is being part of a family most of whose members have long ago left the island. Of being close to them and loving them. Of being so far away from them and missing them. Of envying them and pitying them. Of hardly being able to understand the accents of the young cousins in the summer. Of being embarrassed by the time warp wherein their parents live. Of wishing they would not speak so loudly. Of being proud, proud, proud of them for what they achieved, and those before them, since Ellis Island, and being dimly yet acutely aware, somehow, that almost all of them have walked a hard emigrant road. Of no-

---

* This essay originally appeared in the October/November 2000 (15th Anniversary) issue of *Irish America* magazine. Reprinted with permission.

ticing, almost with pain, how they have held on to the memory of the island. Of noting, when the old ones come back, how important it is to them to renew their sense of who they were before they became who they are. Of the strength of the links in the chain.

Being Irish?

Is being a One Man Republic, a One Woman Republic, with all the good and all the bad that comes of that. Is being so often the square peg in a round world shaped by forces far beyond the island. Is loving the island with a fierce love. Is hating the island with a fierce hate. Is being Orange. Is being Green. Is sometimes being more prepared to die for the island than to live for it. Is thinking too much about all the Yesterdays and not enough about the Tomorrows. Is owning a head inside which the highways of the mind are sometimes so narrow that the margin briars snarl up in each other; sometimes so wide and free you would get lost on the journey across. With all the good and bad that comes of that.

Being Irish?

Is something which is stronger the further away you are from the home island. Is something which is stronger at the great watersheds of Life, at birthings, dyings, marryings. Is something which draws the islanders so close together wherever they meet across the globe. Is something which has spawned a million wistful tunes and songs. Is something which has danced to a trillion mad jigs and reels. Is something which can darkly make one lonely in the heart of a crowd of revellers; in the best of company when alone amidst old hills. Is something flaunted betimes on the sleeve, betimes scarcely declared at all. Is some organic thing which almost every other race can analyse better than we can. But which you have to be Irish to fully understand.

Being Irish?

Is shamrockery, blarney, roguery, pishroguery (superstition), With all the good and bad that comes of that. Is Saint Patrick's Day and Easter Week and the Twelfth of July and Saint Bridget's Day and Reek Sunday and Puck Fair and Killarney. With all the good and bad that comes with that. Is the All Ireland Hurling Final and the All Ireland Football Final, Sam Maguire and Liam McCarthy, and the full-blooded Garryowen with the ball of the other shape and

Sonia O'Sullivan, Barry McGuigan, Michelle De Bruin. With all the good and bad that comes from that. Is O'Connell Street in Dublin and Cork and De Valera and Michael Collins, Gerry Adams and Charlie Haughey, Ian Paisley and Bertie Ahern, James Joyce and Samuel Beckett, Yeats and Gogarty and Shane McGowan. Is Guinness and Jameson and Bulmers and Murphys and Smithwicks and Tayto and Jacobs, the pint and the half-one and singsongs and "Danny Boy" and the Fleadh and the Giant's Causeway, the Aran Islands and the McGillicuddy Reeks, Belfast brick and Waterford glass and Belleek china. Is the IRA, Official and Provisional and Real. Is the UDR and the UDA. Is Fianna Fail and Fine Gael and the Progressive Democrats. And all the good and all the bad that comes out of all of that.

Being Irish?

Is being proud of it always, but especially now. Being Irish is being fashionable just now. Being Irish is Riverdancing at Lughnasa around the bonfire of Angela's Ashes. Being Irish, being one of those clannish islanders of the Western World, is, in the end, just great craic! And that is what Life is all about.

Inez McCormack

Inez McCormack is President of the Irish Congress of Trade Unions and a member of the Northern Ireland Human Rights Commission.

Photo: GreenGraph

To a woman born in the north of this island from a Protestant background, this question seems to go to the heart of the harsh conflict of national identities in which I have lived most of my life. A lifelong involvement in the civil rights movement, human rights activism, the women's movement, and trade unionism has developed a contribution and view that just relationships are at the heart of real democratic change in any arena. A personal and political perspective has been honed in surviving the visceral anger that is the response of any unjust status quo to challenge and change. Any thriving has come from working with others in exercising that challenge through the practice of participation and right. This has enabled me to witness again and again the capacity for imagination and generosity of those who most need change.

The personal also shapes the political, so here is a little of that. A mother from Huguenot stock who settled in north Donegal in the 1690s and lived on the same land ever since. She was born and grew up in an Ireland undivided by political partition but her loyalties and emotions were partitioned by that history. A childhood in comfortable County Down that excluded any knowledge of conventional Irishness, except as a dangerous unknown. Yet some of that legacy of determined awkward conscience is at the root of a quest for an identity that rests on an inner sense of justice.

Introduction to this discussion was filtered through the civil rights movement, which was about challenging the humiliation of being treated as a lesser being. The first battles of feminism and trade unionism, as in human rights activism, revealed how power when pushed redefines change within the limits of its own comfort and that the powerless are impressed only by changing realities. This has shaped an understanding that to oppose a wrong only when it is acceptable to do so is to support injustice and that in opposing any wrong you have to create shapes of right. All of this has conditioned an approach to what being Irish can mean — not on what it is comfortable and exclusive to be but how capable it is of being uncomfortable, uncertain and inclusive.

At a public meeting during one of the bitterly contested referendums in the 1980s in the Republic on the issue of abortion, I remember making a point that if Ireland did not belong to those women who left in secrecy and shame every year on the boat to Britain, then it did not belong to me. It has been not edifying to hear a recent cross-party, cross-community debate in the new Northern Assembly, with a very few honourable exceptions, demonising such women. An interesting portent of change in that vicious debate was the courage and clear speaking of one woman who is an Ulster Unionist.

The discussion about what it means to be Irish today needs to take another look at the language and content of the Good Friday Agreement. It is far more than a harbinger of peace and political co-operation. It contains the possibilities of new relationships based on a culture of justice, rights and participation. Some of that content came from the long, hard and unpopular struggle to name and challenge religious and political discrimination. Some came from a unique alliance of groups representing different forms of dispossession that had experienced their own journeys of pain and exclusion. They came together to assert their own rights in the context of the rights of others and won the support of all the pro-agreement parties and both Governments in getting those provisions in the Agreement.

The discussion needs to understand that racism, discrimination, and intolerance is rooted in the fear of the "other". While they deeply wound the victim, they also debase the perpetrator. International standards and practices based on the Universal Declaration of Human Rights open for us a way forward to provide criteria, structures and remedies that can help shape a culture of inclusion and change. It needs to work out how to set benchmarks that measure implementation and interaction between civil, political and social, economic and cultural rights. The right to vote without the right to shelter is nonsense, and vice versa. It needs to do all of this in the context of the growing understanding that the concept of participation is crucial to the practice of right.

I am well aware of how difficult all of this is going to be, North and South. There is the brutal politics of exclusion and sectarian hatred to be overcome in the North. There is the cynicism with the political system and the growing insider/outsider society in the Republic. Only programmes of action based upon recognition of the need for a comprehensive response can successfully confront and reverse the trend towards exclusion. Building just relationships between and within these traditions based on the indivisibility and practice of a rights-based approach to participation and inclusion will not be easy or popular.

As President of the Irish Congress of Trade Unions, I have spent a lot of time in the last year talking and listening to workers and communities in all parts of the island. The focus has been on how to make connections between the different struggles that are tackling injustice and trying to build new democratic forms.

This has given many snapshots of the possibilities of what change could be like. At an emergency meeting convened by rights groups to challenge the criminalising and demonising of refugees and asylum seekers, hearing women, exhausted and strong, from inner city Dublin describe their own unresourced initiative to bring "strangers' children" into their crèche. Listening to an encounter between a young Garda and a young Traveller at a conference in Tipperary where one was trying to exercise the acceptance of responsibility and the other was trying to exercise the generosity of patience. In Galway, in Tralee, in Donegal, in Belfast, in Dublin, in Derry, watching groups representing different dispossessions listening with respect and interest to each other's stories and working out strategies for change.

A senior politician puzzling quietly with me about how to make elected democracy connect with this new and bristling civil society. Hearing a tired young man in a rundown building demanding funding to continue the project that is transforming young educational rejects into perky young people beginning to believe in themselves. Standing with young women in Dublin on a three-month-old picket line, asserting their dignity by fighting for the right to be in their union. The Diaspora in action in the form of an Irish emigrant trade unionist bringing me to a meeting in Boston to recruit young Irish workers on building sites into the protection of a union.

At a meeting to discuss implementation of the equality provisions of the Good Friday Agreement, listening to a man from the north, whose son was murdered by sectarian hatred, responding to a politician who was making little of the discrimination which shaped his life and marred his son's by saying, "We can all do better than this." Hearing an ex bus driver demanding that the nation and the government lead the fight against injustice in East Timor thousands of miles away. At a solidarity demonstration, a poet and Nobel laureate finding the words, as poets do, to express the willing and overwhelming response, "We are answerable."

We are no longer the survivors of tragedy and dispossession. Will the creativity and innovation that produced a cultural explosion, economic transformation and political settlement be put at the service of transforming our democratic potential? Can a literature and music, which asserted our humanity through the worst of yesterday, help us to an understanding of being Irish that means an inner sense of justice for and with each other?

It is all to play for in the Ireland of today. We have produced our shining lights in our poets, peacebuilders and presidents who have set worldwide standards for justice, rights and humanity. In this last year alone I have seen, in a thousand small shining lights north and south, democratic possibilities being practised by those whose only affirmation is that of their own conscience. We need to make connections. Until recently, the possibility of justice and equality being at the heart of a political settlement was regarded as an impossible or unacceptable dream. It happened because many people, the likely and the unlikely from the powerful and the powerless, believed enough to make a dream work. That gives me the stubborn confidence to believe that being Irish today can and must mean new relationships on this island, fashioned on the practice of justice.

*Frank McCourt**

Frank McCourt is the bestselling author of Angela's Ashes *and* 'Tis.

The English Catholic martyr, St Edmund Campion, lived in Dublin for a while in 1569 and here is what he wrote about the Irish:

> *"The people are thus inclined: religious, franke, amorous, irefull, sufferable of paines infinite, very glorious, many sorcerers, excellent horsemen, delighted with warres, great almes-givers, passing in hospitalitie: the lewder sort both clarkes and laymen are sensuall and loose to leachery above measure. The same being vertuously bred up or reformed are such mirrours of holiness and austeritie that other nations retaine but a shewe or shadow of devotion in comparison with them."*

If you're Irish you're searching for yourself in Campion's wide-ranging assessment. Are you religious one minute, "sensuall and loose to leachery" the next? Amorous, but still a mirror of holiness?

Much depends on where and when you grew up. If, like me, you were raised in mid-century Ireland you had to think twice before engaging in sensuality and lechery and if you did there was nothing for it but confession on Saturday. My Ireland was known the world over as "poor and priest-ridden". The

---

* This essay originally appeared in the October/November 2000 (15th Anniversary) issue of *Irish America* magazine. Reprinted with permission.

Irish were marrying so infrequently and emigrating at such a rate that an alarmed American priest wrote a book entitled *The Vanishing Irish*.

We *were* poor. We *were* priest-ridden.

And De Valera-ridden.

These were the ingredients of our lives in the lanes of Limerick and, I'm sure, in lanes in every town and city in Ireland.

But especially in Limerick, because this was the one major city in Ireland without a university, a community of independent thinkers and scholars. Dublin, Cork, Galway, Belfast — all enjoyed the social and intellectual benefits of higher education, but not Limerick. There was an intellectual (and spiritual) vacuum — and the church filled it.

There was no political vacuum: De Valera had already filled that with his various obsessions, his dreams of a Gaelic-speaking people digging joyously in the fields by day, dancing in the dusk at the crossroads, Irish dancing only, leaping lads ready to die for creed and country, dimpled maidens so chaste they put the lie to Campion's sensuality and "leachery".

Why go on about this? It's old stuff and haven't the Irish writers, from Joyce to McGahern, exhausted this vein? No, you can't exhaust it because that Ireland with its tricolour, its crucifix, its various blood sacrifices, has affected generations of Irish even unto seven times the seventh generation.

And the irony is that even Irish-Americans may have been affected by the psychological climate of mid-century Ireland. If you live in the United States, especially in the great urban areas, you are literally nagged into reflecting on your ethnicity. It's one thing if you're Irish from Ireland. That's easy to spot: there's the accent. When they say, "Gee what a cute brogue," you have to respond, to adjust. You're in America and you've been labelled "Irish". You didn't have to think about that in Ireland, but you're in the States now, pal.

And when you think about being Irish, what comes to mind? If you're a cub of the Celtic Tiger, will you go along with St Edmund Campion and admit that you are, indeed, amorous and ireful. Whoopee and musical beds and there is Mother Church in the corner, her head hung, weeping.

Irish-American? That's another story. Here is virgin territory for the social historian: not the *history* of the Irish-Americans, but their relationship with the folks back home. Of course, we brought baggage from Ireland, We brought our stories, our songs, our hymns, our sense of place. We barged into the Brahmin enclaves of Boston and never took no for an answer. Daniel O'Connell had told us, *Organise, organise,* and if we were slow to act in Ireland we seized the day in the United States. We dominated politics and the church and set up an education system of parochial schools and universities, which seems to have escaped the attention of our historians. Simply put, we saw power and took it.

All along, we looked back over the years and across the ocean and deferred to the history, the tradition, the land. Look at the richness of Ireland's culture, all that history, all that suffering, and a song for every event, every battle, every lost love, every sailing away, every drop to ease the pain. At any party in the States, the Irish would sing loudly, merrily, endlessly while their Irish-American brothers and sisters served the drinks and in their ignorance of their own achievements wished they'd been hurt into that kind of music.

Then something happened. Damn! Who is this Michael Flatley, this Seamus Egan, this Eileen Ivers, this Joanie Madden and her Cherished Ladies? And who do they think they are, coming to Ireland and, not only sweeping the competition but, talented, pushing their way into the culture of their ancestors. Who is this Mick Moloney, a Limerickman at Villanova University, who gives equal time and grace to the musical traditions of the narrowbacks?

The Atlantic has become a puddle which poets and musicians leap without a second thought. Irish-Americans are discovering their own turbulent and rowdy history and the songs that go with it. They're throwing the overalls in Mrs Murphy's chowder and splashing Finnegan with whiskey to wake him, Michael Patrick McDonald takes us on a heartbreaking tour of his South Boston family while William Kennedy guides us through the heart and soul of an Irish, an American Albany.

So . . . what is it to be Irish nowadays?

It is to live on either side of the Atlantic Ocean, or anywhere else, and to be able to say, *You've come a long way, Michael or Maggie.* You've come singing and dancing and, remembering St Edmund Campion, you may be "mirrours of holiness", "great almes-givers", and "passing in hospitalitie".

Ian McCracken

Ian McCracken worked as a physics teacher in Foyle College in Derry (1961–98) and is currently working as a Development Officer for Donegal with Derry and Raphoe Action. He is a Presbyterian.

"Being born in a stable does not make one a horse."

So said the Duke of Wellington in the House of Commons. While totally logical, the statement is, I feel, not very profound. Being born in Ireland, however, surely does make one Irish.

My earliest recollection of an awareness of feeling Irish occurred when I was about 15 years of age. The occasion was at Lansdowne Road, Ireland v Wales. Ireland won that game and I had the privilege of seeing Jack Kyle dropping a goal from right in front of me as I stood with others, both Welsh and Irish, on the front row of the terrace. I remember clearly the intense feeling of immense pride in being Irish. It was created by the circumstances of the event but extended beyond that as we shared the banter and camaraderie with people from Cork, Kerry, Antrim, Down, etc. To be able to identify with others who, like me, had been born on this island was special. It seemed totally appropriate then, as it has done since, that Ireland should have a rugby team drawn from the whole island. The modern professional game has perhaps removed the genuineness of an Irishman playing for Ireland — without being paid. While inevitable, the change in the structure has, for me, removed a part of the game, a game which united people of the island.

There are many events in Irish history which raise the patriotic spirit. Battles and skirmishes will do that to most people. However, the potato famine of

1845–1847 is a happening which reduced the population of Ireland from eight million to less than half that number. The annoying thing is, it was not just the failure of the crops which led to so many deaths, hardship and emigration. It was the failure of the then government of the land to distribute available food to their people. The population of my native Donegal was 300,000 in 1841. While potatoes were a much eaten food, there must have been plenty of other foods around. And it didn't just happen to the Irish;it also occurred in the lowlands of Scotland and in Wales. Could the event have been a factor in the growth of the intense national fervour found in these Celtic countries today?

In my student days, I worked in Kent at the seasonal work with fruit and vegetables. In the particular firm where I worked, there were students from many nations. I was there for two days before I understood a word the foreman, a decent fellow, said. He was speaking English, and so was I and he had difficulty with my language too. He used to mutter, "I can't understand a word you bloody foreigners say." My reply was always the same: "Oh no sir, I'm not foreign, I'm Irish!" He enjoyed the humour. What impressed me about the student workforce was that those from outside the islands of Ireland and Britain could all converse in their own language as well as English. That convinced me that our Irish language has to be part of our being Irish. I very much welcome the present revival of the language. Some people learn the language as a vehicle for expressing their national feelings. As a people we allowed the language to decline; a greater national feeling would have kept the language alive as the spoken word in everyday use. But, "*is fearr mall ná go brách*".

The culture of a people includes their patterns of thoughts, beliefs, ways of behaving, rituals, dress, language, traditions and customs, as well as their art, music and literature. While many of these components remain constant, the expression of some of the components themselves change, not only from county to county, but also with the passage of time. The days (good old!) when a lad went to a dance on his bicycle, met up with a girl, got too friendly before discovering she lived several miles in the opposite direction from one's home, and took her home on the crossbar of his bicycle, changed to the Cortina with the bench front seat — very sociable. That custom has further changed, in that the country Dance Hall is now obsolete and those who do take young ladies out in the car find each is strapped tightly into their respective seats on each side of the vehicle. Being sociable has to find other means.

I have lived in Ardagh near St Johnston since 1937. My family came to Ardagh towards the end of the nineteenth century. My father was born in 1900 in Gorticrum near Artigarvan, County Tyrone. His family, as tenants, had been moved around the Duke of Abercorn's Estate. He and my mother, a St Johnston woman, lived and farmed through the years of the formation of our State. My memories of influences and home ethos were of being Irish. Perhaps the easy acceptance of citizenship of the new infant State can be understood by the few stanzas of the poem reproduced below, written by my grandfather's brother. The poem was frequently referred to in my home as "Uncle Robert's Poem". It describes the feelings of the tenants dispossessed in the clearance of the estate to make way for the Duke's planted forest which was subsequently blown down in the storm.

Finally, "being Irish" gives me a sense of identity, a sense of pride in my country and a sense of being another link in the chain of history. This would be incomplete without the sense of humour which, while different for each individual, yet has a national identity. As a people, we have the ability to find humour in ourselves. In telling a Paddy Irishman joke, we can, without any loss of being ourselves, identify with Paddy, identify as Paddy. Without our sense of humour and without Paddy, we would be less Irish. Long live Paddy!

McCracken's Poem

I

There's bitter grief in Baronscourt, it's Duke feels sorrow now.
The stern proud look he always wore has vanished from his brow.
The spider has revisited old scenes in his domain
And widespread desolation has followed in his train.
'Tis not the peasant's ruined cot nor homeless wanderer's cry.
The hearth stone cold nor rooftree low that makes his Lordship sigh,
But his stately Larch, his spreading Elm, his Oziers, Fir and Oak —
Blown down before a power more strong than Gladstone's skilful stroke.

III

Like druid in his sacred grove he inspired both fear and awe,
For on his lips hung life or death — his very word was law;
And slaves at will toiled on his land; from childhood they had learned
Their duty was to work and starve and give him all they earned.
The wealth created by their hands half-yearly did they give
To satisfy their needy Lord — and purchase leave to live.
It was hoarded up with anxious care, well did the tenants know
The meaning of those dreadful words — you'll pay the rent — or go!

VII

But now his class seems doomed at last — poor courtly selfish knaves,
They quailed before the power of those they trampled on as slaves;
Now slaves no longer at their feet in wailing suppliant tone
But men erect, united, and demanding back their own.
Men pledged by all their hopes on earth to struggle hand in hand
'Till Landlordism with root and branch is driven off the land.
Let those who toil on Irish soil of every race and creed
Take from cruel Landlords power and their lust for endless greed.

7-11-1894

Geoff MacEnroe

Geoff MacEnroe is Director of the IBEC/CBI Joint Business Council's Business Development Programme. He previously worked with an international firm of engineers and contractors and held senior positions with the Irish Trade Board in Dublin, Brussels and Tokyo.

Until one has the opportunity to travel outside Ireland, it is difficult to understand how one distinguishes one nationality from another other than by language. The first time I visited Paris as a student, I remember being surprised that the black population there was speaking French, not English, and were in fact French rather than American.

When I took up my first job in industry in Birmingham in England, I was very surprised that as soon as someone heard me speak, they knew I was from Ireland. Having been brought up in Dublin, I had assumed I did not have a distinguishable Irish accent. When Nelson's Pillar in O'Connell Street was blown up, I was anxious that my work colleagues would assume that I would not have supported this action.

In the early 1970s, I was sent by the Irish Export Board to open an office in Japan. At that time, the main Irish exports to Japan were dairy products and bowling alley equipment. Even the Japanese, who understood English, had difficulty locating Ireland. When you said you were from Ireland, they enquired, "Do you mean Iceland or Holland?" At a reception for the first Irish Trade Mission to Japan, a Japanese couple who had visited Ireland arrived wearing Aran sweaters. Their interest in Ireland was such that on meeting representatives from Donald Davies, they opened a prestigious shop in Tokyo to sell the Donald Davies ladies wear range.

I was interested to learn that two Northern Ireland products were well known in Japan, Mackie's textile machinery and Moygashel fabrics. When a major Japanese glass manufacturer was launching Waterford Crystal in Japan, it was necessary to transfer the Irish flag indicating the location of the factory, which had been positioned in England, to Ireland.

On my first visit to Korea, I was told that the Koreans were known as the "Irish of the Far East". When I enquired as to the reason, I was told the Koreans liked to drink and there was often conflict in families, with father disagreeing with son and brother falling out with brother.

As suggested above, foreigners who have had contact with Irish people do not distinguish whether they have come from the Republic or Northern Ireland. The way Irish people have welcomed tourists over the past 50 years has meant that Irish people are known throughout the world for providing traditional Irish hospitality. This is one reason why Irish people are welcomed when they travel abroad. During the 1960s, as one of six students from Dublin on a camping holiday in Italy, we were surprised to be invited into the house of a local Italian. We welcomed the opportunity to have a shower in his bathroom and also some breakfast. The reason for the hospitality was that the man had visited Belfast many years previously to see Italy play in the football international and he had not forgotten the hospitality he had received.

On another occasion, when visiting Iran with a delegation from Ireland exhibiting at the Tehran International Fair, I was again reminded of the Belfast connection. Coming home one evening by taxi, we were stopped at a police checkpoint for questioning. As soon as we said we were Irish, our interrogators mentioned the name "Bobby Sands" and we were waved straight through.

In 1993, I was travelling around the US with William Poole, my Co-Director from Northern Ireland, explaining the work of the IBEC/CBI Joint Business Council in developing cross-border trade and breaking down barriers between Northern Ireland and the Republic of Ireland. A number of people we met whose ancestors had emigrated to the US from Northern Ireland expressed surprise that an Irish Catholic from Dublin was both working closely with someone from Northern Ireland and travelling in America promoting the same message of north/south co-operation.

For many decades, the Irish had a low opinion of themselves. This is obviously related to the long tradition of emigration in Ireland. For centuries, Ireland's sons and daughters emigrated to England, the United States and Canada and to many other countries around the world. They left because there were no opportunities for work at home and whenever they went, they were determined to succeed; whenever there was an opportunity to do so, they took it. Today, there is an Irish Diaspora throughout the world of more than 50 million people of Irish descent. A noteworthy mark of the Irish character is the way they retained their Irish identity. It is interesting to note that in places as far apart as Argentina and Newfoundland, even today, there are strong Irish communities where the people have retained their strong regional Irish accents.

Irish people have always had a particularly outward-looking attitude. The work that members of the Irish religious orders have carried out on the missions in many under-developed countries has left a very favourable impression of Irish people in these countries. Many Government and business leaders in these countries are proud to say they were educated by Irish priests and nuns. The fact that Ireland was never a colonial power has been an advantage to Irish exporters of products and services when developing distant markets.

As we enter the twenty-first century, Ireland has been transformed. The Irish have achieved a great deal in the past 15 years. Ireland is the fastest growing economy in the European Union, employment is growing rapidly and living standards have improved beyond recognition compared to the gloom and doom of the 1970s and 1980s. Ireland has justly earned the reputation of the Celtic Tiger economy. The portrait of the Irish today is that of a young well-educated workforce with the confidence to successfully compete with any other nation. With the positive developments in the Peace Process, further prosperity can be enjoyed by the Irish throughout the island of Ireland.

Ann McGeeney

Ann McGeeney works for the ADM/CPA Peace Programme in the border counties of Ireland. Her interests include rural development and women's issues. She is married to Jimmy Murray and has three young children, Daisy, Holly and Ardal.

The Green, the Orange, the Guinness, the Shamrock, the kiss of the Blarney, the turf, the drunk, the Quiet Man, the "top of the morning sir", the GAA, paedophile priests, Yeats, U2, the no-warning bomb blast and 30 years later, and now; now, the Celtic Tiger. So what is Being Irish?

The notion of Being Irish first dawned on me when I was around seven years old. It was the early 1970s when the British Troops descended on us and began tearing around our local roads in their green lorries; which I later learned were called Saracens. These guys were exciting and strange, great crack altogether and many's the day we carried cans of sweet tea and loaves of sandwiches to these foreign men as they struggled to pull one of their heavy lorries out of the local boghole in Cornonagh, my homeland.

Suddenly these English soldiers were no longer our friends and when we asked why we were told that they were the ugly Brits who had come to steal our land – Irish land. It didn't mean much to us as children except that we were Irish and they were strangers, English and that meant they were bad.

Through the 1970s when I went to the local secondary school, I had little exposure to anyone different from myself: Catholic, nationalist and Irish. Outside of school, I socialised in the south of Ireland where I danced and sometimes courted. Politically, we may have been from different countries but culturally we were more or less the same, Irish.

It wasn't until the 1980s when I went to Queen's University in Belfast that this issue of Being Irish came back again. The difference this time was that although some of these people looked like me, were the same age and at university for broadly the same reason, they were different. They were my Protestant unionist classmates. They were very much Northern Irish with their allegiance and for many their identity British; mine was not.

No one had prepared me for the cultural shock of meeting the people so very much like me but at the same time not like me. Many were and still are my close friends but their beliefs on the issue of Being Irish were poles apart from mine. In our radical enlightened student fashion, we had regular discussions on the subject. I even listened to one woman boast of how her father considered himself a great Irishman and him in the B Specials! A very different perspective on Being Irish.

In the 1990s, I took myself off to England to experience the London scene. At that time I came into contact with a number of English people whose limited experience of Ireland and the Irish was either as presented by the English media or unfortunately as the stereotypical drunken beggar on the streets. I spent a considerable time trying to convince them that being Irish was no big issue or banner to wave. Ordinary people doing ordinary things from a country which has tragically had its fair share of extraordinary experiences. However, come St Patrick's Day in London, the ordinary firmly takes a back seat. Almost everybody seems to insist on Being Irish for the day.

Cajoled and intoxicated, I was persuaded to take them to an Irish event in Battersea Arts Centre on St Patrick's night. Mary Coughlan was singing alongside Fairground Attraction's Eddie Reader; the Fleadh Cowboys were in full flight and all in all the night showed the very best of the Irish and "wannabe Irish" enjoying themselves. Or so it seemed. At the end, some drunken guy with an English accent (thank God) commandeered the stage and started raving about how downtrodden we Irish were and about rebellion, and whose fault was it – the English of course! As we stood there looking at this eejit, all that raced through my mind was how my friends would have all their stereotypes about the Irish confirmed by this one act of stupidity. As he straightened his rose-tinted spectacles and reflected on the fair old land, it was with some relief that he collapsed and was manhandled off the stage. Despite the hot tears stinging the back of my eyes, I could just about hold them back and reflect that this person must not have been in my Ireland for some time. He wasn't aware of how things were moving on and changing — this was a guy who in my view wanted to stay put and hold onto some misguided and powerless image of Being Irish.

Those days spent off the island were for me some of the best times to be Irish — they provided the opportunity for me to argue the good bits of Being Irish and listen to what the downsides were. They also provided me with the opportunity of considering where I really wanted to be. This, of course, was back at home in Ireland where I felt I could really contribute meaningfully to Being Irish.

Barry McGuigan

Barry McGuigan is former boxing champion of the world. He is now a sports commentator and journalist. He is married to Sandra, and is father of Blain (17), Nika (14), Jake (13) and Shane (11).

I was born in Monaghan, raised in Clones. Living so close to the border with Northern Ireland, the Troubles were as much a part of the landscape as the soft, green hills.

I was lucky. I was born to parents who preached tolerance and understanding. They were owners of a grocer's shop which supplied goods to both sides of the religious community; discrimination never made sense. But more than that, as a family, we never felt that way inclined. By nature, my parents were open-minded and brought up all their children free of prejudice. Though a Catholic, my father, a musician by trade, used to perform all over the North to audiences of both religious persuasions. He, too, saw no sense in making judgements about people on grounds of belief, colour or creed.

This liberal upbringing informed my thinking when I began to box at the age of 12. By my teens, I was competing further afield and soon became the champion of Ulster. Clones is in one of the three counties of Ulster which lie in the Republic. Though technically in Ireland, I was able to compete in the Ulster championships and later fought for the Commonwealth title. This meant that I transcended religious and political division and represented the whole community. But this was not a matter of expedience. It reflected the way I saw the world. I am aware of the issues, of the sensitivities of all in Ireland, north and south, Protestant and Catholic, but always had a vision of how life might be. I carried this around with me and aspired towards it. Still do. I believe the future is there to be shaped and that the forces of change will eventually allow divisions to heal. There is an optimism and will for change among the young that is tangible. There is certainly no future in looking back.

My own family is a case in point. My childhood sweetheart, Sandra, lived across the road. She was a Protestant and educated in the north. I am delighted to say, after three and a half years together she agreed to be my wife. We were not alone in marrying across religious traditions. Of course, the pressures on us are not quite so great living across the water in England. But as sons and daughters of Ireland, the old country has never left our house, nor will it. Our children are almost as Irish as us in that respect. They, too, see only people when we go home. When my eldest son Blain was barely three years old, we stopped off after one of my fights in a country pub in the north. Sat next to us was a young family with a boy roughly Blain's age. As youngsters do, they spoke spontaneously, mostly nonsense. My daddy's got a Volvo, my daddy's got a Mercedes and so on. When imagination dried up, the other chap screeched, "Well I'm a Protestant." To which Blain responded by turning to me and saying, "Daddy, what's a Protestant? Have we got one of them?" One child with prejudice engrained, another blissfully ignorant of such issues.

While there are some for whom religion remains divisive, the majority are learning to move on. That is how it has to be. When I think back about my career, it is not so much the great victories that I recall but the tremendous support I received from across the board. The atmosphere at my fights was so electric it is hard to put into words. There was such a bond between supporters from across the religious divide that they used to say, "Leave the fighting to McGuigan." The King's Hall in Belfast where I had so many great nights was particularly special. As were my "homecomings" to Dublin and Belfast after my world title wins. The streets were thronged with thousands of people, all joined in their passion for boxing and support of me. Fantastic moments; so much so that when I watch old videos of those times, I rarely pay any attention to the fights, just the old faces at ringside, spotting the characters who stood by me through good times and bad.

I feel that I represented everything that is Irish both north and south of the border. To me, there never was a border, metaphorically speaking. No barriers, no divisions. The Irish are a special race. There is a camaraderie between the people that is almost unique in these isles. We are a very compassionate lot, for whom the family is paramount.

I was reading a travel piece just the other day which featured Pete McCarthy, presumably a son of Ireland a few generations removed, travelling around the Emerald Isle. One evening, he popped out of his B&B for a quick pint in the local. Four hours later, he was a few doors down the street enjoying the hospitality of a family he had not known when he entered the pub. That sums up the old country for me. Hospitality the like of which you will not see anywhere, given on trust with a generous heart, north and south.

When my work is done in England, I'll be heading back to end my days among the people who made me the man I am. We have our faults, of course. In my case, punctuality can be a problem. I can't give you a time when I'll return. But I'll be back. No question.

Martin McGuinness

Martin McGuinness MP, MLA is Minister for Education in the new Northern Ireland Executive and was chief Sinn Féin negotiator at the talks that led to the Good Friday Agreement.

I was born and raised in the Bogside area of Derry City in the North of a partitioned Ireland. One of seven children, my mother is a Donegal woman and my late father a Derryman. Therefore I am the product of a cross-border institution. I am Irish. I readily accept that had I been born in Oslo I would have been Norwegian; in Paris I would have been French; but if I had been born on Belfast's Shankill Road, I may have proclaimed myself British.

Something I could never fully understand is how the British establishment were able to instil such detest of all things Irish in a section of our people that they deny their Irish identity.

I suppose the environment into which we are born shapes our sense of identity. And if the establishment can succeed in controlling that environment, then it can determine what we identify with. The influences that we are exposed to, unless we have a very strong individualistic character, can predetermine the path we follow in many aspects of life. Family, friends and community can have a very potent and formative effect on the choices we make and how we portray ourselves. For instance, my grandfather worked in an iron foundry, my father worked in the same foundry and if the foundry had continued in existence and the political situation had remained the same, I too could have followed in that tradition.

By accident of birth, I came to my new world in 1950 in Derry City, Ireland. The community that received me identified with the country in which they were born — which is the accepted norm in every other country in the world — it was natural. Therefore I am Irish.

The fact that I was born in a part of the island of Ireland that is occupied by a foreign power cannot change the fact that I am Irish anymore than the occupation of France or Poland by Germany during the Second World War made the population of those countries any less French or Polish.

This brings me to "what it means to be Irish in today's society". For centuries Irish people, both in our own country and throughout the world, were portrayed by the British colonial power as an inferior nation. Because of its superior physical strength, the British Empire — with some brave and notable exceptions — was able to subjugate the Irish at home and abroad into passive acceptance of a second-class existence.

This all changed when the generation born between the pre-war years up to the late 1940s entered the phase of life when they were looking for careers or starting to raise a family. This generation were better educated than previous generations and were unwilling to accept the role of second-class citizen. They began the struggle for justice, equality and freedom. Out of what began as a campaign for proper housing, jobs and an end to gerrymandering grew a reawakening of our own ability and identity. A pride in our Irishness began to grow and gain acceptance in almost every section of our people at home and in the Irish Diaspora worldwide.

The post World War generation in Ireland spoke; they asserted themselves, they demanded recognition and the world listened. No longer do Irish people anywhere in the world, but particularly in our own country, have to accept anything less than equality.

To travel to many parts of the world and see the admiration in which other nationalities hold not just Irish people but all things Irish fills me with a tremendous sense of pride. That is when you come to realise "what it is to be Irish in today's society". I wouldn't change it for the world. The tremendous warmth with which we Irish are received in the four corners of the world today should not be allowed to draw us into a sense of complacency, thinking that the job is finished. It is not. There is still a section of our people that has yet to be reconciled and persuaded that they are an integral and cherished part of the Irish nation — those of the Unionist tradition. We must work to show them that their traditions and cultures will be respected and accepted on a basis of equality in the new Ireland that we envisage. That they will not have to give up anything that they wish to preserve — including their British citizenship — in what will be a multicultural, multiracial, multilingual secular society.

There is another section of our people who also feel unwanted and who also must be brought in from the sidelines to share in the building of the new Ireland. They are the poor and the less fortunate in society. One very worrying fact of life in Irish society today from which none of us can derive any pride is that a third of the population is living below the poverty level. The Celtic Tiger has passed them by.

We must endeavour to remedy that situation. We must fulfil the promise of the 1916 Proclamation to "cherish all of the children of the Nation equally". That means sharing the wealth of the nation equitably. It is our responsibility not just to continue saying that these sections of our people are a part of the Irish nation but to make them feel and want to be a part of the nation. Working towards that goal is also "what it means to be Irish in today's society".

The Irish Peace Process has created space for new ideas, new opportunities and new relationships to be explored and realised for the good of all of our people. It is my view that the work of peace will continue to impact positively and powerfully on the issue of identity — Irish and British — for the foreseeable future.

As I write, prospectors are beginning to dig for diamonds in the hills of Donegal and a 6,000-year-old Neolithic habitat has been uncovered at the site of Thornhill College in Derry. Yet I believe the richest vein we have struck in the past hundred years is the vital cross-community, all-Ireland support for change and co-operation. I'm happy to identify with this innovative concept as we travel forward with increasing hope and confidence.

Tommy McKearney

Tommy McKearney, a former political prisoner, was reared in the County Tyrone village of The Moy. He now lives in County Monaghan and works for EXPAC (Ex-Prisoners Assistance Committee), one of many projects supported by the Special Support Programme for Peace and Reconciliation.

Legendary traditional musicians The Chieftains settled themselves to play a tune that I had never heard before. The piece was called "Guadalupe". It was fabulous and it received a magnificent reception from the audience. Unknown to the musicians, though, that tune helped me answer a tormenting question — what does it mean to be Irish today?

It appears a simple enough question at first glance, but the devil emerges with a little reflection. Too many people have an annoying tendency when addressing this type of question to create a satisfying self-portrait, a cosy wish-list or — worst of all — a caricature of ourselves. If the exchequer had a pound for every time the Irish were described as fighting, poitín drinking, racehorse loving raconteurs, the Minister for Finance could reduce income tax to five per cent.

The old *Punch* cartoon send-up of the Irish has always been an offensive misrepresentation. We are not a barbarous people. At the same time, the kinder, dewy-eyed picture conjured by *The Quiet Man* treatment was and is inaccurate. Ireland is not a Dostoevskian nightmare. Neither are we a land of happy, artless peasants.

Indeed, to the casual observer, being Irish today appears not unlike that of being part of many other English-speaking countries. We watch the same television programmes, listen to a lot of the same music and admire/detest the same economists. At a pinch, it might even be possible to imagine us as north-western Europeans. Our clothing, our housing, our education and nowadays even our eating habits are not noticeably different from a lot of other parts of Europe.

Yet in spite of all this, we are different. The differences though are subtle. And that gentle subtlety was beautifully illustrated when Paddy Moloney with his uileann pipes, Derek Bell on the harp and Kevin Conneff on the bodhran were joined by Keane, Fay and Molloy in a splendidly, uniquely Irish interpretation of a Mexican melody.

The venue where I listened to this arrangement was in Armagh City and the largely local audience had come to hear the very best in live Irish music. I looked around the crowd as they clapped in approval. A good cross-section of the community in terms of age, gender and income was present. In truth too, it could have been any country town in Ireland. And still they revelled to the sound of a Latin rhythm played on the uileann pipes, the bodhran, a harp, and all done in a distinctly Irish style.

It struck me then that this is perhaps what being Irish means. We accept the world and put our own *blas* on it. Maybe it has ever been the case. A medieval Celtic Church which was not quite Roman. An Anglo-Irish aristocracy which was never quite either. A population which was never quite quiet. We even produced a football game that is neither quite soccer nor rugby.

At its worst, it might be described as a form of obstinate perversity, but in reality it is a wonderful uniqueness and it would be a pity if we were ever to lose it. Nor do I think for a moment that we ever will change. Look at what is around us now in the newly prosperous economy. Things are not perfect, but there is an improvement over the not too distant past.

Yet recent economic success has come as a result of a policy that has no real origin elsewhere. The social partnership came too at a time when the received wisdom was altogether different. When the major producers talked of stringency and allowing managers to manage, Ireland developed a partnership that worked through consensus. The current reality has its flaws but the Irish have learned a very powerful lesson. We know now that prosperity is possible here and that it is a manmade condition.

There is a long way to go before we can feel content about Ireland's new-found affluence. Too many people remain in relative or actual poverty. Too many people control excessive wealth. The point now is that we known we can change things and that we can at least shape if not totally control the remedy.

This is heady knowledge for a people long adept at insidiously moulding their surroundings into something quietly and uniquely Irish. We are not dramatically different from other people. We are just persistently distinct.

As the man says: "Take her away there Chico Moloney."

Anne Madden

Anne Madden is one of Ireland's foremost painters. A member of Aosdana, her work is exhibited internationally and is represented in over forty public collections. She and her husband, Louis le Brocquy, recently returned to live in Ireland after living in the south of France for forty years.

Both my Irish father's and my English mother's families lived in Chile, South America, from the 1860s, where my parents were born. After the Crimean War, my paternal great-grandfather Denis Madden made his way from the Crimea to Chile where he acquired two farms near Valparaiso, San Antonio and San Pedro. My maternal great-grandmother and father sailed to Chile from England on their honeymoon in search of rare plants and then settled there. Mining and farming were their occupations.

My mother and father left Chile for Europe when I was four years old. I have in my mind a snapshot collection of vivid images of early childhood in that country. From then on my life was spent between England and Ireland, and it was in Ireland that I formed a deep attachment to the glaciated limestone wilderness in County Clare known as the Barony of Burren. I rode horseback, cycled and later drove its intricate web of roads until they were mapped in my mind; I roamed the synclines and anticlines of its stone hills and the expanses of limestone pavement; fished and rowed clinkered boats on its lakes and gradually discovered many of the monumental traces left by man since Neolithic times. The Burren excited my imagination and informed my early paintings, became a touchstone in my life, giving me an indissoluble feeling of being part of it. My adult life (mainly spent in France) with the painter Louis le Brocquy did not change this. Although I have been itinerant, one thing is constant: my Irishness, grounded in the rock of the Burren and in the consubstantial identity with its nature and substance.

Martin Mansergh

Martin Mansergh is Special Adviser to the Taoiseach on Northern Ireland, Economic and Social Matters. He studied at Oxford University where he became an authority on eighteenth-century French history. He is married to a Scotswoman and runs the family farm in Tipperary with his brother.

Being treated as Irish, at school in England in the 1950s, was to feel different and proud of it, despite exposure to derogatory comparisons. Spending summer holidays with my grandmother on my father's farm in Tipperary on the edge of the Golden Vale was to experience fitting happily into the deeper roots of extended family and parish. I took a ride by donkey and cart to the rural creamery each morning, and once a week accompanied the farm manager, a member of the Old IRA, round the fields. But there was a lot of visible poverty which led to heavy emigration, and that too had long been part of being Irish.

For many people, identification with and pride in county is as strong as nationality. Tipperary meant Ireland. As a teenager, I was inspired by Yeats, as was my father, and by Irish history, which he taught. Going back and forth across the Irish Sea, I followed keenly the progress being made by Lemass's Ireland.

All young people have to decide for themselves who they are, as well as where they are going to live and work. Pádraig Pearse spoke of his parents' marriage being the coming together of two widely remote traditions, English and Gaelic.

All second-generation Irish, especially those of mixed parentage, have a potential dual identity. Religious difference, and on top of that the notorious ambivalence around the Anglo-Irish tradition, were, in a South of Ireland context, further complications in my own case. Being Irish meant identifying with the people, and empathising with the values and traditions of the great majority, without losing sight of the contribution that could be made by a positive-minded minority.

Being Irish, or any nationality, is a mixture of law, descent and choice, for there are subjective factors, such as how you regard yourself, and how you are regarded by others. Law is simple. Anyone born in Ireland or a child of an Irish-born parent is an Irish citizen by right, as are some others of Irish descent or who are married to an Irish spouse. Apart from residence and registering as a voter, citizenship is explicitly affirmed by taking out an Irish passport, which I did after Bloody Sunday.

Article 2 of the Constitution now states that "the Irish nation cherishes its special affinity with people of Irish ancestry living abroad who share its cultural identity and heritage", a clause appreciated by Irish communities abroad.

In the early years of independent Ireland, there was a tension between the vision expressed by Young Ireland, the Gaelic revival and the 1916 Proclamation, and, on the other hand, a narrower form of cultural nationalism which, ignoring Northern Protestants, wanted to exclude what was left of Anglo-Ireland from a nation viewed as overwhelmingly Catholic and ideally Gaelic. Euphemistic phrases like "less characteristically Irish" were an uneasy compromise used to describe famous writers like Yeats and Synge, an attitude that did not survive much beyond the 1950s. There was also a greater tendency to apply political tests to people outside the mainstream, before accepting them as Irish (to Elizabeth Bowen to this day, for example, in some people's minds, despite her decision to be buried with her husband at Farahy in her native Cork). W.B. Stanford, in response to such attitudes in 1947 put it better, when addressing his own: "if you are a true Irishman you love Ireland before all countries".

Over the past 30 years, progressive and conciliatory thought has laid stress on respect for two traditions, though in reality there are many more. This runs the danger of typecasting people and cementing divisions, rather than softening them, but it represents in Northern Ireland the predominant political reality with which one has to come to terms. The recent revision of the Constitution has neatly squared the antithesis between the traditional one nation theory and two nations thinking. By asserting that everyone born in Ireland is entitled to be part of the nation, it respects the choice of those who do not want to be, such as those who see themselves as not Irish but Ulster British.

To be Irish today is something to be proud of. It is to be part of a stunningly beautiful country that is a success story on many fronts, the peace process, an economy driven by technological innovation, as well as much cultural and sporting achievement. The resources exist at last to tackle outstanding social problems. Emigration has been reversed, yet history and mobility have attracted to nearly every country self-confident Irish communities. Our young people look outwards. We can use our new-found strength to broaden our identity, so that it is ready to accommodate, on the basis of what is democratically agreed, and to the extent that they so wish, those on this island who express more affinity to the land mass that lies across the North Channel than to a country that transcends the border.

Paddy Moloney

Paddy Moloney is the founding member of The Chieftains, who have been together for 38 years. They have won six Grammy awards and one Oscar.

I grew up in Donnycarney on the northside of Dublin where a number of well-known pipers lived, including my tutor Leo Rowsome and Dan Dowd who often lent me his ancient set of pipes for recordings. I spent many wonderful musical evenings with Dan, but it was when I heard Leon Rowsome, son of Leo, play his pipes that I began to beg my parents to have Leo make me my very first set.

Each evening, our house in Donnycarney would be filled with the sounds of music, song and dance. My parents came from County Laois in the midlands of Ireland, a small farming family. We holidayed in Laois with my grandmother in the Slieve Bloom Mountains and again the farmhouse was filled with music and storytelling each evening.

I was always fascinated by the success of Irish performers in other countries, such as John McCormack and Delia Murphy. When the Clancy Brothers and Tommy Makem had huge international success with Irish songs, I felt I should do the same for our wonderful folk art of traditional Irish music.

I first felt the overwhelming strength of our Irish identity when we played the Royal Albert Hall in London in 1975, to a full house, everybody dancing in the aisles to Irish music. This was at a time when our music was not in fashion and it was a difficult time for the Irish living in London.

For over 30 years, we have been travelling to countries where our only form of communication is through music. It amazes me to this day how effective it is as a form of language. As soon as you begin to play, another musician understands what you want to do and joins with you. We have made many successful collaborations this way in South America, China, Italy, etc.

Having received an incredible reaction to our music all over the world for almost four decades now, it makes us very proud to be ambassadors of Irish music. In the early days, we did come across some "over-greening" as we call it, especially on St Patrick's Day in New York where the only tunes played were "Did Your Mother Come From Ireland", "Mother Mo Chroí" and all of those other tearjerkers, but I am happy to say that the real music has since taken over. There is a great interest in the history and tradition of the music.

The Irish are known for our cultural heritage and I wish and hope for further recognition for our music, songs, poetry, film, and all forms of Irish art in the twenty-first century.

Paddy Monaghan

Paddy Monaghan is married to Anne, a counselling psychologist; they have four young adult children and live in Dun Laoghaire. He is Secretary of the Evangelical Catholic Initiative in the Republic and also works as a financial consultant.

Being Irish for me means that I identify with Ireland and with all the achievements and blemishes within the Irish character and with all our past history and future potential.

As a teenager growing up in Meath, my identity was defined more in terms of what I wasn't — I wasn't English! As a student, I took part in the march on the British Embassy after Bloody Sunday. I felt hostility, anger and hatred towards England, the symbol of all that had oppressed us as a nation. A year later, I came into a personal faith in Jesus Christ and experienced real repentance for my hatred. I had a desire to build bridges of friendship with Protestant Christians and between North and South, Ireland and England. I began to see that my identity as an Irishman was not as important as my identity as a Christian, which now enabled me to move beyond that which was Gaelic and Catholic to embrace my "British" Protestant fellow Irishmen and women.

Among the 250,000 Protestants within Northern Ireland who would identify themselves as Evangelical, some 100,000 would not accept that it is possible for a practising Roman Catholic to be a committed Christian. For many of these, being Roman Catholic is nearly indistinguishable from being Irish. Encountering these evangelical Christians brings, initially, the inevitable painful realisation that they do not accept me as a Christian. I have, however, found that the mutual sharing of our personal faith in Christ establishes a basis upon which we can talk, without rancour, about the major difficulties they have with the Catholic Church. I identify myself as an Irish evangelical Catholic. By evangelical Catholic I mean those Catholics who have come to know Jesus as personal Lord and Saviour, those who have responded to

> *"Jesus' call to conversion. It is a radical reorientation of our whole life . . . a conversion to God with all our heart . . . a turning away from evil and the . . . resolution to change's one's life, with hope in God's mercy and trust in the help of his grace." (Catholic Catechism, section 1430/1)*

As part of the outworking of this identity in general and the focus on reconciliation in particular, my colleague, Eugene Boyle, and I published 29 evangelical Catholic testimonies in our book, *Adventures in Reconciliation*, which has encouraged others to build bridges of friendship. The book was warmly commended by many senior clergy in the Catholic and Protestant Churches and, thanks to a grant from the Community Relations Council in Belfast, was sent to all Protestant Clergy (over 3,000) in Ireland, North and South.

Over the years, as the IRA campaign gathered momentum and more policemen were murdered, I felt it important to express repentance, not just in words, but also in action. So I attended the funerals of policemen and other victims. It was always appreciated that I, as a Southern Catholic, came to "mourn with those who mourn". After the IRA murder of four RUC men at the border, I drove to Newry RUC Station with a bouquet of flowers. It deeply touched the murdered men's colleagues that a Southern Catholic would come with a token of the genuine sympathy of fellow Catholics from Dublin. It also helped them realise that being Christian for me was more important than being Irish, where there was a conflict.

I believe in the power of forgiveness and am so thankful that Tony Blair issued an apology for Bloody Sunday and, more importantly, set up an independent commission, some 27 years after the event. My wife, Anne, and I had the privilege of being invited to a garden party in Hillsborough last June, where we were introduced to Prince Charles. I took the opportunity of saying,

"I apologise for the murder of your uncle (Lord Mountbatten) in my country." Prince Charles was deeply moved by this and thanked me very much.

In my opinion, our nationalistic Irish music from the past needs to be purged of its militaristic themes and words. For example, I can no longer sing our national anthem with its outdated and hostile lyrics; the words fail to capture the more positive views of Britain now emerging within the Nationalist psyche and they exclude the ethos of the Protestant Unionist tradition in the north of Ireland.

I am deeply saddened that our flag, which is a beautiful symbol of reconciliation (orange for Unionist, green for Nationalist, white signifying peace between them) has become a symbol of division. Many Northern Ireland Protestants think the colours are green, white and yellow, not orange. Do we not need to be reminded that Meagher, when launching the flag in 1848, said:

> *"The white in the centre signifies a lasting truce between the orange and the green and I trust that between its folds the hands of the Irish Protestant and the Irish Catholic may be clasped in generous and heroic brotherhood."*

I recently attended the Munster/Northampton rugby match in Twickenham. I was certainly proud to be Irish when the 30,000 Munster fans stayed behind not only to cheer their own team, beaten by a point, but to heartily applaud the winning Northampton team. The ability to be gracious in defeat is a wonderful trait.

I value the creativity, artistry and imagination of our Catholic Irish heritage. I also value the hard-working, no-nonsense reliability of our Irish Protestant heritage. I'm ashamed of the reputation we have abroad because of the "Troubles", whereby we are known as a nation where Catholics murder Protestants and vice versa. This has brought great dishonour to the name of Christ and the name of Ireland. However, I believe passionately that God can and is bringing about change. I see it happening through the Anglo-Irish Agreement, which brought a real healing in the "anti-Brit" attitude of many in the Republic, and through the Good Friday Agreement, which, when we see its full outworking, may well become a model for the resolution of conflict in many places abroad. *As real Christianity leads us to reach out the hand of friendship and build meaningful relationships, Catholic and Protestant, North and South, Irish and English, Ireland can again become "a light to the nations".*

Austen Morgan

Austen Morgan was born and grew up in Northern Ireland. A barrister in private practice in London and Belfast, he is the author of The Belfast Agreement: a practical legal analysis, *available through http://www.austenmorgan.com in November 2000.*

Personal Identity

Asked recently by an Irish diplomat how I saw myself, I surprised him by answering: "Irish, British and European" (normally I preface the term with "white" in cosmopolitan London); Irish because I was born in Ireland, though not the Republic; British because I come from Northern Ireland (though have long chosen to carry an Irish passport); and European, because the Commission in Brussels, if not the Parliament, will shape the context of my future.

I have never had any doubt about who I am or where I came from (visiting periodically the recently abandoned house where my father was born). Perceptions of my identity (this I understand) shift with time and space, the observer, Irish and otherwise, deploying his or her own mental map in social interaction. Identity is fluid, not fixed; it flows with the course — courses — of human history. When it does not, it becomes fundamentalist, nasty and dangerous. This has been the case, in my experience, in Ireland, with the strong relationship between identity, nationality, citizenship and nationalism.

Identity in Ireland

I have long rejected involuntary membership of the Irish catholic community. This is principally because of its historic inability to integrate with Ulster Protestants during the modernisation of Ireland, even aspirationally. Anglophobia, romanticism, ambiguity about violence, and, yes, catholic sectarianism (especially in Northern Ireland) have characterised a mean-minded nationalist culture dominated by an inferiority complex.

Irish Nationality

In the nineteenth century, "Irish" referred unproblematically to Ireland (then one of the four nations or regions of the United Kingdom); the 1892 Ulster unionist convention in Belfast, for example, proclaimed *"Erin Go Bragh"*.

This was to reckon without Irish cultural nationalism (dating mainly from 1848), the Gaelic Athletic Association, the Gaelic League, and mainly Dublin literary and artistic endeavours. On the eve of the 1916 Rising, the Irish Republican Brotherhood took over the Gaelic League. Sinn Féin shaped the new state in 1922, and civil war politics — plus cultural nationalism — came to dominate the new polity.

The separatist phase of the Irish state (the 1920s to 1950s) is now readily dismissed by the new Europeans. Though rejected by most real Irish people, the nostrums of Gaelicism have been challenged less than Catholicism.

Northern Ireland

The Northern minority, in the context of an uninterested UK government and an opportunist Irish one (the grievance of partition), adopted a hesitant abstentionism vis-à-vis the new devolved administration. Cultural nationalism became an aspect of this continuing catholic defenderism.

Such a counterproductive strategy began to break down in the 1960s, when I was at St Columb's in Derry (and, though it is difficult to believe now, a young teacher called John Hume was perceived as a new, non-sectarian voice). The promises of that decade for Northern Ireland, including the civil rights movement, were devoured by republican militarism, the province being plunged into nearly three decades of what the Irish Free State endured in 1922–23. Not surprisingly, cultural nationalism thrived. Field Day sought to recreate the nationality of the 1890s. And west Belfast was proclaimed Ireland's newest Gaeltacht.

The Belfast Agreement

Insofar as this is a product of the 1985 Anglo-Irish Agreement (which excluded the unionists) and a direct result of Hume–Adams, I would not wish to affirm it. However, politically and legally, that text of 10 April 1998 promised a historic compromise between nationalism and unionism, including on questions of culture and identity. The 1937 Irish territorial claim was ended, the concept of consent was affirmed, and Northern Ireland — it was agreed — was an integral part of the United Kingdom. The peaceful road to a united Ireland was also reaffirmed as the only possible one.

Northern nationalists, however, with Sinn Féin leading the SDLP increasingly, and the Irish government aiding those it once called subversives, have tried — perhaps fatally — to press a joint sovereignty, or authority, interpretation on the Belfast Agreement. The key event was the Patten report on policing of September 1999 (which, ironically, preserved an integrated police force against nationalist demands). However, some cod constitutional theory of the chairman's, and symbolic liquidationism, stimulated catholic triumphalism.

This encouraged Sinn Féin, in office, to wage war on the union flag, citing contradictory principles: neutralism (which is not in the Belfast Agreement), meaning no flags; and parity of esteem, which does not mean joint sovereignty, implying the union flag and Irish tricolour together.

Less attention has been paid the Irish language lobby. Basically, republicans (the SDLP is not interested) and the Irish government have followed article 8 of Bunreacht na hÉireann (Irish as the national language), despite the Agreement specifying Irish, Ulster Scots and the languages of the various ethnic communities. Secondly, the operative legal text is the European Charter for Regional or Minority Languages, which embodies a very different set of values.

Conclusion

I will continue to refer to myself as White, Irish, British and European. However, by Irish I mean the historic Ireland (a Norse name), the fashionable "island of Ireland" being "government of Ireland" gobbledegook. If, however, the Belfast Agreement continues to be appropriated by nationalism, I can always — by way of protest — trade in my Irish passport for a British one.

Jane Morrice

Jane Morrice MLA was elected to the Northern Ireland Assembly as the Women's Coalition member for North Down. She is the former head of the European Commission Office in Northern Ireland. By profession she is a journalist.

Being Irish . . . a case of "mistaken identity"

This was possibly one of the most difficult essays I have ever tried to write. It was only after several attempts that I finally understood why. The fact is, I have no idea what it is like to be Irish because I am not.

Ask a Canadian what it is like "being American" or a Portuguese what it is like "being Spanish" to see the reaction. Some may laugh, recognising an honest case of "mistaken identity". Some may see it as cultural imperialism and inflate their own sense of identity in defence, while others may simply correct the mistake, aware that the issue of identity is one of the most sensitive, most complex and possibly most divisive questions facing modern society.

International examples such as these serve to illustrate the mistaken assumption that everyone who lives in Northern Ireland knows what it is like to be Irish. The assumption is based on geographical fact. Yet geography may have little influence on cultural identity. From my own experience, I would contend that politics, religion, education and social circumstance have a far greater influence on cultural identity than physical geography.

Let me explain. I was born in Northern Ireland — a country on the edge of the European continent sandwiched between two great cultural identities — British and Irish. Both have spent many years attempting to woo me into their own "identity zone". Neither has managed to succeed.

I spent my teenage years living with violence, hatred and bigotry and I could not accept it. If this was my culture, I wanted none of it. My country and its people were tearing themselves apart. The only thing left to love was the landscape. Unable to identify with this "culture of intolerance", I chose to disengage, and start searching for a new culture which would accept me for who I am, not what I am.

The result is a "hybrid", absorbing those parts of the British/Irish culture I respect, disowning those I reject and continually embracing new influences with which I can identify. When asked, I say that I live in Northern Ireland, hold British citizenship and describe myself as Northern Irish and European.

There is no doubt that my early identity was shaped more by British influence than any other. Carnaby Street, Shakespeare, the Beatles, Margaret Thatcher and fish and chips had a far greater effect on my life than Grafton Street, James Joyce, the Boomtown Rats, Charles Haughey or corned beef and cabbage. Holidays in Donegal allowed me to experience Irish culture at first hand but, when I needed a job, London, the capital, was where I looked.

In my later years, I developed a fascination for all things foreign, indulged my passion by learning to speak French, Spanish and German so I could read their literature, sing their songs and understand their people. I chose "European Studies" as my degree course. Obviously, with hindsight, I was preparing my escape.

I left home in 1977 and spent ten years travelling and working abroad. During a year in New York, I flirted with the "American dream", but only momentarily. The culture shock was electrifying. The "anything goes" attitude gave me a confidence I could never have mustered in the dark, dour, "fear of failure" society back home. I met more Irish there than I ever met in Donegal.

I moved to Brussels and followed the "European ideal" with interest. I appreciated the opportunity it offered to give me a new identity to which I could relate. Unlike the pressure I felt back home, I felt no pressure to become a European. It was a mantle I chose for myself. My own identity was enriched by contact with different cultures and I learned to respect people who were different.

I also learned that there is very little real difference between the peoples of the US and Europe and even less between the people of Britain and Ireland. We may have different flags and different allegiances but we have the same love for democracy and hatred of fascism. We may have different traditions but we share a similar desire for our rights to be upheld and respected by others. We may speak different languages but we know we need to communicate. We may have different religions but we share the same God.

My travels also taught me that it is impossible, no matter how hard the circumstances, to forget our "roots". That is undoubtedly why I returned to Northern Ireland to settle, bring up my family and help contribute to a change in society in the hope that it will eventually lead to a new "culture of tolerance". It is also why I will always describe Belfast as my birthplace, Van Morrison as my favourite musician and Northern Ireland as my home.

Bruce Morrison

Bruce A. Morrison was until recently Director and Chairman of the Federal Housing Finance Board in the US. From 1983 to 1991, he represented the Third District of Connecticut in the US House of Representatives, where he played an active role in promoting Irish interests in the United States. He is currently Vice Chairman of GPC/O'Neill & Associates, an international public affairs and public relations firm.

Being Irish came somewhat more recently in my life than some other touchstones of my identity. I was adopted as an infant, and being an adopted child often raises more questions of "who am I" than faced by others. But it also opens up early the possibility of being part of more than one heritage.

So, while being Irish was a less important part of my youth, it has become a very important part of the last 20 years for me. And that has a lot to do with the welcoming nature of the Irish American community as well as the things I have done. My name, of course, is of Scottish origins, and it is often found among Catholics as well as Protestants in Northern Ireland. It is from Northern Ireland that my father's father came — Scotch-Irish we called him. He was Protestant, with little use for Catholics, except that he married one. And she was an American of English heritage, just to make the ironies a bit richer. Most of my father's siblings became Catholics as well.

My father grew up in a largely German first-generation immigrant community in the Queens borough of New York City. My mother, a German Lutheran, lived there, too. They met in high school and married in their early twenties. I entered the picture 15 years later, the first and only child. We were Lutherans, and I was more likely to think of myself as German American, rather than Irish, and certainly not English.

Most important, though, was being an American. Thus, my first lesson about nationality was one of choice, not birth — belief, not blood. I came to regard my birth as an American to be the great gift of forebears who had joined a nationality by choice. They chose to become part of a nation based on a charter of democracy and human rights — the US Constitution and its Bill of Rights. In a world of ethnic hatred and strife, I have grown to cherish the very idea of a nationality that is independent of ethnicity and dependent on a respect for the rights of individuals.

I grew up in suburban America of the 1950s, and ethnic heritage was largely being left behind in the cities. Kids spoke of "what they were", but it was the melting pot, not the mosaic that defined my experience. In short, I missed out on the other half of the magic of the nationality by choice during my youth. That "other half" is what allows us to be Irish Americans or German Americans without any doubt of our political loyalty to the United States.

The celebration of our cultural heritages is an enriching, not a competing loyalty. This magic has been doubted by some throughout our immigrant history, usually in the form of questioning the loyalty of the newest heritage to arrive; some of that persists today. But the good news for me has been that the experience of ethnic identity came alive as I pursued the ideals of my American identity through politics.

When I was elected to Congress in 1982, I got to decide the things I would work on. Active Irish American constituents talked to me about Northern Ireland and about the plight of a new generation of Irish immigrants without legal status. I took up these causes — human rights for Catholics in Northern Ireland and legalisation for Irish immigrants to America. With these causes, I began to explore my own Irish identity and how it fit into the history I was now seeking to alter.

The Irish American community laid out the welcome mat. There were more and more occasions for me to enjoy the fruits of Irish culture and history, with regular opportunities to travel to Ireland. Some cynics might say that it was just politically convenient to "become Irish". But that would be completely off the mark. As much as my infant adoption gave me a family for life, awakening my Irish connections has given me a heritage for life.

Northern Ireland has challenged me for almost 20 years. Given my Ulster Scot grandfather and my Protestant religion, I never had the same background as many Irish Americans. I knew it wasn't about religion in some doctrinal sense. My grandfather came from no ruling class and didn't think of himself as British either. I came to feel a special need to contribute to a solution.

The genius of the Good Friday Agreement is the recognition that the two different nationalities in Northern Ireland must exist in parity of esteem. It provides the political structure for the constitutional arrangements to change in whatever direction the two traditions choose to evolve and integrate in the years ahead. To me, being Irish has been a choice and it should be one for the people of Northern Ireland as well.

Immigration was also an unexpected cause to adopt. It was the plight of the illegal Irish that was my impetus. But it became a speciality that absorbed much of my energy for the past 15 years. It captures a lot about who we are as a country and who I am as a person. A nation of immigrants is a nation by choice, of self-selected strivers from around the world, a nation always in danger of shutting the door on the new strivers in favour of the "real Americans" who are already here. For me, being Irish means remembering an immigrant heritage that changed who and what I could become. It means sharing with the world the magic that exists in lifting nationality from the bloodlines of ethnicity to the lifelines of human rights.

We Irish have now come full circle, as a nation of emigrants becomes host to new immigrants. It really isn't new, of course. Ireland has absorbed many waves of conquerors for two millennia at least. The wonder of Irish achievement across so many fields is testament to the good fruits of that process. Now it is not about conquest and absorption, but about choice in a mobile world and a global economy. Some say the newcomers can't be Irish; they don't look like us. To me being Irish, like being American, is a choice of allegiance, the best kind of nationality. For me, being Irish has involved a choice to breathe life and breadth into one part of who I am. It has answered the fear of the adopted child of not having a real heritage. I learned the lesson that the best identities are chosen, not given. And thanks to the Irish and Irish American communities, my choice has been honoured and embraced.

Liam Mulvihill

Photo: Inpho

Liam Mulvihill is Director General of the Gaelic Athletic Association.

An old friend once said that to appreciate what it meant to be Irish one had to go abroad to meet the Irish. That was not meant to be a criticism of the Irish in Ireland. Simply, those who have been lucky to stay at home take their identity for granted. They live in a naturally Irish environment where the attitudes and habits that are distinctly Irish are everyday things.

It is changing, as Ireland is gradually becoming a more cosmopolitan society, bringing with it all the differences, advantages and problems that have been apparent in larger nations in the past. But it is when abroad, in centres where the Irish have congregated in numbers, that one can sense what it is to be Irish. The Irish psyche lies somewhere between the volatility of the Latin and the reserved discipline of the West European. It is a simmering passion that constantly bubbles. Sometimes there is an eruption, a demonstration of unrefined emotion that can be triggered by any aspect of life.

The passion is often misunderstood. Because the Irish demonstrate their passion unashamedly — the *craic* as is it renowned worldwide — it is often seen as frivolity. But the "*craic*" is merely an extension of the demonstration of passion and is not confined to social outings. It can be found in politics, religion, music, drama and sport.

Sometimes in Ireland, being Irish is more difficult. We can be self-conscious, reluctant to manifest ourselves to our neighbours. It is part of living in a confined space, where everyone seems to know everyone else and there are few strangers. The Irish abroad have no such inhibitions, displaying their culture and identity with great pride to those of different ethnic origin.

Ireland and its people have emerged as a modern nation from a difficult history. The Irish have been a repressed race, beset by disasters, natural and man-made. An island race was forced to spread around the world, leaving behind the things that they valued most and never forgot. Today, third and fourth generation Irish as far away as Australia and North America retain a sentimental attachment that can only be explained by the specific Irish psyche. No matter how far the remove, there is still a simmering passion for the heritage.

The enforced departures from home shores, which continued until very recently, brought a new dimension to the Irish nation. The contribution of Irish men and women to the development of the western world has been phenomenal. In every facet of society, the Irish can be found to have been at the centre of growth.

It has created a greater Ireland. As an entity, Ireland remains an island. But as a nation, it stretches throughout the world. The impact on the latest generations of Irish in Ireland has been huge. They now travel and live in the world with great confidence and strength. Oppression is long past and the Irish live comfortably as a worldly people.

In the Third World the Irish, initially through religious orders and more and more today through charitable organisations, have been to the forefront in battling the appalling difficulties that face the peoples of those tragic lands. There is a particular resonance to that work. The tragedy of the mid-nineteenth century, when the Great Famine decimated the land and the population, has never been forgotten. It has not, however, shackled the Irish. Rather, it has ensured that there is a sense of responsibility among our people to ensure that no others should have to suffer as our forefathers did. We do not live in the past but use the past as a means of generating a better future.

At home we are becoming accustomed to embracing other customs and other peoples within our shores. This change is the most dramatic of modern

Ireland and has presented great challenges, as well as forcing us to face up to certain difficulties.

Today, being Irish does not mean rejecting the European ideal or identity. It means that through pride in our own identity, through our games, our music and our dance, we are situating ourselves at the centre of our own culture rather than at the margins of others.

Dervla Murphy

Dervla Murphy is an internationally renowned travel writer, whose books include Eight Feet in the Andes, In Ethiopia with a Mule, South from the Limpopo *and* A Place Apart — *the last about Northern Ireland.*

Being Ashamed of Being Irish in 2000 AD

During the night, from my city centre hotel bedroom, I could hear an odd sound, a sharp discordant flapping noise. Next morning I observed its source, as a gusty wind romped with vast plastic sheets insecurely draped over the façades of nearby bomb-ravaged six-storey buildings. The place was Belgrade, the date 18 October 1999.

The previous day, on arrival in post-airwar Serbia, I had soon discovered that, then and there, "Being Irish" was helpful. Whenever I addressed a stranger in English — to ask directions, to order a beer in a bar, to change money at a key-maker's kiosk or enquire about train times at the station — hostility showed. Occasionally extreme hostility (even hatred), sometimes a silent stare of disgust before the person moved on, most often a contemptuous dismissive shrug. This was unsurprising; the Serbs are not unfriendly people, I knew from previous experience, but they cannot be expected readily to identify an Irish accent. To preface all encounters with the explanation "I come from Irska" might in normal circumstances be considered eccentric but it almost always worked among the well-informed urban folk of Belgrade, Niš and Novi Sad. Later I was told that during the airwar, Irish journalists found themselves in a privileged position, being frequently granted permits denied to their NATO-tainted colleagues. Tito was a founder of the Non-Aligned Movement and many Serbs were aware of Ireland's honourable record as a non-aligned State. They had not yet heard the bad news.

While thus taking advantage of my country's reputation, I inevitably felt hypocritical, knowing that within weeks Ireland was to join NATO's Partnership for Peace (PfP). Only when this mortal blow was dealt to our independence did I fully appreciate how closely my pride in "Being Irish" was entwined with our non-alignment and consequent freedom to speak out on such issues as Tibet and nuclear weapons. As a PfP member, Ireland is tightly tied to an Alliance that remains openly devoted to its nukes and is led by the only country in the world which has actually used nuclear weapons. Nowadays, NATO representatives may often be heard referring to "the decisions of the international community" when the decisions in question have been made in America by Americans to protect America's worldwide interests. During the "airwar", Michael Byers, an American law professor, pointed out: "States representing half the world's population and three of its seven declared nuclear powers disagree with NATO's Balkan policy." Several NATO members and Partners also disagreed with it, but their governments could not say so out loud. Now, shamefully, we Irish have consented to being similarly silenced.

The general use of "neutrality" rather than "non-alignment" is unfortunate; Irish neutrality can only be described as a long-dead sacred cow with a bad smell. During the Second World War "downed" German airmen were incarcerated while "someone" enabled their British equivalents to slip quietly across the Border. Tens of thousands of Irish men and women fought with the British forces or worked in British armaments factories — not normal behaviour for citizens of a "neutral" State, but commendable in the context of a war against Hitler. (Post-war, some naive American politicians proposed that certain senior Irish army officers should be decorated in recognition of their co-operation with the Allies.) Yet during the disjointed and muted debate that preceded our joining PfP, it proved impossible to separate a parochial obsession with the mirage of "Ireland's neutrality" from the real issue. This grievously weakened the anti-PfP case. We should have opposed joining PfP, not to preserve a phoney neutrality, but because the Partnership links us to a ruthless military alliance that maintains a symbiotic relationship with the international armaments industry (known to its friends as "the defence industry"). NATO also insists not only on retaining nuclear weapons but on developing new ones and as a result of its defiance of the Nuclear Non-Proliferation Treaty, that treaty is no longer taken seriously by anyone.

Repeatedly, we have been assured that PfP membership will enhance the Irish army's peacekeeping skills — a disingenuous ploy. We are rightly proud of our soldiers who, over the years, have distinguished themselves as UN peacekeepers in many sensitive troublespots. An "enhancement" of their capability sounds desirable — until we realise that this involves Irish taxpayers spending many millions on NATO-style military equipment, thereby adding our mite to the armaments industry's profits. In fact, as Partners, our future peacekeeping operations will be less effective; worldwide, PfP members are perceived, correctly, as American pawns who cannot be trusted to act impartially. We are now "enhancing" our military power at the cost of out past political acceptability in unstable regions. And the Irish army's ethos can scarcely avoid being damaged by its association with an alliance that favours the brutal use of "superior military technology" to solve enormously complicated problems.

In March 1999, Ireland's government, if as loyal to the UN as it claims to be, would have protested vigorously against NATO's rejection of the alternatives to the airwar and its snubbing of the Security Council. Four weeks into the airwar, Mary Banotti, MEP, called on the government "to suspend its decision on joining the NATO-led PfP for twelve months until the people of Ireland have had a chance to fully explore the issues involved in our membership". She was of course ignored, though in 1996 Bertie Ahern had said, "Any decisions involving a closer association with NATO would represent a substantial change in defence policy and must be put to the people in a referendum." Had the PfP decision been postponed and the promised referendum taken place, it is possible that the Irish would have voted to retain their independence and dignity on the world stage.

NATO's bloody blundering in the Balkans was terrifying — the Alliance's lack of any intellectual grasp of the political situation or any comprehension of the historical background, which led to its failure to foresee Belgrade's wholly predictable (and predicted by many) reaction to an attack on Serbian territory. NATO, by its reckless insistence on expanding to the very border of Russia, could well be the catalyst for the new century's first major war. As we peace-niks tirelessly point out, the possession of weaponry does not satisfy the boys who own the toys. Eventually, the urge to use those toys prevails and non-violent methods of conflict resolution are discarded. That is the underlying logic of the militarism now tightening its stranglehold on every continent.

The accusation that being anti-PfP implies being insular and backward-looking exasperates me. Vividly I remember returning from then-remote Baltistan in April 1975, and stopping for a few days in Paris and feeling — "Now I'm home!" For 50 years or more, being Irish has merged, for me, with being European. Yet not until that morning in Notre Dame did I fully realise that my European-ness, my Irishness and my West Waterford-ness form equally important layers of my identity as I perceive it.

Niamh Murray

Niamh Murray is a highly regarded lyric soprano, nationally and internationally. She has performed extensively in operas, operettas, oratorios and stage musicals, and has won numerous awards for her singing. She is a guest presenter on Lyric FM and is also a prolific recording artist.

A number of years ago, following a concert in which I was the guest soprano, an American tourist came up to me and, while complimenting me, suggested I was not a real "Irish Colleen". Expressing my surprise, I asked him why he should think this. His answer amazed me — he told me that I was not a real "Irish Colleen" because my hair was not red! This reply set me thinking and wondering just what it does mean to be Irish.

I've always believed that there are particular traits which are peculiarly Irish. We tend to be good conversationalists with a wide variety of interests in numerous subjects and topics, well versed and quite knowledgeable in world affairs. We have a particular sense of humour which delights in the absurd and the ridiculous — laughing at ourselves but not necessarily too happy when others laugh at us! We are a proud people but sadly, perhaps, inclined too often to begrudge the success of others, slow to praise and quick to chide. As a nation, we have enormous talents and potential, if only we could believe in ourselves and not rely on the opinions of outsiders to decide whether something is good or bad!

Of course, I'm Little Miss Perfect, exhibiting none of the above negative traits . . . I jest! Where did I come from and what influences helped form the Irish woman I am today? Well, my parents came from very rural backgrounds, my mother Mena from Carraroe, County Galway and my father

Ciaran from Killashee, County Longford. Mum's family was steeped in Irish culture, surrounded by the Gaeltacht and revelling in the Irish language. *Ceol traidisiúnta* was very important to the family. My grandfather Luke was a sergeant in the Garda Síochána, a great character who was very popular in the locality. Agnes, my grandmother, was a schoolteacher, a highly educated and classy lady. Dad grew up in a family of six children. His father, Jack, was a school teacher and was very involved in music and drama. His mother, Hannah, was a talented violinist and was President of the Longford-Westmeath Federation of the ICA.

When my parents married in the 1960s they brought together a myriad of colour, personality, talent and exciting life opportunities from both families. Shortly after their marriage, my parents travelled to Nigeria where they taught for a few years in Calabar with St Patrick's Missionary Society. During the 1940s, 1950s and 1960s in Ireland, many young couples went abroad to work with the wonderful missionary orders before settling down to married life. Thus, religion has always played an important role in my life. I've often wondered how my mother coped so bravely in Africa — she who had never been abroad before this adventure.

My parents often related their experiences of Nigeria to us — its heart of darkness, the soldier and sugar ants, the mosquitoes, the wide religious and cultural differences, geckos, snakes, wild monkeys (particularly the one that jumped into my playpen and nearly killed me in its enthusiasm to play!). Dad contracted malaria and when I was born, both my parents were hospitalised — Dad with malaria, Mum with me.

On the return journey to Ireland, I had my first birthday in Rome, little realising that, years later, I would be back to sing in a historical broadcast from the Eternal City on BBC's famous religious programme *Songs of Praise*, and that my father would be granted a Papal Award, the Benemerenti Medal, for his services to Church music.

Anyway, all of this background has formed me — the "Irish Colleen" from Nigeria — who has always felt a little sense of displacement, being unable to visit her place of birth. Like my parents, I became a teacher but gave it all up to pursue a career as a classical singer.

It's impossible to write about what it means to be Irish and to reflect on Irish identity without considering my family, immediate and extended. Calling to one another's homes, leaving doors open to welcome guests, were part of the fabric of Ireland not so long ago. What has happened to all of this simple human interest and interaction? What has become of the tremendous devotion which Irish people had to their religion? Where has Ireland's true identity, which was so evident in its culture, gone?

Enough of this rambling and reflecting on what it means to be Irish. I'm Irish and I'm proud of it — good, bad or indifferent. I'm proud of my parents and four brothers Fiachra, Cormac, Fionnan and Ronan. By the way, maybe some day I'll satisfy that American gentleman and dye my hair red!

Julia Neuberger

Rabbi Julia Neuberger is Chief Executive of the King's Fund, an independent healthcare charity seeking improvements in health and social care. She lectures on and writes about Judaism, women, healthcare ethics and dying well, the title of her latest book. She became a Rabbi in 1977.

I'm not Irish, though I hope that one of the (much less important than other) results of a final peace agreement in the North will mean that people like me can hold dual citizenship. After all, all my grandparents were German Jews, and all acquired UK citizenship. My father fought on the British side in World War II, but my maternal grandfather fought on the German side in World War I; my paternal grandparents were that now often-sneered-at group, economic migrants — though they might not have been sneered at too much, because they were comfortably off. My mother was a refugee from Nazi Germany, who found a warm welcome in Britain, first in Birmingham and then in London. So I am British, and grateful and proud to be so.

So why Ireland for my second country, my adopted home? The connection is far from obvious, because there is none by blood or belonging. Ireland is my other home by choice. I'm a "blow-in", one who has tried to make a contribution — I owe the Irish that for the warm welcome we have received — but a "blow-in" nevertheless. We came for a holiday many years ago, and we have never quite left since.

So what is it? At first it was the charm, the humour, the literary quality of everyday talk, the celebration of the land, the sea, the beauty. I was beguiled. And then I began to be more involved and less easily won over. The strong sense of belonging that all Irish Americans feel could also exclude people like

me. The attitude to state support for denominational education in the North —
strongly held to be an essential by Nationalist and Protestant alike, despite the
clear popularity of integrated education — makes me feel an outsider. One
summer, our children attended the Protestant school in Ballydehob, very
briefly, by the great generosity of the authorities, because the Catholic school
would not accept our Jewish children, however temporarily. Protestants and
Jews together — the also-rans? That can make me feel uncomfortable too.

And yet the use of memory, the recording of the Famine in literature and
now in museums, the sense of peoplehood, the restoration of the language, the
pride in Irish food, clothes, glass and design — these are things I warm to, I
even love. Increasingly, my clothes are Irish, made by people I know, or sold to
me by those who know them. I have had few more pleasurable moments as
Chancellor of the University of Ulster than giving honorary degrees to fashion
designers and racing magnates. I have loved the celebration of Irish cheeses in
the United States, and rejoiced in the successes of Irish theatre in England and
the US, and the Irish novel worldwide.

So much for the love affair. It may not always be reciprocated, and I have
certainly had my share of unpleasantness in Ireland — over integrated education in the North, and over my support for and pleas for generosity towards
asylum seekers, when I have cited the generous welcome I and my family have
received. But what I feel deep down is something beyond the attractive, the
warm, the cosy, the charm. For there can be begrudgery, hatred, land battles
and long held feuds, and there are many unpleasant stories to tell. What I feel
most strongly is what I learned from that formidable professor of Irish Studies
at Boston College, Adele Dalsimer, whose recent death is so lamented. It was
she who made me see a parallel between Jews and Irish, a passion for memory,
a passion for learning, a way with words, a love of the law (!), and an understanding, albeit often unexplored, of what religion can really be about. Adele
was a Jew, and an honorary American Irish person. She it was who set up the
Irish-Jewish Passover Seder, remembering the Exodus from Egypt, the Famine, the Holocaust, the emigrations, celebrating longing for return, and praying for liberation for everybody.

For me, Ireland at best is the new confident and accepting face of Europe. And the Irish are able to welcome, to succeed in all they do, teach, learn, and create a new series of overlapping identities that can include all of us who want to be a part.

That means that we can be Irish by birth or Irish by ancestry; Irish by choice or Irish by accident; Irish with strong British links, or Irish with a link across the Atlantic, or even a bit of both; Irish by association or Irish by nationality; Irish in looks or Irish in voice, or neither of these, but Irish by choice. It's a more inclusive notion of Irishness than used to be the case, but as Ireland's confidence grows and as Irish people are successful the world over, there's no reason why it should not be the norm. Much of the time, it already is. And I hope, and pray, that it will become the universal view — and that the new Ireland will include us all, and make us its own.

Doireann Ní Bhriain

Doireann Ní Bhriain is a broadcaster and arts manager. She has worked as a presenter and producer on RTE television and radio. She was Irish Commissioner of l'Imaginaire irlandais, a festival of contemporary Irish culture held in France in 1996; organised the 1997 Celtic Film and Television Festival; and is currently general manager of Millennium Festivals.

I can only think about being Irish now in the context of what it has meant to me to have been Irish at different stages of my life. Oddly enough, despite qualifying in terms of lineage, with both parents having a long line of Irish-born antecedents, I wasn't always comfortable with my Irishness when I was young.

Brought up by Irish-speaking parents in a middle-class Dublin environment in the 1950s, I was thrown into conflict the minute I stepped out the door. At home, Irish was the language we spoke. In my grandparents' house up the road, it was Irish too. My grandfather, Peadar Ó hAnnracháin, an idealistic and impressive Gaelic Leaguer and one of the legendary *múinteoirí taistil* (travelling teachers), had cycled the length and breadth of Ireland as a young man teaching eager students of all ages the language their parents had lost or been forced to abandon. He was a writer and a nationalist who was utterly devoted to the revival of Irish, and though I may find some of his views somewhat narrow in retrospect, I am quite humbled by his idealism and deeply grateful for his transmission to me of the language his parents chose not to speak to him, although it had been their first language.

Outside my home, Dublin's middle classes were trying to shake off the dust of the past, and that included the language. My classmates had very little interest in Irish and indeed were often hostile to anything to do with the language or with its cultural expression. I was the only child in the whole school whose name was written in Irish, and I distinctly remember being called "the Irish girl" when I was still in primary school. I was embarrassed at being "Irish'" and hated my parents speaking Irish to me in public. It wasn't until I went to university, and discovered that Irish was beginning to be cool, that I finally felt comfortable about my identity. I fell in love with Irish traditional music and wore my Irishness comfortably, alongside my growing fascination with other languages and cultures.

Even then, however, I really only knew one way of being fully Irish and that was in the Irish-speaking, Catholic, Gaelic world in which I had grown up. I absorbed a perception that Protestants weren't completely Irish. Neither were people whose accents were described as English and, had there been any black people in Ireland then, I would have excluded them from my definition of being Irish too. I find this shocking now, but for all the liberal attitudes I developed about sex and religion and politics, it was some time before I began to interrogate what being Irish really meant. And it wasn't until I got to know Northern Ireland and its people well that I earned the right to call myself fully Irish.

At a visceral level, I see Ireland as the ground in which I grew. Its sounds, smells and images and the lives that have been lived in it are like cells that inhabit my body and my soul. I am lucky enough to have had Irish as my first language, so my roots spread deeply into that ground and draw enormous sustenance and wealth from it. However, a Nigerian, a Spaniard or a Chinese person could probably say the same of his or her place of origin.

After all, being Irish makes me no better — or worse — than anyone else on this planet. To tell the truth, I often get irritated by our national smugness. Aren't we great? Aren't we so welcoming and friendly? Doesn't everybody love us? I don't deny that as a people, we seem to have an easygoing and attractive way about us, but we have only to look at the revelations of rottenness in public and private life in recent years to see how much that can mask.

The choices we have made about our behaviour and our priorities in recent times often make me uneasy about being Irish. I don't like belonging to a soci-

ety where greed and self-aggrandisement are lauded, where frightened people
who cannot build a future in their own countries are derided and belittled,
where adults can destroy the lives of children in their care and where vulner-
able people are not loved or protected. What appears to be endemic political
corruption and the inequitable distribution of our new-found wealth leaves me
even more uncomfortable with the notion that being Irish is good.

But I will not despair. There are good, kind, imaginative, open-hearted
people in every corner of this island. They found a voice to force change in
Northern Ireland. Their voices and their constructive lives echo through communities up and down the land. They come from a variety of cultural and religious backgrounds, and are enriched by contact with each other and with
those of different races whose arrival has opened new doors. I am excited
about getting to know more about the people whose circumstances have forced
them to make a home here, and about those with whom we have shared the
island, but whose ways of life we have not valued. Together, we will challenge
the old and create a new Ireland. And that's when I'll be able to say with conviction that I'm proud to be Irish.

David Norris

David Norris is a member of Seanad Éireann, a conservationist, a lecturer and a keen Joycean scholar. He campaigned successfully for the decriminalisation of homosexuality.

Some years ago, when I was being introduced as an after-dinner speaker by the then Dublin City Manager, Frank Feely, he said, "Well now David, we know that you are a real Dub and passionate, especially about the north side of the city and its Georgian core, but I am not sure whether you were born on the north side or the south side of Dublin. Would you like to start by telling us where you were born?"

This was a bit tricky for me, as I wasn't born in Ireland at all but on the equator in Central Africa, where I spent the first six months of my life. Moreover, my father wasn't even Irish but an Englishman, although on my mother's side I can trace my ancestry back to the crack of doom. So to the purist, the very notion of my being really Irish might be called into question.

In addition to this I don't possess what is normally regarded as a real Irish accent, and because I don't employ the brogue I have occasionally suffered the consequences. I remember speaking at a meeting of the General Council of County Councils in Ballybunion and because I gave the councillors a dose about section 4 planning permissions, I was rewarded by the first questioner asking me, "What part of England do you come from sonny?", and then suggested that I might profitably make my way back to the home counties.

The Ireland in which I grew up in the late 1940s, 1950s and 1960s was indeed an apparently homogeneous place. There was an unspoken assumption that to be Irish you also had to be white, Catholic, heterosexual and Republican. Since I only fitted into one of these categories, I did at first feel rather dislocated from the surrounding culture. My childhood echoed to the loudspeakers of Corpus Christi Processions and the political rhetoric about the 700 years of brutal British oppression. The Easter of 1966 is a particularly unpleasant memory, as the religious significance was eclipsed almost entirely by a celebration of Patrick Pearse's notion of blood sacrifice.

But I grew to discover that Irishness was a little more complicated than might at first appear. Pearse himself was half-English so that occupying the General Post Office and employing terms of racist abuse against his father's countrymen had to be seen as a form of overcompensation. Several of the other prominent Republicans were also less fully Irish than one might have assumed. James Connolly was born and spent the early part of his life in Scotland, speaking ever after with a strong Scottish accent. Cathal Brugha certainly seemed to be genuinely Gaelic until you realised it was a translation of Charlie Burgess. While even Eamon Ceannt was really Eddie Kent, than whom it would be impossible to sound more English even if you were George Gloucester, the King's younger brother.

The simplistic nature of the way in which we regarded ourselves was also reflected in our reactions to sexuality. I certainly remember the return of the supposed bones of Sir Roger Casement in the 1960s but it was regarded as a matter of treason to suggest that Casement, who certainly was a hero in his defence of the human rights of the Putumayo Indians in Brazil and the native people of the Congo, was anything less than a full-blooded heterosexual. And, of course, the infamous Black Diaries were forged. The only openly gay couple visible in Dublin, the late Michael MacLiammoir and his partner Hilton Edwards, were simply explained as being "theatrical".

However, shortly before his death, Michael MacLiammoir made an impassioned plea on the radio for the reform of the laws criminalising homosexual behaviour between males and when a few weeks later he died, the President of Ireland Cearbhaill Ó Dálaigh made a significant, though discreet, breakthrough in being seen on television approaching Hilton Edwards, to shake his hand and say, "I'm sorry for your trouble, Hilton," the traditional greeting to the bereaved spouse.

The other side of the coin is that we did in those days have a grudging respect for the institutions even when we might have felt them to be oppressive. The Roman Catholic Church was still securely recognised in the Irish Constitution as having its special place, a position remorselessly exercised by the Archbishop of Dublin, Dr John Charles McQuaid. The legal profession and judges were above suspicion, the word of the priest was law in the land and no one had heard of paedophilia; banks were pillars of secular rectitude and politicians were regarded with admiration and respect. One might disagree with the views of Mr De Valera or Mr Cosgrave but they were still figures of a certain presence. Writers were held in great regard and they seem to be the only group to have survived more or less unscathed. Nowadays, indeed, their public behaviour at least is a good deal less Bohemian, so that they as artists are still swimming against the tide. Dublin indeed was full of literary characters whose doings were recorded not just in the newspapers but in the popular imagination, even though censorship was still a live issue.

We have come painfully into maturity. We have also less painfully started to experience something of an economic miracle. The one thing I regret about the Celtic Tiger is that we seem to be in danger of moving from being an unthinking Catholic country to being an unthinking materialistic nation, which in my opinion would be considerably worse. Our self-congratulatory image of ourselves as "Ireland of the Welcomes" has certainly been seriously challenged by the arrival of refugees and asylum seekers. We were the most generous people when we had nothing. But then it's always easy to be generous when you have nothing and we are showing considerable signs of selfishness, intolerance and racism now that we are expected to become both pluralist and multiethnic.

For this reason, we have all cause to be grateful to those sterling people like Tom Hyland, an unemployed bus driver from the working-class suburb of Ballyfermot, who single-handedly brought to the attention of the Irish public the outrage of political genocide being perpetrated by the Indonesians against a small defenceless people of the island of East Timor. This at least showed that individual ordinary Irish people could have an impact, not just on national but on international politics.

James Joyce, from being an unread blasphemous and pornographic writer, has become part of the Irish pantheon: Bloomsday is celebrated with ever-increasing Joyceanity throughout the island. Homosexual behaviour has been decriminalised and a measure of civil rights accorded to the gay population of Ireland. Censorship is virtually gone and the once despised Georgian architecture of eighteenth century Dublin, sizeable chunks of which were demolished during the 1960s, is now officially cherished and paraded for international visitors. On balance, the Ireland of the new millennium is a better place, but it is certainly more complex and presents each of us with a challenge.

Barbara Nugent

Barbara Nugent is Chief Executive of The Sunday Business Post. *She was part of the original team to launch* The Sunday Tribune *in 1983. She is also Chair of the Board of the National Museum of Ireland.*

Being Irish puts few demands on you. It allows you to be as cultured or as batty as you wish. It gives you a freedom from expectations. People don't feel threatened by you but rather entertained by you. Neither our ancestors nor ourselves have ever colonised or waged war on anyone, so we are judged at face value and I like that. The fact that we have the fastest-growing economy in Europe and still don't take ourselves too seriously has enhanced our reputation.

I love the fun we Irish indulge in, the talk, the debate, the closeness of family and friends, the silent understanding and sometimes even the intrusion into one's personal life from our more robust friends. I love our ability to laugh at pretty much anything, our storytelling, our literature, our music and our turn of phrase. To me, it is all bound up in our language, which has been lost to most of us, but is still an integral part of the way we express ourselves. It makes for a wonderfully colourful existence.

I love our curiosity and thirst for knowledge and the fact that we tend to be outward-looking. Our interest in the politics and policies of other countries, our adoption of an American-style technology and business culture, our interest in being Europeans and our reduced dependence on Britain all display our ability to grow and yet feel distinctively Irish.

I love the fact that we are impulsive and a little bit eccentric, argumentative and passionate and that a party can burst out at any time. I love the fact that you can have a deep discussion on any subject and take a stance that might well be argued as strongly by you from the opposite angle the following night — just for the hell of it!

I love the richness of our countryside, its colours and its silence. I love the sea that surrounds us, and I'll never tire of the "crying wind and the lonesome hush". I love the spirit that has brought us through our difficult history un-daunted and sent us out to the four corners of the globe to learn and succeed.

I love my Dublin. It's small and personal but has a city feel to it. It thumps with energy and laughter and when the sun shines I can think of very few places I would rather be.

But can we continue to enjoy, with modest pride, our identity? Can we hold onto the carefree generosity that was ours? Are we beginning to show cracks in our cultural strengths now that we are being put to the test? Is the taste of suc-cess too much for us to don without changing the very qualities that differenti-ate us from others?

Our growing selfishness, evidenced by our treatment of asylum seekers and economic migrants, is testing us. Can we continue to love, enjoy and celebrate our Irishness while this trait, hidden thus far, now rears its ugly head? How have we forgotten what it was like to need help so quickly? Is skin colour blinding us to what is our true nature, or what I believe it to be?

We have faced challenges before and our spirit has brought us through, but these were from external forces. This is the first time we have had to face the challenge from within. After our shabby start, will we dig deep into ourselves and find the openness and generosity once shown to us?

I believe we will, for how can I go on loving the Irishness within us if we are so deeply flawed? I have always been an optimist. I believe we Irish have the ability to embrace change. The human qualities that saw us through our terri-ble times are still within us. Once we scratch the surface of our new-found prosperity, we will find them.

Earlier I wrote about my love of literature. Of all the lines that have been written by the great Irish scribes, none could be more appropriate to end this piece than this one penned by W.B. Yeats:

Tread softly for you tread on my dreams.

Brendan O'Carroll

Brendan O'Carroll is a playwright, comedian and author of four novels, including the "Mrs Browne" trilogy, one of which (The Mammy), *was filmed as* Agnes Browne.

Kiss me, I'm Irish

Comics throughout time have made a meal of our Irishness, regaling us with tales that reflect what we believe is our particular and peculiar way of approaching life and the universe. These idiosyncrasies have collectively become know as "Irishisms". Allow me please to give you some short examples.

During the Civil War here in the 1920s, a group of ten guerrillas were laying in wait to ambush an Army convoy that passed this particular spot at 8 p.m. every evening on patrol. At 8 p.m. there was no sign of the convoy; at 8.10 not a sound could be heard and the waiting attackers were getting uneasy. By 8.30, one of the soldiers crawled to his commander and whispered, "What's the story?"

"I don't know," replied the chin-rubbing officer. "They are very late."

"Aye," says yer man, and adds . . . "Jesus, I hope they haven't had an accident."

In the 1950s, my mother Maureen O'Carroll was the only female member of the Irish Government. During this time, she was appointed to a police commission to investigate the possibility of closing down some of the stations in the smaller towns and centralising the Gardaí in the bigger towns. She went from station to station all over Ireland and her diary of that time makes for hilarious reading. In one tiny village in Cavan, the station had a Sergeant and five Gardaí. She asked the Sergeant, "Do you really need six Gardaí in this village?"

The Sergeant replied, "No, but if we didn't have them we would."

In another village in Donegal, she opened the "incident" book to find it completely blank. She quizzed the Garda.

"This is blank," she exclaimed.

"Aye, 'tis," the Garda confirmed.

"But anything unusual should be written in this book," my mother added.

"Aye, but sure divil a bit unusual happens around here," he replied with the assurance of a man with his finger on the pulse.

My mother was not giving up. "Let me ask you, Guard, what would you call unusual?"

The Garda thought for some moments. "Well you'd have to see it to know."

Mammy persisted, "If an aeroplane landed in the Main Street, would you call that unusual?"

"No," the policeman replied.

My mother was aghast, "Then what would be unusual??!"

"If it took off again, now that would be unusual," replied the Garda with a wink.

Call me old-fashioned, but those tales warm the cockles of my heart. And now as I experience being Irish in the new millennium, I take great pride that although the economy is booming, and we have shed our old inferiority complex, that we have reversed emigration, and have embraced being European, that communication between any two places is mobile, rapid, and our country is becoming one of the most modern in the world, somebody somewhere in Ireland is saying to someone else, "Divil a bit happens around here."

Is it any wonder that no matter where in the world my career takes me from time to time, the highlight of every trip is coming home?

Conor O'Clery

Conor O'Clery opened the Irish Times bureau in Moscow in 1987 and in Beijing in 1996, and is preparing to launch the first Irish Times New York bureau early in 2001. He is the author of a number of books, including Melting Snow, America: A Place Called Hope?, The Greening of the White House *and* Ireland in Quotes, a History of the 20th Century.

Beijing Irish

As a foreign correspondent, I often have to declare my nationality on immigration forms at airports. I always write "Irish" with something of a flourish. It's a good nationality for western travellers to have in the developing world. We are a small nation, not threatening anyone, with no colonial baggage, and possessing an empathy with the underdog that makes Irish people exemplary aid workers and UN peacekeepers. We tend to fit in well in foreign parts at a personal level, with an informal, easy-going approach.

Being Irish sometimes means being patronised, especially in the United States. The response, "Oh my God, you're really Irish," has opened some doors for me as a journalist, so I've no problem with that. But being patronised comes in different forms. In Moscow, where I opened the first *Irish Times* bureau in 1987, the blue-rinsed mother-in-law of a British diplomat asked me incredulously at a cocktail party, "You're from the *Irish Times*? Are people in Ireland really interested in what's happening here?" Her idea evidently was that the Irish were all maids and labourers. Actually, if she only knew, they were just as curious about the fall of the Soviet Union as her bridge partners, a point brought home to me by an elderly farmhand with trousers tied up by string whom I encountered when on holidays in Leitrim, and who asked me, upon hearing where I worked, "Is it true collectivisation is fucked?"

But I knew I had to show I was as serious as other long-established corre- spondents in Russia. I was breaking new ground, as I did later in China, in setting up an Irish media bureau in a world capital where there never had been one before. It had long been standard practice for Irish national newspapers to send reporters overseas only on brief assignments, while taking the real news from agencies and foreign newspaper syndications. We had a provincial men- tality in those days which affected the whole country, and which spawned the syndrome of "sure it will do", rather than "we can be the best".

We've grown away from that now. Joining the European Community was the turning point. It transformed our relationship with the UK, making Ireland less economically dependent and more of an international partner, and hence changed our image of ourselves, one which we shared with the American dip- lomat who once famously described Ireland as "small potatoes".

The incredible growth of the 1990s became a great source of pride to people like me who grew up in Northern Ireland, where one had always to be defen- sive about the impoverished "Free State", especially when the per capita GDP in the south came to exceed that of the UK for the first time. In my hometown of Newcastle, County Down, the culture which assailed us every day on radio and television was that of Britain. We grew up with *Coronation Street* and the *Last Night of the Proms.* If portrayed at all, the Irish tended to be literary drunks, "thick" paddies, or romantic incompetents in movies with diddley-aye music. To embrace Irish literature was almost an act of rebellion to the other side.

In my early days, I was heavily involved in a cross-community amateur dramatic society, but it fell apart after a bitter row over whether we should stage a John B. Keane play or a silly London farce; those of us who argued for John B. Keane were tarred as dangerous subversives. Today Irish writers are regarded as international and not just national assets, Irish performers and dancers have taken the world by storm, many Irish companies have gone global, there is an Irish pub in every big city in the world (even several in communist China), and Irish people, so long denigrated as the fighting Irish, define themselves by not being soccer hooligans.

I often meet colleagues from Australia, Canada and the United States who tell me they envy the strong sense of belonging and identity which Irish people like me have. They also would like an Irish passport, and some have managed to get one through Irish ancestry. It certainly proved useful to be Irish when reporting on the siege of the British embassy in Beijing after the NATO bombing of the Chinese embassy in Belgrade in May 1999. Assailed by furious Chinese protesters who wanted to beat me up as a NATO-loving westerner, I managed to extricate myself by telling them, "Hey, we've been fighting the British for 800 years." Which, on the day, was as good a way as any of defining what it meant to be Irish.

Niall O'Dowd

Photo: Irish America

Niall O'Dowd is Founding Publisher of The Irish Voice *and* Irish America *magazine.*

Back to Where I've Never Been

On a plane flight back from Ireland a few years ago, I found myself committing a heresy. The lights of New York had just hove into view off the right side of the plane and for the first time ever I thought, "I'm home now."

It was an involuntary thought, not something planned in advance. It was the moment after almost 20 years in America that something fundamental had changed in my psyche. Ireland was no longer home.

All those years, no matter where I lived in the US — Chicago, California, New York — Ireland was always home. Indeed, the more I embedded myself in American life, the more the thought of "going home" for my vacations or on business appealed to me. Back then, as the plane descended into Shannon or, later, Dublin, it was hard to hold back a feeling deep in the soul that I was back where I belonged.

Pete Hamill, the wonderful American writer, described his first visit to Ireland in memorable terms. He said it was "going back to where I've never been". I felt some of that in later years, as the Ireland I had known and left in 1978 changed beyond all belief and the friends I had through school and college all drifted away and got on with their own lives. It was a different Ireland with an unfamiliar landscape I was returning to. In that time, too, I missed all my nephews and nieces growing up, and the many family occasions which are so woven into Irish life. Yet I didn't need any of that directly to feed my soul. Just being in Ireland was enough. I feel it most intensely in Ballydavid, County Kerry, some ten miles or so from Dingle, where I have a small cottage not two miles from where my father was born and raised.

My father and his father and his grandfather walked these roads all their lives. I never did except as a young child, too small to remember, but I could feel at one with them now. I could walk the same roads they did, view the same incomparable vistas of sweeping mountains and dashing seas, stand on Ballydavid Strand as they did and watch the fishermen land their daily catch, linger over a sunset out by Blasket Sound and contemplate the beauty of the earth as they surely did.

My cousin Padraig, who lives in the old family farm, told me stories of the old days, of the young woman from my father's family who died during the Famine. She was buried in the fields, because they were too weak to take her to the graveyard; I could almost weep at the memory.

I could stop in Kilmakeadar cemetery and see the graves side by side of my grandfather and grandmother, one vaguely remembered, the other not at all, yet feel a kinship and connection with them that defied any rational logic.

That sense of being Irish, of belonging somewhere, is heightened by my exile. As an emigrant to America, you are forced to think about who you are and regret who you might have been if you had stayed. As Barry Moore so beautifully put it in his song "City of Chicago":

"In the city of Chicago
as the evening shadows fall
there are people dreaming
of the Hills of Donegal"

Many a night we exiles dream of the Hills of Donegal and Kerry and all points in between. But we are aware, more and more as we get older, that it is a dream, and luckily for us one we can replenish and live out several times a year if we wish. What must it have been like for those generations who never again saw their homeland or kith and kin after they left? The heartbreak must have been truly devastating.

This year, I brought my new-born daughter home to Ireland for the first time. Alana O'Dowd won't remember it, but she too, was going back to where she'd never been. I took her to my father's grave and there I took a photograph of her at his graveside. He never knew her, but she will know him when she gets older. She will be American, but Irish too, just like her father has become now. One of the greatest gifts I can give her is to help her understand that sense of herself, of being Irish as well as being American. She deserves to have that.

Josephine Olusola

Josephine Olusola is a journalist and playwright, currently living in exile in Ireland. She is Editor of The Voice of Refugees, *the newsletter of the Association of Refugees and Asylum Seekers in Ireland (ARASI).*

"Hello Paddy!"

At first, it made no sense. Here I am, on O'Connell Street, waiting for the bus (No. 122) to take me home, when an elderly fellow — smartly turned out — approached me. I had noticed him making a beeline for me even before he approached me; you are more aware when you are of colour or a foreigner in Dublin these days, what with the increase in drug-related crimes and racial attacks, whether verbal or physical. Hence it is always safe to be on the look-out when out at night.

Having prepared myself for, at worst, a verbal onslaught and, at best, a "Hello", I was pleasantly surprised when the man stopped, bang in front of me, and repeated his greetings. "Hello Paddy," he said. Unsure of his intentions, I reluctantly muttered a greeting of some sort. "I called you Paddy because you are one of us and are welcome," he explained, stretching out his hand in friendship. I took his hand in mine and shook it firmly, gave my warmest smile and said, "Thank you."

The gentleman was obviously Irish and I am not, obviously.

Over the three years that I have lived in Ireland — seeking the protection of the State, because mine had failed to — I have witnessed, firsthand, the generosity of the people as well as the ugliness that comes with bigotry. One thing I had never been called is a Paddy!

The word "Paddy", just as any other racially differentiating word or the word "race" itself, can have different connotations depending on when or how it is used. It is a well-documented fact that, not so long ago (perhaps still in some places), these words were used to cause offence to people.

Not so long ago, I was at a concert in the grounds of Dublin Castle to see Tracy Chapman play. Her supporting act was a chap by the name of . . . Paddy Casey! I was so high on the music — acoustic guitar and folk songs, his first then hers — that I was screaming his "name", or so I thought. You see, none of us had heard of Paddy or his music before, so my friends and I arrived at the gig late. So it was only by chance that I overheard some people shout, "Go on, Paddy"; I thereby assumed that his name was Paddy. I joined in revering a great man in the making — only to notice that, every time I called out to Paddy, the couple next to my party were giving me some seriously offensive looks. Evidently, they did not know his name so assumed that I, a black woman with a foreign accent, was taking the "Mickey" (!) — or at least being racist. I ignored their conceit and carried on as only an honorary Dubliner can, screaming, "Go on, Paddy!"

To some people, the name Paddy has come to mean everything positive about this Isle. The post-modern Paddy is green, peaceful, friendly/jolly, ambitious, achieving and proud. And the Ireland of the new Paddy is cosmopolitan and still welcoming, or is it? Of my many discontents with my "Ireland", the plight of refugees and that of the homeless, poverty and any other form of exclusion, top the list.

I am a Nigerian woman living in a post-Famine, post-Depression, affluent and prosperous Ireland. Yet in the new millennium, thousands are sleeping on the streets, homeless and despised by the rich who think the homeless are to blame for their predicament. The Ireland of a "thousand welcomes", where refugees seeking asylum are treated and regarded with contempt and disbelief. Coming from a majority world country, where corrupt leaderships and poverty are the norm, yet homelessness is not, I cannot understand why this is so in this land of plenty. Nor can I understand the neglect, on the part of the Irish leadership, of the underclass and the poor. But then I am not an economist; I am only a refugee.

Under all human rights conventions, all humans are born free and equal in rights and in dignity and must be provided for, if they are unable themselves to do so. Everyone has the right to sufficient provision for his or her well-being. No one should have to sleep on the street because they cannot afford otherwise, whether one is a citizen or alien. Everyone also has the right to seek asylum.

I have repeatedly used the term "refugees" for people seeking asylum, because we are just that. People become refugees the moment they are compelled — usually by forceful means or the threat of force, detention or even death — to flee their homes. Once in their country of sanctuary, they only seek the recognition of their status as refugees from the State.

I went to a Catholic school in Nigeria, where my early academic and scholastic achievements came from Irish nuns. I was also encouraged to love all humankind, the earth, and sport — maybe not necessarily in that order — and I was told many a thing about this country. Having said that, the fact that I find myself seeking asylum in Ireland is merely a coincidence.

I am proud of my Irish heritage, I am proud of my present one as a southside Dubliner (in the making!). I am also proud to be a "Paddy-Nigerian" and I thank "yer man" for recognising me as such!

Amal Omran

Amal Omran is a lecturer at the University of Gezira, in Sudan. She is currently completing a PhD in Equality Studies UCD and has been living in Ireland for four years. She is an active member of the Irish Black Migrant Women and Muslim Women organisation.

I wish I had never come to Ireland; her love grew in me. I love the people, the sun in the summer and the snow in the winter and the rain all the time. I want to live in Ireland and I want to live in Sudan — they are both my homes! It is wonderful to have two homes; then it does not matter where one lives.

Being here has enriched my life; I have spent wonderful years here. When I first came, I was a timid shy girl who was very curious to know and understand the culture of this part of the world. The Irish were nice to me; no one called me names! When I finished my Masters, I wanted to do my PhD but it did not cross my mind to go elsewhere, as I did not want to be anywhere but Ireland. If someone asks, "Do you miss home?" I say, "Ireland is my home now; I have good friends here."

I was in the right place at the right time, to meet wonderful Irish people. I wanted to thank all the Irish for the wonderful time I spent in their country, so when I met Mary Robinson I gave her a little present, a beautiful wooden elephant curved in Abanous. She said, "That is very thoughtful." I met Gerry Adams and he said, "Good luck", and that is what I need to survive in Ireland.

But it was not always fun. I did not like my picture on the front page of *The Irish Times*. This is how it happened. I went to a conference and a journalist took my picture. I felt flattered. When he came over to me to get my name, I said to him, "Do not print my picture and say REFUGEES INVADING IRE-LAND! I will sue you." The next day my housemate came rushing home, shouting, "Amal, you are in the papers! Front page, nice smiley picture!" I could not believe it — when I saw my picture I wanted to drop dead! It looked silly. I felt like buying all the papers in town and throwing them in the bin! I wrote to the editor to tell him how I felt. He sent me back an apology that made me believe I made the right choice of stay to study in Ireland.

I was born into a Muslim family. Being a Muslim means believing in one God, the lord of mankind, who created the heavens and the earth, whom all creatures need, the most merciful, most forgiving; there is nothing like him. A Muslim is someone who submits their will to God and Islam means peace. I never understood what being a Muslim meant until I came to Ireland, where many are searching for the Truth. As a Muslim, Ireland has given me the chance to live that experience of peace of mind with knowledge of the purpose of life through my religion, which I came to appreciate more. However, being a Muslim woman in Ireland is not easy. I was once asked why I have to wear my veil here, as my family was away and could not see me! I feel I need to explain my culture to the country and the people I love so much.

I have seen big changes in the last few years. I have seen Irish people questioning me with their eyes — what am I doing in their country? Some have the courage to ask me, some verbally shouting it in my face! But why? Because I look like an alien, with my skin colour and the way I dress. However, there are always those who are there for me to wipe my tears, and they are also Irish.

John O'Shea

John O'Shea is a founder member and director of the relief and development agency, GOAL. A keen sportsman, he worked for 24 years on the sports staff of the Evening Press.

Y̶ou'll never beat the Irish!" the Irish supporters chant has been heard in sports grounds all over the world. And it's true, you never will!

Back in 1992 when GOAL was working in Baidoa, the cockpit of the famine in Somalia, I had to get back to *The Evening Press* in a hurry. I hitched a lift on an American cargo plane returning to Mombassa after it had delivered the first consignment of food. The only other passenger was a doctor who was working for the Arab League and we got talking. The inevitable questions were asked about what each of us was doing and where we were from. As soon as he heard I was from Ireland he said, "Ah, Ireland — the caring nation".

I consider that to be one of the most significant comments concerning the Irish that I have heard in my 22 years' involvement in the Third World. He didn't mention Gaelic football or hurling or green grass or drink or music or fighting or Northern Ireland or Eurovision or anything else. No, he associated Ireland with caring and that is the single most important aspect of the Irish identity as far as I'm concerned.

Even in my days in the Simon Community in the early 1970s I realised that the Irish have a deep commitment, even a passion, for helping those worse off than themselves. I'm referring here to the rank and file, the ordinary person on the street. He and she really care.

It was only when I became immersed in Third World activity, when I needed assistance by way of money and volunteers from the people of Ireland, that I appreciated just how phenomenally different and humane the Irish people are. That is probably the most important difference between the Irish and any other nationality.

I have been to many western countries where that humane attitude appears to be absent; people just don't seem to care. Of course, I have also been to many Third World countries where the wealthy ignore the poor and where organisations such as GOAL have to come in from outside to try and bring hope to a tragic situation.

This generous side to the Irish should never be underrated. It may not be reflected by our government's performance in the area of foreign aid but hopefully that will change in time.

The second phenomenon that has always struck me about the Irish is their love of sport. As a sports journalist and a sportsman myself, having attempted a variety of sporting pursuits, I have had a unique opportunity to experience that commitment. I have witnessed Irish men and women spending long hours talking and arguing about sport and the merits or demerits of different sportsmen and sportswomen. This passion for sport and the love of talking about it is a salient common denominator that makes the Irish very easy to get on with.

We Irish are something of a contradiction. We still retain the village mentality in the sense that the population of one village will do all they can to beat the next at football or hurling or whatever. However, when it comes to helping the people of Bangladesh or Ethiopia or wherever the latest disaster occurs, we all rally around and are capable of a global attitude. I find this seeming contradiction, this dichotomy in our makeup, a feather in our collective cap. I would consider myself a global type of person yet I too retain that village mentality. I would rather play for Kerry in an all-Ireland football final than to win a gold medal in the Olympics.

I think it was Mary Robinson who first popularised the phrase "The Irish Diaspora" during her Presidency. Many of the people who were in that Diaspora might not have heard the word before but they liked the sound of it! Oth-

ers of course, especially the Dubs who have a habit of dropping their t's, just
misheard and thought that Mary was calling us despera' names altogether!

The Irish, dispersed or not, are famous for several things, mostly of a sociable nature such as singing, drinking, sport, jokes, culture, religion and
fighting — not necessarily in that order. But what strikes me wherever I go is
the understanding the Irish seem to have for the plight of the underdog. I don't
know whether it is because of our history or just something in our national
psyche but we constantly seem to produce concerned people who are not
afraid to put themselves out to come to the assistance of fellow human beings
in trouble.

In particular I am reminded of that extraordinary group of people, the
many thousands of Irish missionaries, nuns, priests and brothers, who down
the years have dedicated their lives to bringing help to the poorest of the poor
in the world. They brought their medicine and their education and all types of
support to forgotten people in some of the remotest places on earth. A friend
of mine, a doctor cum priest, has worked for 40 years in the Turkana desert;
another, a nun in Calcutta, has been there for over 50 years educating the deprived. There are legions of these unsung heroes who still have to beg for
money from the Irish Government, which is pathetic. I remain in awe of them.

In the past few years, Ireland has changed probably more than it has in the
previous couple of centuries. Young Irish people have proved themselves to be
particularly adept at the use and development of computer technology. I over-
hear conversations on trains and in pubs between these young electronic wiz-
ards and my head reels. People of my generation might not understand all this
new e-commerce and dotcoms and megabytes, but it certainly seems to be
working because Ireland has gone from being a relatively poor country to becoming very prosperous in a very short space of time.

The economic tide has certainly come in, but I hope that this will not alter
the Irish persona too drastically. I hope that in this scramble for more and
more wealth, we will not lose our love for our fellow man. It has been my experience that if someone is getting rich it is usually at someone else's expense. I
hope that this national rush for wealth does not leave us blind to the needs of
others, either at home in Ireland or in the wider world. We must take time to

make sure that the tide lifts everyone at the same rate and that nobody gets left behind.

Reports emanating from the various tribunals currently grinding their way to God knows what sort of conclusions are far from encouraging on this score. The lurid tales of secret transfers of brown envelopes full of money given by people of wealth to people in positions of power is worrying to say the least. It is certainly disgusting and very disappointing, but most of all I find it worrying. I worry when I think of the signals that this type of behaviour sends to the younger generation, the people who will one day be in positions of power themselves. Will they be able to make the fundamental changes that are necessary? Will they be able to see that there is something much more important than the acquisition of wealth? I believe that they will, because basically people don't change. I don't think any amount of computers or corrupt politicians can alter the basic good nature of the Irish people. Intrinsically, they will always care for those in need or in trouble.

This blight of corruption will have to be rooted out because it simply does not reflect the generality of the Irish people. It is a cancer eating away at Irish society and the politicians have a duty to extract it themselves because otherwise they are going to suffer where it hurts them most — at the ballot box. Of that there can be no doubt.

Over the years, I have had the pleasure of working with hundreds of nurses, doctors, social workers, engineers and others who have selflessly given of their time and energies to travel to some of the world's least hospitable places to give a helping hand to others. Many have turned their backs on lucrative careers to do what they knew to be right and I have the utmost respect for them. What is more, so do the Irish public. This is evident because every time GOAL mounts an appeal in response to the latest tragedy — and sadly this is becoming more and more frequent — the Irish people never let us down. Their generosity is prodigious.

No, you'll never beat the Irish.

Andy Pollak

Andy Pollak is the director of the Centre for Cross Border Studies in Armagh. Formerly religious affairs and education correspondent of The Irish Times, *he was co-ordinator of the Opsahl Commission in the early 1990s.*

My name is from Poland; my father was a Jew from the Czech Republic; my accent is from England. My Irishness is the result of an accident of birth (in my mother's hometown of Ballymena, County Antrim) followed by a passionate and lifelong attachment. Ever since I was a book-devouring small boy growing up in a dull south London suburb, I have wanted to be Irish. Whether it was the Kerry of Muiris Ó Súilleabháin, the Dublin of Joyce and James Plunkett, the Sligo of Yeats' early poetry, or the Protestant Belfast and Fermanagh of Robert Harbinson, this was the fractured island and nation I wanted to belong to.

And because I was born a Northern Presbyterian, the Protestant and dissenting face of Ireland has always been particularly important to me. My pantheon of heroes is full of the kind of Protestant and socialist oddballs who validated my existence as an Irishman: Jonathan Swift, Jemmy Hope, Charles Stewart Parnell, Roger Casement, James Connolly, John Hewitt, Hubert Butler. It was the internationalist George Bernard Shaw's "wild and inextinguishable pride" in being "a patriotic Irishman" which inspired me, rather than the narrower "green" rhetoric of traditional Irish nationalism (although in my younger days it too had its attractions).

In the 25 years I have lived in Ireland, I have felt that broad multicultural current rising around me in all sorts of ways: the end of inward-looking isolationism brought about by the enthusiastic embrace of all things European; the success of an Irish soccer team managed by an Englishman and starring people with Nigerian and Italian fathers; the miracle of the Good Friday Agreement, with its recognition that the only way to peace is for the Irish-Irish and the British-Irish to start to learn the difficult compromise of living side by side with as much equality and justice as a bloody history will allow.

I am not blind to the violence, dishonesty, greed and hypocrisy of much of Irish life. After declaring his pride in his nation, Shaw goes on to point out, quite rationally, that "if you put an Irishman on a spit, you will always find another Irishman to baste him". But I have found a sense of community on this island, and an acceptance and generosity from its people, that is a real gift in the soulless, self-obsessed, money-driven late capitalist world that passes for Western civilisation. I hope with all my heart that the new prosperity of the Celtic Tiger economy — in effect, the belated arrival of that late capitalist world in Ireland — will not completely drive out the old communal and humanistic values of the *meitheal*.

Amid the joy and comfort I have come to feel in being an oddball Protestant Irishman, there is one source of great sadness and one source of great shame. The first is that the Protestants of the North, limited by the "narrow ground" of their history of conquest and siege, have not been able to identify more with their Irishness. There was a time, until a little over a hundred years ago, when many Northern unionists could cherish Irish culture, music and language alongside their British political identity. Understandably, 30 years of being battered by the Provisional IRA has turned them away from all things Irish. I understand and respect that they treasure their Britishness above all things (together with their Protestantism), but I believe that by denying their rightful place as a constituent part of the Irish people, they have cut themselves off from great personal rootedness and cultural richness. Often when I sit in a traditional music session in Belfast or Armagh, and conclude that I am probably the only Protestant in the room, I am sad that so many people in Northern Ireland cannot experience the sheer delight of such an occasion.

My sense of shame comes from the way in which a small influx of asylumseekers has provoked such xenophobia in a people who should know better because of their own history of poverty, oppression and emigration. I blame the "ordinary" Irish less than their leaders, politicians and powerful figures in the media, who from the time the first significant trickle of refugees started appearing in our streets, put out the message that these poor people were "spongers", criminals and undesirable aliens who were not wanted in our cosy little country. I had hoped that the Irish, because of their personal generosity and collective memory of past suffering, would have learned the hard lessons of racism from the experience of other nations. I was wrong. We are no better or worse than any other white, rich European people, and our politicians and media — with a very few honourable exceptions — are shown to be as lacking in moral leadership as any on this continent.

For in the end, although I am deeply proud of the historical accident that, in John Hewitt's words, "conscribed me of the Irishry forever", my first responsibility is to try to live as a citizen of the world. Nationality comes easily. Citizenship is the difficult thing.

Terry Prone

Terry Prone is the Managing Director of Carr Com-munications and the author of 14 books, including Racing the Moon. *She lives in Dublin.*

An Improvisation in Search of a Certainty

The late sixties. A group of young actors at a master class given by one of the greats of Irish theatre, Ray McAnally. He requires the girls to do an improvisation. No words. He just wants us to act the part of a very beautiful woman.

One by one, we climb onto the stage and shimmy across it. One slowly smoothes imaginary clingy satin over her hips. One tosses back her hair and consults a non-existent mirror. One prances to a couch onstage and flounces into it as if the other pieces of furniture weren't up to her at all. When the last has gone through the exercise and returned, red-faced, to the group, the old man of the theatre lets us down gently.

"A very beautiful woman doesn't get out of bed in the morning and preen," he says. "Her beauty isn't a surprise to her. It's a given. An *assumption.*"

Being Irish should be an assumption, but, for me, it's a constant improvi-sation, exploration and reconfiguration. I am less sure of it the older I get.

In my teens, I had the whole thing worked out. To be Irish was to own a continuum of complaint. Nothing much could be expected of a nation with so many strikes against it, so when "poor little Cat'lic Ireland" came through on any front, we expected a kudos upgrade. We might not be much, economically, but look at Tintawn. Tintawn was a gruesome distant cousin of carpeting. It had the sensual appeal of a distressed sack, but it resonated with self-sufficiency and frugal patriotism.

Every area of Irish life had its Tintawn story of survival and triumph over adversity. Bord na Móna's early peat briquettes, each like a long damp brick encased in a hairy old sock, exemplified sturdy independence of overseas fuel suppliers. Every salmon lashing up the Shannon via the ESB's weirs demonstrated the skill and vision of those manly engineers portrayed by Keating. The Abbey Theatre, with its riots and fire, its legendary actors and writers, not to mention its Irish language panto at Christmas, was best of all, because it had achieved international fame, thereby giving reflected glory to its home territory.

While you could be proud of these things, being Irish precluded *enjoying* them. And boasting was completely out. The best way to handle praise was with self-deprecatory humour. Shrugging, smiling, self-serving self-dismissal allowed us to gain even from the restrictions of a closed society. My parents' generation – the more liberal of them — bought banned books on trips to the North or to Britain. Listening to them promising to lend each other their copy of the latest Behan or Edna O'Brien, I was struck, as a child, by the blessed freedom provided by tight constraint. Swapping banned books created a togetherness of mutual affirmation, a benign conspiracy of civilised people forced to live within these ridiculous rules, but empowered thereby to make these little gestures of pseudo-samizdat defiance.

To be Irish, at that point, was to be happily behind the eight ball and permanently, instinctively, against the establishment. "Give 'em hell," was the motto, although if a Noel Browne gave 'em hell and had the dogs set on him as a result, there was little tangible support coming from those who ostensibly approved his actions. The best person to give hell to the powers-that-be was someone like Brendan Behan, who, as a writer, was entitled to be outrageous, who could be relied on to be funny and — even better — might be drunk when he did it, so the rest of us could simultaneously delight and deplore.

Having survived Peig Sayers (the woman who arguably caused 60 years' worth of national emigration) the suburbanites among us hoped that life in rural Ireland had improved to the level portrayed in John Hinde postcards, just as we hoped our parents' suspicions about processes like planning were unfounded and apologias like "it's not what you know in this country, it's who you know" unjustified.

In one decade, all those hopes were swept away. The conspiracy theories turned out to be right and it transpired that clientilism and cronyism had been more efficacious than the most paranoid had ever imagined. Peig proved to have confabulated some of her spectacular miseries, and John Hinde was revealed to have dickied up the colours to make rural Ireland look a hell of a lot better than it did in reality.

Simultaneously, Ireland's economy boomed, emigrants returned, Dublin became the cool capital of Europe and when people overseas talked warmly of Irish culture, they meant *Riverdance* rather than *Riders to the Sea*. My definition of Irishness got shot full of holes.

For my son's generation, steeped in irony and options, competence and confidence, being Irish is an assumption, a given.

For me, it's an improvisation in search of a certainty.

Janet Quilley

Janet Quilley is a member of the Religious Society of Friends. She worked for the Quakers in Belfast for six and a half years. She and her husband have recently returned to England to be closer to their family.

When I moved to Belfast in 1993, my first clue about what it means to be Irish lay in the discovery that I was a "blow-in" — a new word for me, which helps to define Irishness by identifying those of us who are not Irish-born. We blow-ins are not rooted in the community of shared experience which is Ireland. It hardly matters that closer scrutiny reveals serious religious and tribal fault lines in that experience, developed over centuries, which are sometimes geographical but are also deeply rooted in the mind.

When, however, the inhabitants of the island of Ireland look at the blow-ins — or when they venture abroad and see themselves in the context of the rest of the world — it seems that the fault lines lose their significance; they are first and foremost Irish born and others are different.

I am frequently struck by the generosity and commitment of people from Ireland in the context of the wider world; in the warmth of their hospitality and genuine personal interest and concern for visitors; in the striking level of voluntary and charitable activity concerned both with local need and the needs of the developing world. Mary Robinson in her UN role epitomises these characteristics for me but it is surely no accident that other prominent Irish names spring to mind: Bob Geldof and Live Aid; Mairead Corrigan-Maguire and East Timor; Adi Roche and the Chernobyl Children's Project.

I appreciate this warmth and energy emanating from the Irish sense of community, so often generous in its acceptance of others into its fold — and yet also wary if those others are seen as a threat. This wariness is evident in local communities across the island of Ireland, be they Northern or Southern, Catholic or Protestant, urban or rural. It underlies the age-old conflict between the religious traditions; it is also reflected in the local hostilities which spring up periodically in relation to minority groups such as the Travelling Community and the Chinese; it is seen in the current antipathy towards asylum seekers and immigrants. Such attitudes exist, of course, in other countries, not least in Britain; but the island of Ireland has been exposed relatively late to these effects of globalisation.

A couple of conversations illustrate some aspects of Irishness. There was the man we met in the Sperrins, following a good day's walking. It was New Year's Day; he was slightly the worse for wear and needed a lift down the road. He couldn't understand why we had come all the way to Ireland and the Sperrins if we didn't have relatives there to visit. Since I was English, then surely my husband must be Irish — otherwise what was the point of our being there?

Then there was the elderly Loyalist woman we once chatted to in Belfast. She was trying to explain why Orangemen never go into Catholic churches. "It's all those people they killed," she stated firmly, as if it had happened that week. In fact, she was referring to the 1641 massacres. Long memories are definitely part of being Irish!

Like it or not, the people of Ireland are immersed in history. The archaeological evidence of prehistory seems to lie in every other field: dolmens in the Burren; Newgrange at the winter solstice; the Beaghmore stone circles guarding their secrets in the mists of the Tyrone hills. All contribute to the landscape, which forms and informs the character of the people.

Many people identify Irish music as a defining characteristic of Irishness, although in so doing, they usually ignore those who, sadly, cannot forget its political connotations. I find more striking and more inclusive the value placed by the whole community on literature and poetry. Summer schools seem to be a particularly vibrant aspect of Irish cultural life. Time and again the poets and playwrights encapsulate the political and social experience of the community and people identify with what is written.

And that brings me back to the fault lines that are an integral part of the Irish identity. Stewart Parker, in his play *Northern Star* about the United Irishmen and the events of 1798, puts into the mouth of Henry Joy McCracken a perceptive rhetorical question:

> *"[In 1798] we never made a nation. Our brainchild. Stillborn. Our own fault. We botched the birth. So what if the English do bequeath us to one another some day? What then? When there's no one else to blame except ourselves?"*

This question looms before the people of Ireland as they seek to resolve the issues that divide them. Being bequeathed to each other means inheriting the rich diversity of other traditions and experience. It means accepting the responsibility for accommodating difference and not pushing that responsibility back onto the British or any other outside authority; it means getting rid of that familiar habit of blaming the Brits. It also means being able to expand people's understanding of difference to include new minorities within the compass of the Irish identity. It is likely that Irishness in the twenty-first century, like Britishness in the twentieth century, will acquire new ethnic dimensions, which must be taken seriously if a healthy and diverse community is to be maintained. Perhaps it will become less easy in the future to label outsiders as blow-ins, but I hope that the fabled tradition of Irish hospitality will not be lost in the process — that would be throwing out the baby with the bath water!

Ruairi Quinn

Ruairi Quinn, architect and town planner, is Leader of the Irish Labour Party.

Being Irish today means many things. It involves having an international language, English, and a shared history. It contains a love of our new diversity involving different faiths and racial origins. It also means having a pride in the old diversity of Gaelic and Anglo-Irish culture. It is about the immense attachment to the island of Ireland and a recognition of the achievements of the Irish State. It is about being a citizen of the European Union of Irish nationality, as well as being a member of a scattered people, the Irish Diaspora.

My grandfather was born in County Down, moved to Liverpool in the 1880s and returned to Newry in 1908 with six of his ten children, including my father who was born in Bootle. My eldest brother, who died at infancy, and my sister were born in Newry before my father moved to Dublin to escape internment during the Second World War. The five surviving brothers in our family were born in Dublin. One has lived in Canada for the last 19 years with his Kerry wife and three Canadian children. Another brother, recently returned to Dublin, has worked most of his adult life outside of Europe. My eldest son was born in Greece and one of my other nephews was born in London. Our story is a common and shared one with the rest of the Irish people.

Nationality and nationhood get mingled together, sometimes dangerously. Europeans, in particular, have over the last 200 years insisted on linking territory to nationality as the delineation of nationhood. The results have been ugly. World wars, ethnic cleansing, along with cultural intolerance and religious sectarianism have been the shared experience. Ireland remains affected by the consequences of this particular European disease.

A generation of European visionaries, political and social, tried to rise above it all by abandoning the concept of the nation and suppressing nationalism in the hope for a tolerant and benign cosmopolitanism or internationalism. It did not work. It confused national identity and national culture with the nation state. Yet the Irish or the Greek identity and culture developed independently of whether there was a separate political state. In some cases, the coming into existence of the nation state resulted in the suppression of diversity within the national community of either language or religion or both.

The centralisation of the nation state was also characterised by frontiers, customs posts, national armies and national currencies. In times of economic hardship, open trade between national economies was subject to tariffs and boycotts at the behest of national companies, in the belief that it would protect the national economy and so the nation. The sad and brutal history of the first half of the twentieth century is in part the legacy of that kind of nationalist ideology.

The recent transformation in the technologies of information and transportation have been the scientific forces which made the globalisation of the world's economy possible. The limits of political nationalism and protectionism, particularly after the end of the Second World War, provided the impetus for the global world economy of today. The collapse of communism in 1989 simply accelerated an existing process.

At a regional level, the European Union is the first step in what I have previously described as a post-federal sharing of national sovereignty. The common market, the common currency and the common foreign and security policy are the new building blocks of this union. It is no coincidence that they were once the unique components of the nation state. The culture of nationality will prevail in the emerging European Union, liberated from the necessity to be confined to the boundaries of the old nation state. Regional diversity will once again begin to flourish in the larger European countries.

For the Irish, a unique experience is now unfolding. The scattering of the Irish people over the last 300 years was, at the time, a human tragedy for the vast majority of them. Being Irish in Britain, the United States or Australia was not just to be poor but to be ridiculed as inferior outcasts as well.

The many efforts of struggle for social progress, respect and recognition by the Irish are well known. But that they have come generally to fruition at the end of the twentieth century and the beginning of the era of the global economy is a new-found treasure. Speaking an international language with considerable style and skill, the Irish are now the most scattered and successful European tribe in the world. Smaller only in size to the Chinese Diaspora, the Irish are connected by a common and diverse culture around a rapidly shrinking world. So important is that identity to them that over 73 million people worldwide describe themselves as Irish in their census forms. I am both proud and delighted to be one of them.

Mary Reid

Mary Reid is a community worker, writer, teacher and researcher.

On an intergalactic station in deepest space, two astronauts of Irish descent greet one another in the time honoured Irish manner: "My grandmother was from Cork" being met with "My grandfather was from Belfast".

Being Irish means being attached to the idea of Ireland, to the extent of identifying with a place in Ireland. Being Irish involves a parallel worldview, a world wherein a cherished place is punctuated by events in time. Being Irish reverses the tide of change — as the decades stride past, the more we are inclined to return to our point of departure. Myth has been described "as the penultimate truth". Being Irish is to be predestined to return to the land of eternal youth. Being Irish means that, always and everywhere, we will seek the fair land.

We all do it. The ageing factory worker in Coventry, the computer whiz-kid in California, the staunch Orangeman in the bastion of his farmstead. We all do it, because Ireland's grip on our hearts and minds is faster and deeper than our ephemeral awareness of our own being. The blind seer of Dublin fled "the sow who eats her farrow", the better to feed himself to Anna Liffey alone. Myth is the penultimate truth because the ultimate truth cannot be told. Nonetheless, let us try.

By virtue of being Irish, we belong to pre-antiquity. Before Greece and Rome, we were the people who came to this land to fall in thrall of its lakes and shadows. Before hieroglyphs or gospels were inscribed, we were the people who came to this land and marked our signature on its mountains and hills. Before the Book of Kells or Magna Carta proclaimed, we were the people who came to this land and declared:

> *Who announces the ages of the moon?*
> *Who teaches the place where couches the sun?*
> *(If not I)*

Being Irish is to dance at Finnegan's Wake. Before Osiris was born in Horus or Christ rose from the dead, we were celebrating the triumph of light over darkness, celebrating the tomb as a womb. From Beltany to Sliabh Gullion, from Sliabh an Chaillí to Uisneach, from Brú na Bóinne to Knocknarea, from coast to coast, hill top bonfires blazed the message "to end again is to rise". Being Irish, how could it be otherwise?

Being Irish is to discover that while time and tide wait for no man, and that truly the bell will toll for us all, the life of the spirit is another matter. For all the different drums we often march to, being Irish inevitably marches us towards the drumbeat of the soul.

Being Irish means knowing that someday you will go home. We will return to a land that will live and breathe long after us. Ireland claims us because Ireland itself is a myth. We feed Ireland because Ireland feeds the world.

Adi Roche

Adi Roche is Executive Director of the Chernobyl Children's Project, which helps children suffering from the radioactive fall-out from the Chernobyl reactor explosion in 1986. She was Irish Person of the Year in 1994 and was nominated by the Labour Party in the Irish Presidential election of 1997.

What does "Being Irish" mean to me?? Now there is a question. How much time have you got? Well to start at the beginning, or at least my beginning, the events following my birth on 11 July 1955, and the trauma over what to name me, somewhat typifies "Being Irish".

My mother Chris was expecting another boy when she was carrying me. She was going to name me "John Coleman" after some famous Fenian in the family history (known locally as "The Galtee Boy"!). So when I came along, a dilemma presented itself. If she was to follow the path of naming me after an Irish hero, you could now be reading about Countess Markeviecz Roche, or maybe not! So to get over this problem, my mother took refuge in that other great Irish pastime, religion. She had been reading about the only English Pope, Pope Adrian, and so what did she do? She dropped the "-an" and replaced it with "-enne" — Adrienne. The family doctor proclaimed, "Ah, she'll never be short of a job with a Protestant name like that!"

Somewhere along the way, I became Adi, my sister Helen became "Len" and my brothers became Duck (Dónall), and "Con" (Conchubhar).

So, I have covered nationalism and religion, two subjects which, when talking about "being Irish", simply cannot be ignored. What about language, I hear you ask! In my family, the Irish language was big on the agenda. My parents, brothers and sister all speak very good Irish/Gaeilge, as does my husband

Seán. My Father, the other Seán in my life, still speaks fluent Gaeilge and still sings many of the Irish songs that he sang years ago at *feiseanna*, despite the fact that he is now in the twilight world of Alzheimer's Disease. I still love to hear him sing in his quivery voice. But I am sorry to say that I struggle with my "*cúpla focal*". The words are there buried somewhere in the back of my head, but when faced with an Irish conversation, I seem to panic, lack confidence, and make some excuse like, "I had it in school, but it is all forgotten now" or "*Níl aon ach cupla focal agam*". My husband Sean . . . *gabh mo leiscéil* — Seán (the *fada* over the "a" is vital). Without the *fada* it means "old" and I suppose it is not good to be referred to as such, especially when, as in the case of my husband, it is not true! Anyway, where was I . . . Seán wears a *fáinne*, a pin that tells others that he is willing to converse with them in Irish. In how many other countries do people wear a "label" to show that they speak the native language?

I left Clonmel at age 17 and went to Dublin, "the big smoke". It was such an exciting time for me, 1972 — discos, fashion, boys, my first job, the thrill of being "on the tear" and being a part of it all. Those were somewhat carefree times, and I wouldn't change them for anything. It wasn't until 1978, however, that my "awakening" took place.

My brother Dónall was living in Pennsylvania near the Three Mile Island Nuclear Plant and told me of the great dangers of nuclear power — radiation, CANCER etc. I emphasise CANCER, because it struck a deep note with me. At age 16, my dearest childhood friend Anne had died from leukemia. The thought of this "source of energy" cutting short the life of even one more human being spurred me into action. The Irish Government at the time were proposing to build a nuclear power plant in Carnsore Point in County Wexford. I got stuck into the campaign to prevent this happening, and I haven't stopped since.

I believe my work with the Chernobyl Children's Project gives me a great understanding of what "being Irish" means. I believe the spirit of giving to others worldwide, which so many Irish practise today, relates back to our ancestors who suffered so much in famine times. It reminds me of a story told to me by Don Mullin about a group of Choctaw Indians in Oklahoma at the time of the Irish Famine. Despite having very little themselves, hearing of the Irish plight, they sent a consignment of grain to Ireland.

The people who influence me are varied, but to me are Irish in the sense that they are my brothers and sisters. My parents, my brothers and sister, my "comrades" from Carnsore, Petra Kelly, Christy Moore, Nelson Mandela, Maureen Kim Sing, Martin Luther King, Joan Baez, Bruce Kent, Irish CND, Greenpeace, etc. — these are the people who shaped me, who shaped my "Irishness". Up Clonmel, Up Tipp, Up Cork, Ireland Abú! Like the Choctaw Indians, I believe my brothers and sisters are everywhere, and no land border will ever tell me that these people are not my "Irish" brothers and sisters.

Brendan Parsons, Earl of Rosse

Brendan Parsons spent 18 years working with the United Nations Development Programme, starting as a volunteer in West Africa, rising to principal officer successively responsible for co-ordinating disaster relief in Bangladesh, running the programmes of both UNESCO and UN volunteers in Iran, and of UNDP itself in Algeria. He has worked on the Government's Advisory Council on Development Co-operation. On inheritance as Lord Rosse, he founded the Birr Scientific and Heritage Foundation, as the basis for Ireland's Historic Science Centre, now being developed at Birr. He was recently awarded hon. fellowship of the IEI and hon. life membership of the RDS.

When, nearly half a century ago, my father was invited to open a festival in Cork on behalf of the first Arts Council, to which he had been appointed by none other than Eamonn de Valera, General Tom Barry publicly objected that he was not Irish enough to fulfil any such role. This brought forth a retort which made quite a stir in the press under the headline: "Earl maintains if he is not Irish, there is not an American who is not a Red Indian". Though this would obviously be rephrased in a more politically correct style half a century later, what my father was saying was that our family had been in Birr since long before the Mayflower had sailed with the first colonists for the New World, in the early seventeenth century, and had previously come from the same County Cork as General Barry anyway.

My father quite often retold the story with a mixture of sadness, at the bitterness of the general's attack, and conviction that the time would come when all of us in Ireland would rise above this petty vivisection of our past. How happy he would have been to live to see the ever-increasing inclusiveness of our society over at least the last few years, when the light in the window in the Park has not just tempted back into the fold many of the Diaspora scattered by the winds of the famine, and all the years that followed, but given many more, who never left, a confidence to seize new opportunities built on partnerships with those we might not have even wanted to know before.

Having myself served for nearly 20 years in different countries of Africa and Asia under the blue flag of the United Nations Development Programme, I had my Irish nationality in brackets after my name for far too long for me or anyone else to give it a second thought — until I came home. Then only, in the 1980s, did I start getting requests to describe in interviews, for the press or RTE, what it meant to be "Anglo-Irish", which was not frankly something I had ever considered being before. Irish as well as British possibly, for historical reasons, but that scarcely makes me a good member of the Anglo-Irish, whose sporting traditions of hunting, shooting and fishing are just too normal for a family like ours.

My father was born simply British, as were all those born before the foundation of the state, and chose to retain the passport which he had always had. That, however, no more prevented de Valera from nominating him to the first Arts Council than it prevented his great-great-grandfather, Sir Laurence Parsons, from fiercely leading opposition to the Act of Union with Britain in the Irish House of Commons, or fighting for the establishment of a Chair of Irish at TCD, as executor of the will of Henry Flood. Such forbears had few doubts about what they might have seen as their Irishness. Indeed this was often strengthened by the loneliness felt in London, when they went over to attend sessions of the Parliament to which they had been elected, and found themselves not easily assimilated because of their Irishness. I myself have experienced just the same in London, where I once even had an invitation to dinner withdrawn by a hostess who explained my presence at her table would embarrass her guests on an evening following one of those horrendous London bombings.

To me, though, Irishness is very much less a statement of nationality, as shown by my passport, than a feeling of belonging to the land of my home, the home where all my forbears have been reared for nearly all the four last centuries. This feeling is one of identity with the land itself, for which I feel as passionately as any Irishman can, not just for the fields, but the woods, the mountains, the bogs and the Burren; for the poetry and plays and particularly the music inspired by our land: on our old family harp, as played by Kathleen Loughnane; the tin whistle played by Sean Ryan from the neighbouring castle of Leap; Micheál O'Súilleabháin in the Concert Hall of the University of Limerick; or even (yes, I mean it) *Riverdance* on a world stage. Just listening to and watching any of these gives me greater pride in Irishness than maybe all else — except perhaps listening to Enya on a tape in a remote village in Southwestern China, where no one had the faintest idea where Ireland might be, but everyone just loved the sound of that voice.

That's it, for me: what makes me love and feel part of the land of my home, the land of my forbears.

Dana Rosemary Scallon

Photo: Graeme Macklin

Dana Rosemary Scallon MEP was Ireland's first winner of the Eurovision Song Contest in 1970. She ran for election as an independent candidate in the Irish Presidential election in 1997. In 1999, she was elected as a Member of the European Parliament for Connacht-Ulster.

I was raised in Derry in Northern Ireland. From my earliest days, I have always had a keen awareness of my Irish identity. The love of music, within my hometown and within my family, nurtured by my parents, Robert and Sheila Brown, is a hallmark of Irish people throughout the world. I have vivid memories of family and friends sharing musical evenings in the front room of our house in the Creggan estate and the many community musical events we took part in, from the *Feiseanna* to the Christmas shows in St Columb's Hall. It instilled in me a great sense of family, the memories of which remain with me to this day, and which my husband Damien and I continue to share with our children.

I believe that one of the greatest honours for any person is to represent their country on the international stage, and I was blessed with that honour in 1970, when I represented Ireland in the Eurovision Song Contest in Amsterdam. It was a unique and momentous occasion in my life and in winning for Ireland, for the first time ever, I celebrated together with the entire country. In the 30 years since that event, I have travelled the world, proud of my Irish upbringing. From London to New York and from Australia to Paris, I have shared many a night of song with fellow Irish men and women. There's a tremendous joy and comfort to be experienced when people who are virtual strangers, save for national identity, are brought together, united in song, as they rekindle memories of their homeland.

I am constantly amazed, though not surprised, at the continued tremendous world contribution of Irish people in the many fields of business, art, music, literature, film and theatre, to name but a few. From George Bernard Shaw and W.B. Yeats to Brian Friel and Séamus Heaney and from *Riverdance* to U2, Irish people worldwide celebrate a passion for life in conversation, stories, laughter and song. Our Celtic past, which is rich and diverse, and the ability to overcome many hardships, have gifted Irish people with a unique sense of adaptability, humour and perseverance.

Having trod the well-worn path of emigration for a number of years, we decided, in 1999, that it was time to return home. Today I am happy to share in a new and prosperous Ireland, one that is rich in tradition and plentiful in opportunities and still capable of retaining the values which were carried by past generations throughout the world. When we had little economically, we had a values system and family support that endured the greatest hardships of famine and poverty. In this paradox of old and new, the family still provides the nurturing foundation for Irishness and Irish life. For my part, as an Irish parent, I seek to pass this on to my children and have faith that they will pass it on to theirs.

As a newly elected Member of the European Parliament, I have the honour, once again, of representing Irish people in Europe. I have found that as a nation we are greatly respected and welcomed. In being Irish, we are strongly identified with love of family and with genuine warmth. We are also recognised as having contributed much to the world, both in the past and in the present, and we continue to have much to contribute.

Elizabeth Shannon

Elizabeth Shannon is the Director of the International Visitors Program and the Trustee Scholars Program at Boston University. She grew up in Texas and lived in Dublin for several years with her late husband, William Shannon, who served as US Ambassador under President Jimmy Carter.

Contrary to a commonly held belief in Ireland, it *is* possible to grow up Irish-American in the United States without any sense at all of being Irish. That was my experience as a young woman growing up in San Antonio, Texas, where it was far more important to be Texan than to be Irish . . . or any other nationality.

Although there were thousands of Irish immigrants who came to Texas in the 1830s and 1840s and onward, and although my father's family of McNellys were proud of their Irish roots, there was not the celebration of Irishness that existed in cities like Boston, New York and Chicago. There are various explanations for this. In his excellent history of *The Irish Texans*, John Flannery offers one:

> *"The Irish who came to Texas came to a different world than did those who landed on the north-eastern seaboard. On the American frontier, a man's religion and place of origin was far less important than his ability to handle a rifle and his support of a neighbor. The Texas frontier did not yet have the established social, political, religious and commercial institutions that feel themselves threatened by newcomers of a different national original, religion or economic status . . . newcomers to Texas were welcomed and accepted for*

what they could contribute to a new order. The social and economic bars by which an established order strives to protect its status and privileges were not raised against them because there was no established order."

The "ghetto" establishment that existed in north-eastern cities within all newly immigrated communities as a reaction to discrimination simply did not exist in Texas.

My ancestors came to the United States from Warrenpoint, in County Down, in 1832, first to raise sheep in Virginia, and later, in another generation, to raise cattle in Texas. They looked for ex-neighbours from County Down in Texas, and when they found them, they married them! The Rooneys and Whites and McNellys, all from a little crossroads in Warrenpoint, all intermarried in West Texas!

Some of the early Irish settlers in San Antonio played an influential role on the business and political life of the city. Bryan V. Callaghan, a County Cork man, served as mayor of San Antonio in 1845. His son continued the family tradition and served nine terms as mayor. One hundred years later, a descendent of the first Callaghan was mayor, continuing a family dynasty and displaying the usual Irish talent for politics. The Catholic religion bound the Irish together, but there was not the abundance of Irish fraternal, social and cultural organisations that exist today.

It was not until I married my husband, the son of Irish immigrants from County Clare, that I began to understand what "ethnicity" meant in the United States. I remember being surprised and puzzled that in Worcester, Massachusetts, where he grew up, families and friends were identified as Greek, Italian, Irish, Armenian . . . and later, Asian and Hispanic. I remember telling my brother-in-law once that I couldn't identify the ethnic background of any of my close friends, girls I had grown up with. He had a hard time believing this, but it was true. I think back now: Who among them was Irish? German? Czech? Or any of the other European immigrants who came to Texas?

When *The American Irish* (William V. Shannon) was published in 1964, it was one of the first serious, scholarly introductions to Irish-American history and culture in the United States, and it was my own personal introduction as well. It made me aware of the enormous contributions my kinfolk had made to the United States. I also gleaned an understanding for the first time of what it had meant to be poor and Irish and unwanted. I began to understand the generations of psychic damage done to the Irish-Americans by feelings of alienation that were part of the immigrant experience, and I was grateful that that had not been my experience of growing up in Texas.

When I moved to Ireland and lived there for four years, I discovered, to my amazement and delight, that there, among the Irish, I felt a close and natural connection. I finally felt Irish. Just as the chemistry between two people in love is hard to define, that kinship I felt — and continue to feel — for the Irish is amorphous. Humour is an important element. I laugh much more in Ireland than I do in the United States. I like to stay up late and talk and so do my Irish friends. The Irish inability to suffer fools and their skill at cutting down an unfortunate creature whose pronouncements even hint at pomposity delights me. Their caring for the less fortunate sets a good example, which I try to follow.

Finally, when we moved back to Boston, this most Irish of all American cities, a place that always reminds its Irish visitors of Dublin, I came home at last with real Irish credentials, and a deeper understanding of the culture we call The Irish-American. I revel in it now, proud to be a part of it, proud to see economic prosperity come to the Republic of Ireland and to see the fragile peace tentatively arriving in the North. I am especially pleased to meet all the new, young, hard-working Irish who immigrate now to Boston. With a sophistication born of good education and travel, the confidence that comes from having a choice of staying here or going home to a good job, they bring a vibrancy and energy to this old city. They assimilate but also keep their Irishness. That Irishness is cherished now in America. No need, ever again, to feel unwanted and undesirable.

Peter Shirlow

Photo: Nigel McDowell

Peter Shirlow is a Senior Lecturer in the School of Environmental Studies, University of Ulster, Coleraine. He is the author of Who Are the People? Unionism, Protestantism and Loyalism in Northern Ireland.

Irish and British Need Not Apply

At the personal level, I see myself as a hybrid of identities. While being brought up within working-class Protestant stock, the mind was filled with the glories of Britishness and the waywardness of the Irish Catholic. Of course, like many, reading (especially the works of Orwell and Greene), study and meeting Catholics blunted the tales learnt at the knees of the elders and betters. However, this did not produce, as it has among many, a "guilty Prod" syndrome. Instead, adult life has spurned a rejection of nationalism and the forces of hate, myth and prejudice that it thrives upon — the central problem being that nationalism needs to either conceal facts (i.e. the centuries old mistreatment of women) or be against something for it to mean anything. Rarely are labels such as Irish or British used benignly.

More alarming is that any advocation of post-nationalism means the pursuit of a minority and very misunderstood sport. My Republican friends cannot understand how the forces of history do not guide me towards anti-Britishness, while on the other hand my Unionist friends see lundyism in my betrayal of what is true. For me, such myopic patriotism is not the refuge of scoundrels but the enduring force of misdirected devotion. Devotion built upon the sum of selective histories and a failure to question Irishness and Britishness and, more importantly, other oppressive forces within our society.

The comedian (some would use the word cautiously) Jimmy Young once did a sketch based around an Ulster Protestant being ridiculed by his Dublin landlady on the morning of the twelfth. The Ulsterman was at the time working in Dublin and could not get back for the glories (some would use the word very cautiously) of the Orange festivities. She pointed out to him that not only was the Battle of the Boyne fought on the 1st of July, but even worse, the date had been changed by a Pope (Gregory). On top of that, she reminded him that the Pope sided with Protestant William against James as the result of an alliance between William and Pope Innocent XI against Louis, King of France. More harrowing for the luckless Ulsterman was the fact that news of the Protestant victory led to Pope Alexander VIII offering special masses of thanksgiving for such a decisive victory. The hapless Ulsterman could only retort that he was glad "not to be up in Belfast celebrating that Fenian victory".

Jimmy Young had caught the complexity of Irish/British history right in the bud, and in so doing illuminated the mythmaking and historiography which underpin the metanarratives of pseudo-history which make up a lot of what being Irish and British is all about. Indeed, any valid examination of history will show up the fallacy of any Irishness constructed around Catholicism. Pope Adrian IV's Bull Laudabiliter, for example, authorised the conquest of Ireland by England and paved the way for the first Anglo-Norman invasion of Ireland in 1169 — the objective being to quell Brehon Law and enforce Roman Canon Law as legal authority. Furthermore, those Irish who rebelled in 1177, 1319 and 1798 were excommunicated by the Catholic Church, the same Church that called for loyalty to England in 1798 and Britain in 1801. Furthermore, the excommunication of IRA volunteers during the War of Independence also casts a more recent shadow over Church and national identity. The Catholic Church in Ardoyne has to this very day a memorial dedicated to the Royal Irish Constabulary. Such a revisionist list could go on in any challenge to the patriot games.

Even the name "Ireland" and the term "Irish" are English words. The counties which are the basis of Gaelic sport are based upon the administration units brought to Ireland by the English. It was the English who united Ireland. Of course, such subtlety is lost in a romanticised invention of Irish identity. If anything, the creators of Irish nationalism were Protestant, English and Scots whose families settled in Ireland before the plantations of the sixteenth and seventeenth century. Their sense of nationhood, based upon Old Testament scripture, conceived of drawing the Catholic majority into an Irish nation. Could it be that, on hearing how Irishness was created, like the hapless Ulsterman, proud Irishmen and women will state that they want nothing else to do with that "Protestant/British-created identity"?

It could be argued, given the impact of globalisation, the demise of de Valera's Irish arcadia and the slow death of rural Ireland, that without the Protestant state and the heavy-handedness of the RUC and B-Specials, that romanticised and revolutionary Irishness and bigoted Unionism would have, by now, passed us by. Is it now the case that the most "Irish" part of Ireland is in the republican heartlands of Northern Ireland? This complexity of Irishness has recently been observed by the sociologist Jim Smyth in relation to the most Irish of symbols, the harp. As Smyth has observed, Harp lager is no longer sold in the chic bars of Dublin, as it lacks the sophistication of German and American lagers. But a can of this Irish brew can always be seen in the hand of Loyalists at Drumcree.

So what of our collective futures on this island of ours? For the future to work, the truth must out. If identity is about protection and celebration, then we must stand up to all forms of oppression, ethnic exclusivity, violence and mythmaking, and celebrate the fact that we aim to do so. A post-nationalist view based upon new signs, understandings and victimness and opposed to victimhood should be the basis of new identities. Unfortunately, in the creation of new identities, those promoting ethnic forms of Britishness and Irishness need not apply.

Gaye Shortland

Gaye Shortland is the author of Mind That 'Tis My Brother *and* Turtles All the Way Down, *both set in Cork, and* Polygamy *and* Harmattan, *set in Africa. She is editor for Poolbeg Press.*

Having been Irish all my life, I find myself peculiarly ill-equipped for objective study of the condition. I feel rather like a child who is asked, "Where is the pain?" and can only answer, "It hurts!"

It has always hurt and, viewed in a certain light through squinted eyes, my life has been naught but a struggle with my Irish identity. Being called Gaye Shortland in a West Cork classroom, where everyone else was Mary O'Sullivan or Ann McCarthy, made me identity-conscious almost from infancy, gave me an uncomfortable sense of not quite belonging. The course of Nationalist education which was to be my lot for many a long year did nothing to disabuse me of that notion. The flaw in my identity went back two generations: my great-grandfather was English (and a Protestant!) who came to Cork to teach wickerwork to the blind. He met and was enchanted by Irishness in the form of my great-grandmother, became a Catholic to marry her and never went back. I must confess that there was a stage in my late teens when I tried to persuade myself I was English and went off looking for my "roots" in Devonshire.

The nub of the problem was that, as late as the 1970s, in the pre-Bishop Casey era, national identity was still tantamount to Catholicism of a particularly virulent sort. And so I fled my Irishness just as fast as I possibly could and went as far as I could manage at the time: to West Africa (Nigeria) and later the Sahara (Niger). Abroad, I dreamt of the Atlantic rather than the company of Irish people, and for 15 years, I worked hard on becoming a nomadic Tuareg, eventually going the whole hog — marrying a Tuareg and producing no less than three half-Tuareg children.

It must be said that the Irish in Africa had a marked penchant for "going native". A strong democratic sense led them to meet their African fellow-travellers down the post-colonial road in a hail-fellow-well-met mode and the meeting always took place on the common plain of humour: fun, laughter, a bit of *craic*, and our own peasant history breaking out all over. My beloved nomads were like nothing so much as West Cork farmers — an Islamic embodiment of what, perversely, I had fled. Their virtues are best described by those Irish words which sit stubbornly in everyday usage for the reason that English translations just do not embrace the concepts: they are *flaithiúl* (generous, open-handed, hospitable), *grámhar* (loving, warm, demonstrative) and great *craic* (fun, entertainment). Desultory research has led me to believe that the Irishman before the Famine, before the Church got its ghastly grip on his throat, was a very different animal from today's version and even closer to my nomads. For one thing, he had an in-your-face attitude to sex, which even contemporary liberated souls might envy.

A certain Englishman in Africa said to me: "Why are you, who already belong to one exotic tribe, trying so hard to become part of another?" That was extraordinary: being perceived as exotic. I was more accustomed to being viewed by my English friends as a comic turn. That might have been a turning-point, but I believe it was my mother's petitioning of Our Lady that forced me to turn my face to home — my karma at the end of the day being to re-embrace my Irishness.

Back in Cork, I was a voyeur, spying on my own culture. I rode the buses, I queued in hospitals and dole offices, I watched and listened. I was of the culture and yet apart from it, as I asked, "What have I chosen for my African children now? What way of speech, what cast of mind? Is it good? Is it better?" Out of this experience was born my first comic novel, *Mind That 'Tis My Brother*, followed by *Turtles All the Way Down*, encapsulating what to me is essentially Irish (or at least Cork-Irish, which some may argue is a completely different kettle of fish!) in a city where humour is so prevalent that manners demand that commonplace greetings be in the form of a joke. A Portuguese friend put it in a nutshell: "Latin people are warm and tactile, but the Irish do the same thing with their tongues!" He was not, of course, referring to fellatio, but to our everyday currency of social flirtation, a verbal caressing we are hardly conscious of.

I have now come to terms with my Irishness. Looking at my Saharan kids, the imprint of Africa still evident in their behaviour and thought patterns, I can put my hand on my heart and say I adore their startling sing-song Cork accents and wouldn't wish the other half of them to be anything but Irish.

Darina Shouldice

*Darina Shouldice is a teacher in Darndale, Dublin.
She is also one of the founders of Dublin Bay Watch, a
community activist group working to safeguard the
amenities of Dublin Bay. She lives in Clontarf with
her husband and two sons.*

I was born into a family with a Palatine name. Over 300 years in Ireland and
it still sounds foreign today. However, despite his unusual surname,
Grandpa Shouldice from Ballaghadereen on the Mayo/Roscommon border
was, in my childhood memory, the epitome of Irishness. He maintained a lifelong loyalty to the holy trinity of Irish life at the time: the Church, the GAA and
Fianna Fáil. Grandpa was an eclectic mix of country lad and Victorian gentleman, disciplined soldier (old IRA) and romantic idealist, loyal friend and reserved loner, intolerant of the bully and supportive of the underdog. He spent
his youth fighting for Irish independence but couldn't reconcile himself to a
Civil War where friends turned on friends, and families were torn apart. His
home smelled of geraniums, pipe tobacco and rum-and-butter sweets.
Grandpa was good with women, but I doubt if many got close. There was
something deeply private about the man, which charmed some, and alienated
others. He married two strong independent women, and outlived them both. I
used to worry that he was sad when he would dab a white handkerchief at his
watery eyes and adopt a melancholy look. Was he thinking about Grandma
Dilly or his dead wife Cissie, or was he lonely for his little girl who had died of
meningitis aged three? I later came to know that a peculiarly Irish condition
called *nostalgia* runs in the family (and Grandpa also suffered from a wet-eye
condition which he stubbornly neglected!).

Pop Kelly, my mother's father, was a different kind of Irishman. Born in Westmeath, he fled to America like so many others when he was barely a man, aged 16. By the time he returned to settle in Ireland 20 years later, he had absorbed the positive energy and dynamism of the New World and shed some of the Old World baggage that weighed a man down and kept him in his place. He spent his prime in New York City and his peculiar brand of Irishness stood to him there and blended well with the social landscape. He was naturally generous, good-humoured and gregarious. He was an optimist who refused to look backwards or recognise the native nostalgia. He had become more American than the Americans themselves, and it suited him. He never quite lost his New York *twang*, and simply refused to trade the "garbage" for the "rubbish" or the "sidewalk" for the "path". Pop was a big man in a suit and a crisp white shirt, with a perennial tan and laughing blue eyes. His home smelled of fresh paint and roast beef. He thrived in company and relished being the centre of attention. He adored his five daughters but lamented the son he never had. He enjoyed playing practical jokes but couldn't tolerate being at the receiving end. We christened him *The Lord Mayor* because he seemed to know everyone, even when he didn't. He would stand in his front garden chatting to passers-by while tending his roses and wave at passing motorists who would toot their horns in recognition.

I followed Pop's path to the US, but under different circumstances. I was older, established in a career and open to experience without the naivety of youth. I discovered an inner confidence and a quiet pride in being Irish that was empowering. When I met a native Californian (whose family lineage was clearly American in spite of an Irish surname) who experienced a visceral connection to Irish music and culture, I became convinced that being Irish is a spiritual thing — a state of mind. I spent six years living and working in the US, but as soon as our first son was born, we became equally determined to return to Ireland. This was a "quality of life" decision based mainly on the presence of family and friends, and a belief that Ireland would provide a more wholesome environment for childrearing (a decision my grandparents had made years before).

While we have no regrets about that decision, the Ireland we returned to was fundamentally changed. With the growth in prosperity and the breakdown of the traditional value system, Ireland had been propelled into the twenty-first century. The random violence and overt racism on our streets is an aspect of Irish life that our grandparents never knew. The perennial litter problem and our lack of environmental awareness are still a source of national embarrassment. While the essential qualities of *Irishness* remain intact — among them our humour and humanity — we need to take personal and collective responsibility in order to grow as a nation independent of the controlling influences of church and state upon which our grandparents depended. Ireland is no longer in isolation at the western edge of Europe. We are connected to the global community and we are adjusting to change. I believe we'll use our best resources as a people to rise to the challenging times ahead.

Shalini Sinha

Shalini Sinha is an Antiracism and Equality Trainer in Ireland. She lectures and researches with the Women's Education Research and Resource Centre, University College Dublin. She lives with her family in Dublin.

Being an Outsider, Being Black, Being Irish . . .

Sometimes, living in Ireland — struggling, coping, and fighting to belong — I forget how my relationship with this country, this land, and Irishness began. I am an Indian woman, born and raised in Canada. Ireland was nowhere on the horizon of my life as I was growing up.

As a young Indian woman, inheriting the burden of British domination of my people, I was frustrated growing up in a Canada which believed the founding of our nation by British Imperialism was not brutal domination but a passive, neutral "settlement" of "uncharted lands". I felt no kinship with the national identity that shaped the country of my birth. Rather, I rejected that legacy: the glorification of "Europe" and Britain. I identified very specifically as a minority — Indian, post-colonial, and structurally located in opposition to "British". The part of "Canadian" I did relate to and felt I belonged with lay in the one fact often begrudged but never denied — this was a country of immigrants, and *we* were Canadian.

Like my parents before me, I too have become an immigrant. My new home is Ireland. Like most stories of immigration, mine has been a difficult one (not least as a Black woman here). But this was not where my relationship with this island began. My connection to Irishness began with my deepest love — my partner, now husband — an Irishman born and raised here, and while he has travelled all over, has never lived off this island. My introduction to Irishness was by someone who loved his country and people, felt pride for their struggle against colonialism and warmth for all he met — someone who felt totally at home with me. Through the years, it has proven clear just how much we have in common. Given how hard I struggle in Ireland now, it's nice to remember I first met Irishness in love.

We had a lot of hope and anticipation for my move to Ireland. My partner deeply loved his country and me. He couldn't wait to share the two, expecting that Ireland would feel as at home with me and I in Ireland as we did with each other. I expected to share an experience of colonial resistance with this nation that I never did with my own. I anticipated finally being embraced by a country knowing we had in common something that was core to us both — that piece which explained where we fit in this world, now reflected all around me by a nation. It was only logical to assume that here I would finally be at home, not the "other", dissident, odd one out. Unfortunately, we were all disappointed.

For some reason, Ireland – Irishness – didn't make this connection with me. For some reason the people of Ireland believed there was some great difference between them and me. Was it the colour of my skin that did it? Was it that I am a constant reminder of something you don't want to remember?

My partner and I are extremely compatible, although most have difficulty seeing it. They see our colours, cultures, nationalities and even age difference and get confused. But this White Irish man and Black Indian woman have a world in common. We've both stuck our necks out against our oppressions. We've resisted, and despite the pull in both our cultures to suffer in silence, we've both made decisions to resist loudly, publicly. At the end of the day, in our own ways, we both hope and work for a world where we might get things right for each other, and our people. One thing has been clear right from the start: our people have everything in common.

But this is not what is reflected back to me as I make my life in Ireland – as I walk down the street. It is not a loving reminder of "we understand you and you understand us, we're all in this together" that you give me. It is nothing nearly so kind.

What is that piece you say is specifically Irish? Is it that you're White? Often I think so, because of the shock that seems to follow when one remembers Irishness is sometimes Black, too. The difference is that you were White and colonised and I was Black and colonised. We share our histories of brutality, humiliation, death, destruction, strength, survival, and proud resistance. You cannot tell me that the fact of your Whiteness makes you any different to me.

You may not like it, but I have a right to Irishness. I am here and here to stay. I live my life here, I contribute, I am affected by you, and you are most certainly affected by me. How long do I have to live here before you believe that I have something to say, that I have become a part of this nation and this people, and that you have become a part of me? And what about my children? They *will be* Irish — they will have their father who can trace his family here for generations, their mother with her own story of Ireland to tell, and they will believe they have the right to inherit this country. It is quite possible that they will be Black, like me, and they will not accept anyone telling them that half or all of them does not belong here.

Irish people have been in relationships with Black people for a long time. There is not a continent, scarcely a country, where Irish people have not been, either as missionaries, soldiers, Gardaí, UN peacekeepers, development aid workers, politicians, entertainers, students, volunteers, labourers, holiday-makers, or refugees. While most living on this island have never lived abroad, many have learned what Irishness has in common with the Black world — that place where we feel safe and understand each other. This is evident in how common my story is — how many White Irish people have Black, immigrant partners. Mine is an Irish story.

I believe Irish people have a role to play in the world. But I don't think you can play it until you reconcile your relationships with us, Black people. That "special something that is particularly Irish" is the wisdom that grows from surviving injustice with your dignity, spirit and humanity with you. What is particularly Irish is that you've done this and you're White, and you think there is some great difference between your story and mine. There isn't. That spirit — your Irishness — is what makes you more like me than not.

Marie Smyth

Marie Smyth attended Queen's University from which she has a BSSc (Hons) and the University of Ulster from which she has an MSc and a DPhil. She is the author of The Cost of the Troubles Survey.

A t the age of five, I was sent to the nearest primary school, a school that had been founded by the London Fishmongers company, who owned the land at one time. The school served the local Royal Air Force base, and local children — "civvies" — were in the minority. The RAF children — mostly English and one or two Black children — lived in households with a regular income. They had shop-bought clothes whilst mine were home-made, ate chips at home whilst our potatoes were boringly boiled. We civvies spoke what has come to be referred to as Ulster Scots, a dialect of English with idiosyncratic sentence construction and bespattered with Gaelic words such as *brathan* (porridge) — which we ate, whilst the English children ate cornflakes — and *geansai*, the hand-knits we wore, whilst the English children wore machine-knit jumpers. I learned that an English accent both sounded more intelligent and was a social advantage, so I adopted one during the school day. I was a civvy with an attitude.

Civvies were further sub-divided into Protestants, who could go to religious education with the English children, and Catholics who could not. There were no Catholic teachers in the school. Whilst the other children read from shiny paged bibles, with interesting illustrations, we were excluded to the playground. Far from enjoying my extra playtime, I felt I was missing something, a secret of the inner sanctum. Instead, we Catholics went to religious classes on a Saturday to the curate's lodgings. There was no shiny paged bible, and although our prayer books had coloured illustrations, it was the forbidden Protestant illustrations I wanted to pore over. On holy days, the other children watched as we left the school to walk the mile to the local Catholic chapel in a long snake of school uniforms.

At 19 I went to the United States. In the early 1970s, the McDonaldisation of the world was not yet complete, so the US was strange, and yet they spoke a recognisable version of English. My young cousins questioned me, "Do you have cars in Ireland?" "Do you have television in Ireland?" without pausing to wonder how I knew how to drive a car, and how I knew television programmes such as *Greenacres* or *Bewitched*. Whilst my relatives had assumed that I would mind their children in return for my keep, I had anticipated earning money to subsidise my time at Queen's. At 19, I felt sophisticated, a world traveller, and yet I was perceived as a primitive, good domestic servant material.

I left my relatives and went to work as a waitress in a Jewish health farm in upstate New York. We recognised each other, my Jewish friends and I. Being Jewish seemed a bit like being Irish. It was tricky and rich and deep and you didn't always want to own up to it. Irishness for my Irish-American relatives was not like that. Being Irish was something that you could practise, like golf or break-dancing, or going to mass on Sunday. It was a lifestyle choice. They were white people. It was Irishness with a hyphen, and the journey across the hyphen to Americanness made all the difference in this diaspora'ed world. More Oirish than Irish, it felt like the leprechaunisation of my identity, and the racism and anti-Semitism of some of my Irish-American relatives shocked and shamed me. My outward appearance did not reflect how I felt. My African American friends told me that I didn't think like a white person. People mistook me for a white person. Yet the privilege that white people have was suddenly available to me, if I wanted it. I went home.

When I was training in the mid-1970s, I worked briefly in England. In a restaurant one evening dining with a male nurse and his wife from the hospital I was working in, three large Englishmen surrounded our table and directed their comments at me. They had recognised my accent. "When our boys are allowed to do what they should do, scum like you will be dead, the streets of Belfast will run red with your blood." I asked for the bill, and we left. They followed. I became aware that no one would protect me. Not the police, not the other customers, only my diminutive English male nurse friend and his even more diminutive wife. I have never lived in England since. My brother, who joined the Royal Air Force, lives there, and now answers to the name "Paddy" even though his name is Joseph.

As I sit in my middle age, with my Ulster Protestant husband, it seems that Irishness is not a choice for the likes of us, no more than Britishness is. It has shaped our minds and souls. We live with it, we sometimes use it against ourselves and others. Sometimes it is used against us. The odd glorious time, it is to our true advantage, without being at the expense of anyone else, like seeing this stunning Irish landscape and knowing your place in it. Apart from that, it is simply one of the ways that I am, and that I am learning to live with. Female. Middle-aged. Irish.

Nell Stewart-Liberty

Nell Stewart-Liberty is the publisher of Social & Personal, *a lifestyles monthly glossy magazine sold in Ireland, and of* Carleton Varney's Decorating, *an international interiors magazine sold throughout America*

My father was born and brought up in Buckinghamshire; my maternal great-grandmother was Greek; I started life with a British passport but despite this I am one hundred per cent Irish and proud of it. I was brought up on the Inishowen peninsula, to me the most beautiful place on earth. I was born in Derry, but would much rather have been born in Donegal; my father had to arrange to have the border especially opened so that my mother could make the midnight dash from Fahan to the Bayview Nursing Home. Today the border has visually disappeared, but I am glad that it still exists; to me it is a completely natural line, and I have always considered the Republic of Ireland and the people living in it to be very different to Northern Ireland. I would not like to see a United Ireland.

Childhood summers revolved around lovely Lough Swilly, either swimming in it, or sailing on it; the sea was at the end of our garden. We had a continuous stream all summer of English cousins to stay and even then I knew it was different and, of course, better to be Irish. I remember Prudence, an English cousin who went to a very proper English girls' boarding school, telling me how they had lessons about how to put on a bra properly. I was absolutely astonished; we'd never have anything like that at Derry High! England to me seemed a very peculiar place, although I visited Buckinghamshire often to stay with relations, but I knew they thought I was different and they would comment on my very strong Irish accent, whereas at home people often thought because of my accent that I must be English! At a very grand wedding near Ailesbury, my uncle introduced me to a friend, saying "This is my niece, but she's Irish, so she's rather wild." I took this as a huge compliment. Having escaped the ghastly Derry High at the age of 16 I went to Oxford to do a secretarial course and homesickness featured strongly in my life. My most favourite poem has always been Percy French's *The Emigrant's Letter* — "are they cutting the corn in old Creeslough today . . .". Such a sad and mournful piece, which mirrors my feelings about being away from Donegal. The day my (English) husband left me, my mother and I made a sentimental journey for a lunch of toasted cheese sandwiches in a pub in old Creeslough. It completely fitted the mood and although it is not on the Inishowen peninsula, I still have a very soft spot for Creeslough.

Living in Donegal and crossing the border every day to go to school in Derry during the 1960s made one very aware of the politics of the day (my father was the only employer in Derry at that time who employed both Catholics and Protestants). John Hume is a hero of mine and I remember being on the same evening aeroplane from Heathrow to Belfast as John and Lord Molyneux. It was the day John Hume made his maiden speech in the House of Commons and when we entered the arrivals hall in Belfast, my mother completely ignored me and rushed over to congratulate him on his wonderful speech, which, at the time, was a ground-breaking gesture because many people of my mother's background would not necessarily have approved of his politics. I have always been fervently nationalist and at Christmas when we had to toast the Queen, I insisted that a toast also be made to our President.

Today, thanks to all the revelations, tribunals and crookery, I am not so passionate in my politics, but I am still fervently Irish and would never give up my Irish passport, a thing I have used extensively to travel the world, but I have never been to a place I'd rather live than Ireland. The only time I haven't been right at home here was when I had to spend several months in Altnagelvin Hospital at the height of the Troubles in 1972. I was the only patient not suffering from a gunshot wound on the ward. One room was full of wounded British soldiers, the other full of wounded people from Derry. I was squashed in the middle, in my own tiny private room, and felt very much like a buffer zone. That is the only time Ireland seemed like a foreign land.

I feel lucky to be Irish; my parents met during the Second World War, and because my father was the second son, his elder brother inherited his family home in Buckinghamshire. So luckily for me, my parents decided to live in my maternal grandmother's house in Donegal, so I feel I escaped from being brought up in England by the skin of my teeth. When I was a child, we all went to my paternal grandmother's funeral in Buckinghamshire; due to a travel strike, we could not get back to Ireland. I felt completely stranded. I was sitting in my late grandmother's garden with my father and saw a plane high in the sky, "I wish we were in that plane and we were on our way home," I said. "So do I," was his reply. Ireland affects people like that.

Michael J. Sullivan

Mike Sullivan was appointed as US Ambassador to Ireland in December 1998 following a legal career in Casper, Wyoming, and service as Governor of Wyoming from 1987–1995. He and his wife Jane took up the post in January 1999.

Less than a month after assuming the position as the 24th United States Ambassador to Ireland, while standing on the pier at the Heritage Centre in Cobh, the personal complexity and excitement of the journey I would be undertaking during the next two years began to dawn on me. Of course, it was an honour and privilege as well as an enormous responsibility to be asked by President Clinton to represent him and the people of the United States during this extraordinary period of the relationship between Ireland and the United States. But what did it mean for me and my personal relationship with Ireland and my own Irishness? What about the validity of the questions initially raised by some in Washington, Boston, New York and even Ireland as to whether someone from Wyoming, a distant state in the Rocky Mountain West, who had never even been to Ireland, could be sufficiently Irish or ethnically grounded to justify the President's confidence?

Spurred by the solemn nature of Cobh as a place of departure for Irish emigrants, I considered the circular journey that brought me to Dublin's Phoenix Park. My forebears were post-famine emigrants, leaving Cobh or one of the other points of dispatch in the 1850s. They came to America from the copper mines of the Beara Peninsula, the Midlands of Longford, and farms in Carlow and Wicklow. But more importantly, the visit to Cobh caused me to evaluate seriously the courage that carried all of them across the Atlantic, through the

East Coast cities and into relatively unknown and undeveloped parts of Northern Michigan, Kansas, Nebraska and ultimately Wyoming and the cohesive nature of the Irish that, in my case at least, prompted three generations in the United States to marry other Irish. Undoubtedly, it was a combination of family, community, hunger for opportunity, optimism and faith that propelled these generations in their journey. But how much was passed through to each generation and did any real Irishness remain given time, distance and cultural differences? Would this circle join?

It has now been 18 months since that morning in Cobh and it has been a deeply personal time. I was told in New York before leaving the US, "Not to worry Ambassador, before you get your coat off in Dublin you will have a cousin in every county!" When I received a hand-written letter shortly after my trip to Cobh which commenced, "I am your mother's oldest living relative in Ireland", I was understandably sceptical. But the 83-year-old retired physician attached a copy of a letter written in 1930 from his aunt in Ireland to my grandmother in Wyoming. That introduction commenced a series of family connections, though admittedly far removed, that have become a very important part of our time in Ireland. Travelling throughout the country, seeing the villages, gardens, the names of the pubs, dealing with the Irish people, has served to awaken an Irishness that was dormant and which I did not fully appreciate existed. Suddenly I recalled the names of the older couples who came to my grandparents' house for dinner, advice and interminable conversation (before I understood the meaning of "*craic*") — O'Flannigan, Coughlin, Dawson, Monsignor McDevitt, Madigan. And I was reminded of the little old ladies for whom my father as a friend and lawyer cared over the years — Mrs Collins, Mrs O'Leary, Mrs Flynn, Mrs Macken; the small grocery in Laramie, Wyoming where my grandparents lived; Mrs Brady's candy store in my hometown; and my grandmother's unusually beautiful flower garden, despite her relatively poor circumstances, along the railroad tracks. These were not simply friendships or conditions of chance but the tangible reflection of that combination of ethnicity, character and heritage which has acted as a catalyst for the unmatched success and unequalled contribution of the Irish in America, in whatever part of that vast landscape their journey took them. It is, I would submit, that same combination of traits or "Irishness" — the very same carried across the seas with the Diaspora — that has, presented with opportunity, formed a foundation for the economic successes of Ireland in recent years.

On 19 August 2000, after nearly two years of inquiry and exploration, through the assistance of a gentle Irishman who epitomised the generosity of spirit I have come to appreciate in the Irish (and now recognise existed in each of the generations that by their sacrifice and faith afforded me this opportunity), I stood on the Beara Peninsula at the very spot where my great-grandfather was raised and from which his father walked over the mountain to work the copper mines of Allyhies. It was a breathtakingly beautiful place and I knew I could not understand the depth of the despair or the pain of the circumstances which prompted his departure. But I also knew that I better understood his Irishness and my Irishness, that we had been blessed and that the circle of his journey, commenced in a millennium now once removed, had been joined.

Peter Sutherland

Photo: BP Amoco

Peter Sutherland is Chairman of BP Amoco plc and Chairman and Managing Director of Goldman Sachs International. He was previously Attorney General of Ireland (1981–84), EC Commissioner for Competition Policy (1985–89), Chairman of Allied Irish Banks (1989–93), and Director-General of the World Trade Organisation, formerly GATT (1993–95).

I suspect that the Irish are more emotionally attached to a sense of their own nationality than most others. I certainly am. Standing in Stade Français after the glorious rugby match last year, basking in the international recognition of a figure such as Seamus Heaney or even hearing someone sing "Danny Boy", particularly when abroad, I am intensely conscious of what I am. Perhaps it is a misplaced pride (indeed perhaps all national pride is misplaced) but there is no denying the feeling. Nor am I alone in this. A recent survey in the European Union established that we are the proudest people in the European Union. I suspect that this is not a transient phenomenon. Even when things were less good than they appear to be today, the results of a survey might well have been generally the same.

Of course, other nationalities certainly are not immune to similar sensations. No doubt they are accentuated by simplistic images of the history that binds people together but often divides them from others. We are told that the nation state is a modern phenomenon but, for better or worse, the sense of one's own place and the relationship with it is as old as the human race. No doubt having a perception of a shared past as well as the present increases a sense of national identity, even if the facts are very much more complicated.

I cannot claim to be comfortable with much of this. Indeed, one of my strongest convictions is that nationalism has generally led to division and, ultimately, conflict. For me, the most noble political movement in modern times has been the attempt to combine democracy with sharing sovereignty through the process of European integration. A passionate belief in breaking down barriers and borders does not sit comfortably with a sense of identity which, in the last analysis, often stresses a belief in particular national virtues. By implication, this stress on the relative strengths of one's own people often suggests that others do not share them. There is essentially something triumphalist about patriotism.

Much though one might like it to be otherwise, the fact is, one's nationality often does create a starting point for relationships. Of course, the image of historic events shape the perceptions held by other people of us and not merely our perception of them. The fact is, stereotypes exist in the minds of people everywhere, often subliminally, and they influence reactions. People see others, initially at least, as products of societies with certain characteristics and traits and seek, in interpreting their words or actions, confirmation of their conformity to the stereotype. For the moment at least, being Irish seems to be fashionable. Whilst images of being feckless and amusing rather than responsible and profound are sometimes associated with us, our successes in various fields in recent times have left a positive legacy in our current image.

In Britain in particular, where the appalling events of recent history might have been expected to leave a negative image of us, we are treated with a generosity that is sometimes surprising. We are seen as close relatives rather than as more distant ones. Elsewhere in the developed world, the Diaspora generated over the last couple of centuries has created not merely a network of people who feel an association and loyalty to Ireland but also, amongst those with no family connection, a certain affection rather than antipathy. In some places, such as Austria, France and Spain, educated people know of longer associations underlined by the Irish family names that have distinguished histories, such as MacMahon in France and O'Donnell or O'Neill in Spain and Portugal. Who can walk down Calle O'Donnell in Madrid and not be conscious of past and positive associations?

In the developing world, insofar as there is any recognition of our small island, reactions to us are very positive. We are perceived as being a unique postcolonial State in Europe. Furthermore, through the highly visible contributions made by our missionaries and by those involved in aid agencies, we have acquired an image that is incredibly positive. I had firsthand experience of this because when I was proposed for the position of Director General of GATT, and later the first Director General of the World Trade Organisation, the most positive reaction generally came from the developing countries. An Irishman was not seen as a representative of the industrialised states of the northern hemisphere.

A further positive element abroad is the impact of our young people. In general, they seem mercifully free of hang-ups and display a self-confidence and a capacity to relate to others that is truly distinctive. Through my children, I know, for example, that of all the parties given each semester by the young *stagiaires* in the European Commission, the best, and most popular, is the Irish one. It was always thus. This trivial anecdotal evidence, however, is not without relevance. It is no more than we would expect.

I am proud of being Irish and, although I hesitate to express it, I think that I have good reason. One criticism that I do have is related to how self-absorbed we are. In a way, this brief essay is evidence of an excessive focus on ourselves. I often find in conversations involving a group of foreigners that the Irish speak a great deal about domestic Irish issues, assuming that their interlocutors can somehow see our experience as relevant or important for them. At the end of the day, we need to remind ourselves that we are a very small place in a very big world.

Alan Titley

Alan Titley is a writer and scholar. He is Professor of
Irish at St Patrick's College, Dublin.

To say that "being Irish" is an accident of birth is a truism, probably much repeated on these pages. I was cast upon this world and shore and place and why not knowing. Given another soul I would have been suckled in another creed and another clime. But I had no choice about being made a male, and being born in Cork and growing up in the grey fifties and the multicoloured sixties. These were the nets of gender and of history and of geography which encaptured me, and enraptured me. I was only obeying orders.

But because we are one thing, we can be everything else. That one thing must be cultivated because it is related to the whole of creation. Our souls fret and grow in the shadow of all things. My Irishness is the thread that links me to all people at all times, because it is what I have been allotted. It is all I have to sing with.

Irishness is not a "ground" of being, even less a root. Roots are for turnips and vegetables. Roots are stuck in the mud. We are all nomads and itinerants, and our "culture" is our caravan and pack animal. Identity hangs in the air, like a rope that dangles unsupported. We wax on that rope and let it sway. But the rope is real.

The frayed knots of that rope are knobs and lumps of memory. My head burst into consciousness with a jangle of Chuck Berry, black and white American gangster movies, "The Kennedys of Castleross", Gregorian chant, Seán Ó

Sé's "An Poc ar Buile", the voice of Michael O'Hehir on summer eves, ads for Chivers' Jams. . . . How to make an identity out of that?

And there was also a sporting identity, no less eclectic and anarchic. Boxing from my family, basketball from around the corner, bowling from up the hill, soccer from the street, Gaelic football from school. But above and beyond there was and is hurling, the King and Grand Wizard and High Beatitude of all field games, and in Cork as we were told and as we learned and as empirical evidence proved beyond doubt, we were the best of all. This supremacy and arrogance has helped me to understand the British Raj, and the Roman Empire, and the insufferable pride of being on top. I still suffer more on those rare occasions when Cork hurlers are beaten, than all the defeats of the Irish soccer and rugby teams put together, and they are legion enough. But there is also Cork sentiment and slop, the maudlin strains of that most awful song "The Banks of my own Lovely Lee", and the even worser than worse, "Beautiful City", which it might well be, but not because of the song.

So the local is there as a lodestone, but also a load. It becomes subsumed in the national as discovery takes place, because Irishness is always a journey of discovery. We are tourists in our own country because of our colonial past. No point in hiding it. It is painted on the landscape. But we are tourists, because we all are anyway, no matter into what "normal" and "self-confident" society we are thrown. The journey towards Irishness is a journey into what we are and into what we might have been and into what we might yet be. It is everyone's journey, and it is our own particularly.

Irishness bloomed in me because of my discovery of the Irish language, and what we sometimes call the Gaelic tradition. It was as if it was waiting there, to be plucked from the circumnambient stuff. It was as if I had been speaking it all my life, but had never touched its words. Of course, there grew a political dimension, and cultural politics, and postcolonial re-examination, but all of these were back there as noise. They clamoured for attention but never claimed it. They whelmed in, but never overly. Irishness was that voice that was there, breathing from the ground, laughing on the road, the sweet music of expression that had gone underground and lay in the folds of our consciousness as another dimension.

Mystical shite and onions, I know, but true to the last dot and com. Life and being are mysteries, unless somebody out there has a convincing refutation. I drank deep in the language and its traditions and discovered that it bore no relation whatsoever to the cliché-driven reductionist paper tiger of the popular journalistic tradition. I did meet a few walking stereotypes in my time, but they were few and far away. Because Irish speakers in their close or scattered communities can be as holy as Joe, or as corrupt as a capitalist. If Irishness is always a matter of bits and pieces, the shards of the cracked looking-glass, the crumbs which we gather to nibble together what we are, then the Irish language component is what gives me some meaning as an Irish being out of all this jumble. It is a process of discovery as it always was since I first looked into Séathrún Keating's oeuvre, but it also a process of creating, of wondering, of making new. I could exchange the grey skies of Irish Catholicism for the lurid Latin American kind, or even blot out the magic of Darach Ó Catháin in a swop for Blind Willie Johnson, or all the poteen of Conamara for Spanish wine, but the language is stuck in my throat, and I cannot get it out.

David Trimble

The Rt. Hon. David Trimble MP MLA is First Minister of Northern Ireland and the Leader of the Ulster Unionist Party. He was joint winner, along with John Hume, of the 1998 Nobel Prize for Peace.

When discussing identity on the island of Ireland I believe it is dangerous and inappropriate to attempt to integrate existing diversity. One should not try to blend together traditions that are essentially different. We may disagree as to the extent of those differences, but there is little to be gained by trying to meld things together. Instead, our objective should be to find a way in which diverse traditions can be affirmed and enjoyed. We should not be afraid of difference. There are many countries and societies which have within them tremendous diversities in cultural terms, without those differences necessarily resulting in conflict.

It is worth asking whether there are, and to what extent there are, different cultures within the British Isles. I use that term deliberately to avoid yet another pointless euphemism. Within the British Isles we all speak English, though some people in Scotland and Wales and a smaller number in Ireland also speak other languages. Ulster is regarded as being different from the British mainland yet in Ulster the predominant circulation is of national papers. In the Republic of Ireland the difference is more marked, but one only has to look at the size and direction of television aerials to see a clear and obvious element of cultural unity. These points are made, not to deny the existence of differences, but to point out that the differences that do exist are not as marked as in some other divided societies.

The term I use to describe the culture I grew up is "Ulster-British". I do not like using the term "Protestant" because of the sectarianism encouraged by the use of religious labels. One must, however, be honest and recognise that, historically, community identity and national consciousness were very often formed through religion, with the result that the use of religious labels is sometimes unavoidable. Of the alternatives to religious terms often used, the term "Ulster-Scot" is not accurate, if only because it leaves out the not insignificant English settlements in Ulster. The term "planter" is also inaccurate, for only a few of the Anglo-Scottish immigrants were actually planters and, more importantly, it also omits the "native" Irish who were and have been absorbed within the cultural community that has developed in Northern Ireland. The term Ulster-British is also to be preferred because it emphasises the point that those of my tradition do not see ourselves as a self-contained community unique to this little bit of narrow ground.

Particularly in East Ulster, in any examination of culture, identity and perception, the very strong connections with Northern England and Scotland stand out. Around the Irish Sea there is a triangle consisting of Liverpool, Glasgow and Belfast. This triangle is significant in terms of the economic development of those areas: their growth and decline have been linked and the local cultures are also strongly linked. One only has to mention football teams to make the point. So the Ulster-British people are not a separate people but part of a larger grouping, modified or affected by their particular historical experience.

There is still a long way to go before the historical experience of the Ulster-British community is treated in a similar way to that of others. Until I was 17 I received no formal education about Ulster or Irish history — all I knew I learned from my grandmother who, as a person brought up in Derry, was very anxious to see that I had a proper awareness of the great Siege and, of course, one learnt from reading Orange banners and the gossip of children.

There is an asymmetry between the Ulster-British culture and what we could call the Irish Gaelic/Catholic culture. The latter has, in the course of the last century or so, tried to develop, or redevelop, its own self-contained culture. It was clearly bound up with the development of political separatism. It was to be "ourselves alone" politically, culturally and, especially, linguistically. But it has not entirely succeeded, for the reality of culture in the Republic of Ireland is a sort of compromise between Ireland's British heritage and the Gaelic/Catholic cultural aspirations of the separatists. The persistence of British influences in the Republic and the existence of Gaelic/Catholic influences in Ulster can blur the picture. Yet, there is a clear difference between the Ulster-British and Gaelic/Catholic cultures.

The compromise in southern culture mentioned above is an uneasy one for it scarcely exists in the rhetoric of the State, which is virtually exclusively Gaelic/Catholic. The rhetoric and sometimes the practice of Gaelic/Catholic culture has not fully recognised the existence of the Ulster-British culture. It is not just that it seeks to assimilate another culture; it sometimes refuses to recognise even the existence or validity of that other culture, trying to downgrade the divergence to purely religious differences or to merely regional variations within one culture. Too often, it is suggested that if unionists or Orangemen were properly educated or indoctrinated, they would perceive their "Irishness" and even realise the Gaelic culture was "their" culture as well. Any form of co-existence must acknowledge the right of each culture to exist and to perpetuate itself.

Niall Williams

Niall Williams is the author of Four Letters of Love *and* As It Is in Heaven. *He lives in County Clare.*

Being Irish is not something I ever thought about until I went to America in my early twenties. Growing up in Ireland, I did not listen to Irish music. I was not drawn to Gaelic games nor did I feel any particular affinity with the Irish language. I studied French. The books I read then were American and Latin American. I lived in the landscapes of William Faulkner and Gabriel Garcia Marquez, even as I walked around Sandymount. I was like a man in a house with only windows and no mirrors.

Then I went to America. My first job was in a bookshop in a suburb of New York City. Very soon I noticed that often when I was introduced it was as someone "over from Ireland". The customers in the shop knew this too, and comments on my accent, education and manner were soon defining me. I was "the Irish one" to them. What exactly this meant, other than an accident of birth, I was not sure. There were so many kinds of Irish, and mine was not the kind comfortable with the Guinness blarney and shamrock portrait so pervasive in New York. "Are you Irish at all?" one man asked me, when I told him I didn't drink. The truth is that for a long time I wasn't sure.

Partly to find an answer to that was one of the reasons I moved to West Clare in 1985. I think I wanted to find out about the mythical country. I wanted to live for a time in the actual landscape and not the one as perceived through the poetry of Yeats or the prose of Joyce or even the version of the country found in the pages of *The Irish Times* when read on the streets of New York.

So now, after 15 years here, what have I found? I have found that Ireland is a surreal amalgam of many places. Some of them are ancient and historic and traditional, and others alongside them are mega, plastic, virtual and hyper-amorphous. Years ago I stood in a classroom and felt the floor like a tide with those waiting to emigrate. Now the same tide flows back and renews all definitions of towns and villages along the west. So what now is Irish? What does it mean to *be* Irish? Are there times when we are *being* more Irish than others? To me, none of this matters. Being Irish is simply a label. It covers the multitude of my responses to things that act as mirrors and wherein some part of me is reflected. By this I mean the lift in my heart when I walk along the road in Kiltumper, the sight of high fuschia bushes, the song of the cuckoo, Michael Donnellan in his old cabinless tractor going up to the bog with his *slean*, the music of Martin Hayes, the poetry of Seamus Heaney, the tension and excitement in the parish when the hurlers play, Van Morrison, Stephen's Green, turf coming home in trailers with creels, the sea at Spanish Point, Inch, Donegal, RTE radio overheard on summer Sunday afternoons from car windows where men snooze, the evening sunlight when it falls in the fields across the valley in Kiltumper, horses standing and then running, child drovers with lengths of black piping hupping cattle in swarms of flies, 99s, the smells of gorse, heather, honeysuckle, saddles of freckles on short noses, my children on their bicycles on empty roads shouldered with high hedgerows, my wife in the garden, the hundred seasons of the rain. Such things. And many many more.

Des Wilson

Father Des Wilson was born in Belfast and ordained in Maynooth in 1949. He served as a hospital chaplain, a spiritual director and a curate. Since 1975, he has been the Director of the Springhill Community House Educational Project in West Belfast.

Living in a beautiful country, a country so beautiful it has to be shared, with a beauty that by being shared is enhanced and not diminished. Being Irish means that, but there is heartache in it, knowing the beauty, willing to share it, when so often the offer to share is frustrated and even repulsed. It is awful to be told your gift is not wanted, and the greater the beauty the greater the hurt. Being Irish is sharing a history as well as a landscape. So there is a long, long wonderful voyage of discovery — like sitting in a town square discontented because you have seen all the surrounding streets and homes and corners, then realise there is a whole world out there you were not told about. We learned history but it was history which said we had no history, or that we were a people content with defeat. But the voyage of discovery begins and you learn that every Boyne had its Landen, that every monarch was at most met on the battlefield or at least harassed in the mountains. It was not all defeat and where others might lose heart, we did not.

Part of the fun on the voyage to discover who we are is the fun of being proved right — when we said Ireland had mineral wealth, we were contradicting what we had been carefully taught; when we said Ireland had the potential to become one of the most prosperous small nations in Europe, nobody seemed to be listening. And yet it all proved true, along with much else we had been taught to disbelieve.

So the voyage of discovery of a real Ireland is not all new insights and wonders, it is the realisation too that the wonders in our minds are real out there
as well. And with fresh curiosity, we explore why we so often pretended to ourselves that we Irish were unimportant. The Greeks had their myths, which
were the best in the world, and we had not; Caesar was a great man whose
picture and bust graced our schools as if he had done us all a favour. Finding
out about the Ulster Cycle and the other ancient and wondrous myths of Ireland changed all that, just as did the discovery that Caesar was a cheat, a
forger, an adulterer and a military imperialist who destroyed a million of our
ancestors in the eight years of Gallic wars which in school we had been instructed to admire. It was a consolation to learn that when Paul preached and
wrote letters to the Galatians, he was talking to our own people, Celts who
once were strong enough to conquer both Greece and Rome.

Being Irish means not only making that voyage of discovery but being delighted with it. There is a new brilliance now in our greeting people in the
street with names that are the Irish names of thousands of years ago. We think
nothing of it, it is so common as to have nearly become banal, we are after all
an ancient people knowing each other by names which would have been familiar to ancestors so ancient that their mythology is the only other thing we
know about them. The names are an echo of a past which might become banal
if we knew all about it already, but is vitalising because we are discovering it
year by year as that which made us who and what we are. Catching glimpses of
our people whom we had no sight of for ages.

One of the few good things about being colonised is that — like when you
beat your head against a wall — it is wonderful when you stop. The first time
you admit the coloniser was wrong, untruthful, the first time you reach for the
records to find out who we really are, the pleasure is a hundred times greater
than if we had learned about it all from childhood. Such a voyage of discovery
is best made by adults. As children, we might learn about the Code of Roman
laws imposed on us; as adults we appreciate how humane our own laws were
before that imposition and before the Christians entered our people's lives.
The Brehon Laws were more humane than the laws of the Romans or Greeks,
more humane than the Code of Hamurabi and the Old Testament, more hu-

mane than the Chinese law systems, however far back you go. And when we see our people slipping away from the imposed systems and reverting to the customs of the old times — marriage customs, restorative justice customs — we do not blame them for apostasy, we see them quietly returning to an ancient mode of civilised thought which was enlightened because it grew up with our people. Prisons and punishments and death by tyrants were imports into our civilisation, they were not created by it.

Stand on the Céide Fields. Imagine. It will be 3,000 years before the first Christian message arrives; the men and women and children who built the walls and measured the fields two metres beneath your feet had names we still murmur and shout in streets ages after the Christians, the Vikings, the Normans, the Elizabethan adventurers, the imperialists, have done their worst and their best to us. Those ancient farmers' names and ours are still here. We are still here. Rejoicing in the civilisation we used to know so little about but now are greatly loving as we learn to reverence it fully for the first time.

Being Irish is being the inheritor of a great and ancient and culturally rich civilisation. I belong to those fortunate heirs who for the first time may look forward to having the freedom to rejoice in the past and to mould a fitting future for all our people.

Looking to that Irish past and future, could I wish to become anything else but Irish?